TCP/IP Addressing

TCP/IP Addressing

Designing and Optimizing
your
IP Addressing Scheme

Buck Graham

AP PROFESSIONAL

AP PROFESSIONAL is a Division of Academic Press

Boston   San Diego   New York
London   Sydney   Tokyo   Toronto

AP PROFESSIONAL

An Imprint of ACADEMIC PRESS
A Division of HARCOURT BRACE & COMPANY

This book is printed on acid-free paper.

Copyright © 1997 by Academic Press, Inc.
All rights reserved.

United Kingdom Edition published by
ACADEMIC PRESS LIMITED
24–28 Oval Road, London NW1 7DX

Graham, Buck
      TCP/IP addressing ; designing and optimizing your IP addressing
scheme / Buck Graham.
        p.   cm.
      Includes bibliographical references and index.
      ISBN 0-12-294630-8 (alk. paper)
        1. TCP/IP (Computer network protocol) 2. Computer networks.
   I. Title.
TK5105.585.G73   1996   96-35987
004.6'2—dc20   CIP

Printed in the United States of America
      97 98 99   IP   9 8 7 6 5 4 3 2

This book is dedicated to my wonderful wife Julie.

Thank you for giving me
the time and opportunity to write this book.

Contents

Preface   xiii

Section I   Addressing Prerequisite Topics   1

1   TCP/IP Overview   3

The Physical Layer   4
The Link Layer   4
The Network Layer   12
Reliable and Unreliable Transport Services   19
Transmission Control Protocol (TCP)   22
User Datagram Protocol (UDP)   26
TCP/IP Connections   27
Summary   30

2   IP Address Fundamentals 33

    On Names, Addresses, and Routes 34
    The IP Address 35
    Address Terminology, Notation, and Numbering 37
    Determining the Class of an IP Address 40
        Class A 42
        Class B 43
        Class C 44
        Class D 45
        Class E 46
    Unicast Addresses 46
    Subnetting 47
    Subnet Masks 50
    Mask Mathematics 53
    Contiguous Mask Bits 56
    Subnet Terminology 57
    Special-Case Addresses 60
    IP Addressing Revisited 62
    The Straight Skinny of IP Address Space—A Summary 63

3   Network Devices 65

    Hosts 65
    A Reference Model 66
    Repeaters 68
    Bridges 69
    Routers 71
    Gateways 74
    Network Management Systems 74
    Network Analyzers 75
    Summary 76

4   Routing 79

    The Routing Table 81
    The Forwarding Process 85

Determining the Optimal Route   86
Dynamic Routing Protocols   92
   RIP (RIP Version 1)   94
   Open Shortest Path First (OSPF)   101
Static Routing   107
ICMP Routing   108
Direct Routing   111
Hand Tracing a Route   112
Summary   116

Section 2   IP Address Layout   119

Address-Needs Assessment   119

5   Common Topology Addressing   123

Introduction to the IP Address Worksheet   123
Broadcast-Capable, Multiple-Access Networks:
   Ethernet and Token Ring   134
LAN Transit Networks   136
Point to Point (Numbered)   137
Point to Point (Unnumbered)   138
Pooled Dial-In Access   139
Nonbroadcast Multiple-Access Networks:
   Frame Relay   141
Frame Relay (Full Mesh)   143
Frame Relay (Hub and Spoke)   146
Frame Relay (Partial Mesh)   148
Summary   149

6   Addressing for Internet Connections   151

The Internet Connection   151
Private IP Network Allocation   154
Firewalls and Network Address Translators   156
Summary   157

7   Addressing to Achieve Route Table Efficiency   159

    Addressing for Route Aggregation—An Example   160
    Planning for Aggregation   166
    RIP and Route Aggregation   168
    OSPF and Route Aggregation   176
    Static Routing and Route Aggregation   178
    Classless Interdomain Routing (CIDR)   187
        Supernetting   187
        Classless Addressing   191
        Address Allocation   192
    Summary   197

8   Addressing for High Utilization of Address Space   199

    Estimating Address Assignment Efficiency   200
    Calculating Address Assignment Efficiency   202
    Addressing Efficiency and Routing Protocols   204
    Cheating RIP to Achieve Efficiency   210
    Network Mask Deception—Another Trick   213
    Network Address Translation   217
    Summary   218

9   Managing IP Addresses   221

    Addressing for Management   222
    The IntraNIC   227
    Translation of IP Number to Name   229
    Administration Tools   230
    Bootstrap Protocol (BOOTP)   231
    Dynamic Host Configuration Protocol (DHCP)   236
    Summary   239

10   Addressing for Growth and Change   241

    Anticipated Growth   241
    Unanticipated Change   247
    Summary   248

Section 3   Advanced Addressing Issues 249

11   IP Multicast 251

Resource Discovery   252
Conferencing   254
Internet Group Management Protocol (IGMP)   257
Multicast Routing Overview   258
Multicast Packet Distribution   261
  Flooding   261
  Spanning Tree (ST)   261
  Reverse Path Broadcast (RPB) 262
  Truncated Reverse Path Broadcasting (TRPB)   265
  Reverse Path Multicasting (RPM)   265
  Core-Based Trees (CBT)   266
Multicast Routing Protocols   268
  Distance-Vector Multicast Routing Protocols (DVMRP)   268
  Multicast Extensions to OSPF (MOSPF)   269
Summary   269

12   IP Version 6 273

The IP Version 6 Header   275
IP Version 6 Address Representation   279
IP Version 6 Addressing   281
  Unicast Addresses   282
  Multicast Addresses   284
  Anycast Addresses   287
IP Version 6 Address Allocation   287
Summary   288

Appendix A   The IP Address Helper Application 291

Installation   292
Running the IP Address Helper Application   292
IP Address Section   293

Subnet Mask Section 295
Hexadecimal Equivalents Section 296
Miscellaneous Fields 296
Improvements 297

Appendix B   IP Network Number Request Template 299

Appendix C   IP Addressing Worksheet 305

References 311
Request for Comments (RFC) 311
IETF Internet Draft Documents 314
Textbooks and Other 314

Index   317

Preface

Over the last several years I have been designing networks for large corporate clients. Networks these sizes demand routing table efficiency. In order to achieve any level of efficiency, however, it is necessary to have developed an optimal addressing scheme as the cornerstone for building the large network.

More than a handful of technical books deal with the TCP/IP protocol stack and intricacies of a TCP/IP network. Some of these books are no more than recapitulations of the published Request for Comments (RFC) that serve as the standards; others focus their discussion on points of interest, such as routing protocols. Among all of these books I have not found a good reference on how to design an optimal IP addressing scheme while taking into account network growth, address utilization, routing efficiency, and ease of administration.

Often it seems that an author of a TCP/IP addressing book:

- assumes that a reader already has a high level of understanding of IP addressing,

- considers the topic beyond the scope of the book,

- considers the topic as too mundane to be covered in the book, or

- does not understand addressing well enough to be able to present it.

In fact, I have come across books in which the author has attempted to cover IP addressing and presents the topic with significant technical inaccuracies.

In short, when corporate network managers approach me about designing or redesigning their network addressing, I do not have a reference that I can direct them toward that will satisfy their needs. I was compelled to write a handbook that will guide these people through the process of designing an IP addressing scheme. The design should meet all of the criteria that I consider when I design addressing for the large corporate user. In this handbook I wanted to cover a number of topics:

- hosts versus network addressing

- the rules of IP addressing

- special-case addresses

- IP address subnetting (most commonly misunderstood topic)

- routing considerations when designing an addressing scheme

- addressing for optimal route aggregation

- calculating the efficiency of an addressing scheme

- classless interdomain routing (CIDR)

- multicast addressing

- addressing in IP version 6 (future IP architecture)

Lucky for me, I found a publisher that was willing to help me make this happen. I hope that this book is as helpful to you in understanding IP addressing as I had planned it to be.

Addressing Prerequisite Topics

The chapters in this first section of the book provide a coverage of the topics that I consider to be essential to the understanding of the IP addressing discussions in Sections II and III. The chapters in this section can be skipped as appropriate, based on your level of competence. I would suggest that, at a minimum, you scan the chapters and read the summaries. Chapters 3 and 4 introduce key concepts that should not be missed.

Chapter 1 provides an introduction to the TCP/IP protocol stack and builds a communications model from the physical layer to the application layer. Chapter 2 discusses the IP address found in an IP datagram. Class A, B, and C networks, the unicast networks, are discussed, along with the subnetting of networks to achieve greater utilization. Chapter 3 presents a comparison of the TCP/IP protocol to the OSI reference model. Network devices are then presented according to the layer in which they operate. Repeaters, bridges, routers, and gateways are discussed, along with some of their inherent limitations with respect to IP addressing. Chapter 4 discusses the impact of addressing on routing and vice versa. RIP, OSPF, and static routing mechanisms are discussed, with special attention to addressing considerations.

TCP/IP Overview

This chapter provides a general introduction to the TCP/IP communications protocols. It will cover the link, network, transport, and application layers and the network functions that each provide. Illustration 1-1 depicts the TCP/IP protocols and how they relate to one another.

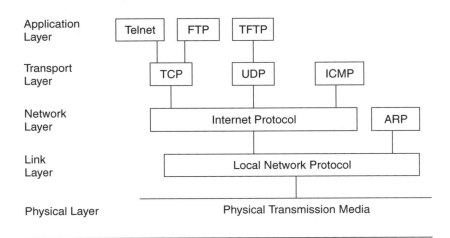

Illustration 1-1 Protocol Relationships

The Physical Layer

The best place to start a discussion of any engineered system is at the fundamental layer, the bottom. For networks, the bottom layer is the physical medium used to carry the signal from point A to point B. The following are examples of the physical network medium:

- unshielded twisted pair (UTP)
- coaxial cable
- radio frequency

In order to support the data services provided on the network, standards for the transmission media had to be created. The physical layer embodies those standards.

The Link Layer

Next up the protocol hierarchy is the local network protocol. In TCP/IP this layer is referred to as the link layer. This could be Ethernet, Token Ring, Frame Relay, PPP, or other media. It really does not matter what the lower layers are as far as the user processes are concerned. At least that was the design goal—to be independent of the underlying topology. In reality the farther you move upward, away from the local network protocol layer, the less evident it becomes what the physical network is or what it looks like. Take a look at Ethernet (Illustration 1-2), one of the most common link layer protocols. Ethernet is defined by RFC 894.

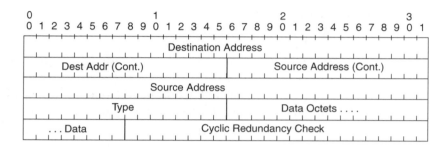

Illustration I-2 Ethernet Encapsulation (RFC 894)

Note that the Ethernet header has a destination address and a source address. The addresses at the link layer are called hardware addresses. These six octet addresses have become commonly known as MAC addresses. MAC is the abbreviation for media access control. This is somewhat of a misnomer, since MAC is concerned with specific aspects of link management on a LAN and does not directly deal with or define hardware addressing on the LAN. It got the nickname "MAC address" by being the address used at the MAC layer, a sublayer of the link layer. This being said, I will admit that I am one of those network folks who use "MAC address" and "LAN address" interchangeably to refer to the hardware address. So scold me.

The bottom line is that Ethernet, Token Ring, FDDI, Frame Relay, and most other network media interfaces have a hardware address associated with them. The exceptions to this are most point-to-point protocols, such as SLIP (Serial Line Internet Protocol) or PPP (Point to Point Protocol). There really isn't much need for hardware addresses on point-to-point protocols, since the hosts on both ends know the other's identity with absolute certainty.

Hardware addresses can be locally or globally administered. A locally administered address is one for which an administrator defines what the address is that is assigned to a hardware interface. Hardware addresses, especially LAN addresses, are rarely locally administered. Ethernet network interface cards (NICs) come preprogrammed with a hardware address that indicates the manufacturer. Table 1-1 is an excerpt from the Assigned Numbers RFC, RFC 1700. Ethernet hardware addresses are constructed with the leftmost three octets reflecting the manufacturer and the rightmost three octets reflecting a serial number assigned to the interface by the manufacturer. Ethernet hardware addresses are most often displayed as a series of 12 hexadecimal numbers, in pairs separated by hyphens, as in 08-00-03-78-9A-BC. You may occasionally see them unhyphenated. Additionally, some network analyzers, such as Network General's Sniffer, give the option of displaying them with the manufacturer's name substituted in place of the first six hexadecimal digits, such as ACC-78-9A-BC. Table 1-1 is only a partial list of all the Ethernet vendor address components.

Vendor Address	Vendor
00000C	Cisco
00000E	Fujitsu
00000F	NeXT
000010	Sytek
00001D	Cabletron
00DD00	Ungermann-Bass
00DD01	Ungermann-Bass
020701	Racal InterLan
026086	Satelcom MegaPac (UK)
02608C	3Com: IBM PC, Imagen, Valid, Cisco
02CF1F	CMC: Masscomp, Silicon Graphics, Prime EXL

080002	3Com (Formerly Bridge)
080003	ACC (Advanced Computer Communications)
080005	Symbolics: Symbolics LISP machines
080008	BBN
080009	Hewlett-Packard

Table 1-1 Excerpt of Ethernet Vendor Address Components from Assigned Numbers RFC (RFC 1700)

Looking again to the Ethernet header in Illustration 1-1, note the field denoted as "Type." That field indicates the protocol that the "Data" field will next be interpreted as. Although Ethernet types are administered by Xerox Systems Institute, Palo Alto, CA, the Assigned Numbers RFC also indicates the legal values that the Type field may have encoded in it (with the caveat that the list is contributed, unverified information from various sources). Table 1-2 is an excerpt from the Assigned Numbers RFC.

Ethernet		Exp. Ethernet		Description
Decimal	Hex	Decimal	Octal	
000	0000–05DC	—	—	IEEE802.3 Length Field
257	0101–01FF	—	—	Experimental
512	0200	512	10 00	XEROX PUP (see 0A00)
513	0201	—	—	PUP Addr Trans
1536	0600	1536	30 00	XEROX NS IDP
2048	0800	513	10 01	Internet IP (IPv4)
2049	0801	—	—	X.75 Internet

2050	0802	—	—	NBS Internet
2051	0803	—	—	ECMA Internet
2053	0805	—	—	X.25 Level 3
2054	0806	—	—	ARP
32821	8035	—	—	Reverse ARP
32923	809B	—	—	Appletalk
33079	8137–8138	—	—	Novell, Inc.

Table 1-2 Excerpt of EtherTypes from Assigned Numbers RFC (RFC 1700)

Again, this list is not complete, and the disclaimer would indicate that the Assigned Numbers RFC should not be expected to be complete. The point that I wanted to make here is that the value 0x0800 (the 0x prefix indicates that the value is in hexadecimal notation) indicates that the Ethernet frame is encapsulating an IP datagram. A value of 0x0806 indicates that the Ethernet frame is encapsulating an Address Resolution Protocol (ARP) packet. Also note that the EtherType 0x809B is used for AppleTalk and that EtherTypes 0x8137 and 0x8138 are used by Novell (0x8137 indicates a Netware Ethernet_II frame). This table illustrates that TCP/IP is only one of many protocols that can run over Ethernet. Lastly note that the values in the range 0x0000 through 0x05DC have the description "IEEE802.3 Length Field." If the value in the EtherType field falls within this range, the frame is interpreted to be an IEEE 802.3 frame, not an Ethernet frame, and the indicator of the protocol found in the frame's payload is the "Type" field in the IEEE 802.2 SNAP header. Please note that the term Ethernet is often used to refer to a CSMA/CD (carrier sense multiple access with collision detection) network running 10 Mbps over Thinnet, Thicknet, or UTP and a variety of other media. Ethernet has a specific frame type, but most people use the term in a general sense and don't differentiate between IEEE 802.3 and Ethernet frames.

I have focused mainly on Ethernet as the link layer protocol. I made a few references to other protocols, such as Token Ring, SLIP, FDDI, and Frame Relay. Don't get too caught up in the link layer, at least not in this book. If you want to examine the nuts and bolts of other media, there are plenty of good books to assist you with them. The point of this discussion is to sketch out a header that you might expect to see at the link layer. For now just accept that each link layer protocol might or might not have a hardware address associated with it. Further, if it is a general-purpose link layer protocol, that is, it does not serve only one master (protocol), it will have some mechanism, such as the EtherType field, to define what the next higher-layer protocol is that is being carried in its payload.

The communications model that we have developed to this point is fairly limited. It looks something like Illustration 1-3. A local network interface card (LNI-1a) sends a packet of data to the other local network interface card (LNI-1b), using a link layer protocol to wrap the data and deliver it with some level of certainty. It works fine if you have a single physical network and all of your devices are attached to that same physical network. Assuming that you had some sort of a directory service so that you could cross-reference a user or a service on the network to the hardware address of the network interface card, you could function quite effectively. The addition of TCP/IP as the upper-layer protocol extends this communications model to look like Illustration 1-4, which shows an application program (don't read more than that into it for now) communicating with another application program.

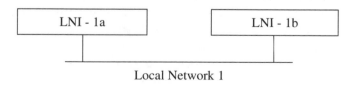

Local Network 1

Illustration I-3 Simple Communications Model

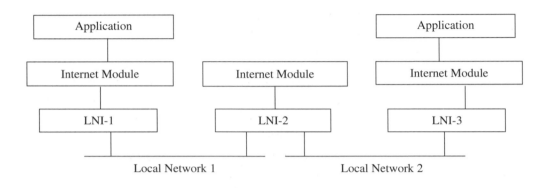

Illustration 1-4 Three-Level Communications Model

For the sake of the following walkthrough, consider that the application on the left is sending data to the application on the right. The data for the application program goes through an Internet module that encapsulates it with an Internet header. This data and its encapsulating Internet header passes through the local network interface, where it is encapsulated into a header specific to the type of network for the local network. It is then transmitted on the local network to the hardware address of the other local network interface on Local Network 1. The receiving local network interface verifies the integrity of the local network header and removes it to reveal the Internet header that is encapsulating the original application data. An examination of the Internet header reveals that the destination of the packet can be found on the other local network to which it is attached. The packet is forwarded through the local network interface (LNI-2), where it is encapsulated for transmission with a header unique to the type of Local Network 2 and sent to the local network interface denoted by the hardware address. The receiving local network interface checks the integrity of the local network header and removes the local network header to reveal an Internet header. The frame is passed up to the Internet Module, where the packet is determined to have arrived at its destination. The Internet header is removed, and the data is passed up to the application program. Transfer complete.

That was a gross simplification of the Internet Protocol. I apologize for the pain, but I wanted to make sure that you understood a few points:

- First, in the example it was not relevant as to what the local networks were. They could both have been Ethernets, or one could have been a Token Ring and the other Frame Relay; it just does not matter.

- Second, the Internet module was receiving data from an application program and passing it across multiple physical networks to another application program via a relay of Internet modules.

- Third, somehow the Internet modules knew how to pass the Internet frame so that it would reach the destination of the second application program. Hold onto those three things.

The first one deals with the issue of transparency of the underlying physical networks. I have discussed this before. I used an Ethernet frame as an example but asked that you trust me when I told you that somehow, some way, the frame would be transmitted across a network to its correct destination and there would be an indication, if necessary, of how to interpret the frame encapsulated within the link layer header. In the case of Ethernet there would be a 0x0800 in the EtherType field, which would indicate that the contents of the Ethernet frame's data field should be passed to a process that we previously identified as the Internet module. The Internet module implements the Internet Protocol (IP) and interprets and constructs IP headers.

Keep holding onto the other two concepts from my diatribe on the gross simplification of the communications model. I will get there eventually. In the meantime this should be starting to take shape for you.

The Network Layer

The local network interface verifies the integrity of the link layer header and strips it off. The bits that are left are supposed to be an IP frame, at least that is what the Type field in the link layer header indicated it was supposed to be. What is it that is left? Illustration 1-5 shows an IP header. I will briefly detail each of the fields in the header, as in Table 1-3. However, all fields that are not relevant to this book are left to you, should you feel compelled to know more than I present.

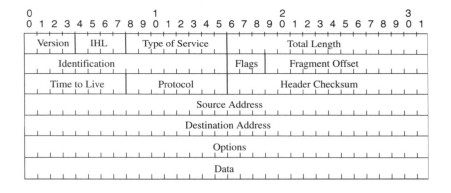

Illustration 1-5 Example of Internet Datagram Header

- *Version:* Had I written this book a few years ago, I would have told you that the value in this field will always be 4. Well, maybe not, but I certainly would not have been likely to go into much more depth than that. These first 4 bits of the IP header are used to dictate how the Internet module should parse the header. Once again referring to my copy of the Assigned Numbers RFC, I find the valid version IDs that can be found in the Version field of the IP header are those which are listed in Table 1-3. The version that you will find in use almost exclusively throughout the Internet and TCP/IP is version 4. RFC 791 defines version 4 of IP (IPv4).

Decimal	Keyword	Version
0		Reserved
1–3		Unassigned
4	IP	Internet Protocol
5	ST	ST Datagram Mode
6	SIP	Simple Internet Protocol
7	TP/IX	TP/IX: The Next Internet
8	PIP	The P Internet Protocol
9	TUBA	TUBA
10–14		Unassigned
15		Reserved

Table 1-3 Assigned Internet Version Numbers (RFC1700)

Now I am going to ask that you trust me. The Assigned Numbers RFC that I used to get the information was published in October 1994. It is the most current as of this writing however, it is still a little out of date. Versions 6 (SIP), 7 (TP/IX), 8 (PIP), and 9 (TUBA) were all subsumed or made obsolete by a new Internet Protocol, IP version 6. IPv6 is the subject of Chapter 12. You will soon be seeing much more of the Internet Protocol that has a 6 in the version field.

- *Header Length:* 4 bits used to identify where the header ends and where the data begins. The IP header is not a constant length. This is a result of the Options field, which follows the Destination Address field and precedes the Data field.

- *Type of Service:* This is actually two fields:

0	1	2	3	4	5	6	7
PRECEDENCE			D	T	R	C	0

The high-order 3 bits are the "precedence" field, and the next 4 bits are the "type of service" flags. These TOS flags can influence how routing decisions are made for the packet being examined. The flags are:

D — Delay

T — Throughput

R — Reliability

C — Cost

They are set in order to bias a potential routing decision in favor of their respective factor.

The 3 bits that represent the "precedence" field influence the treatment of the packet while it is in queue in a router. Congestion in routers results in a growth of queues and delays associated with traversing the queues. The precedence field permits the router to select certain packets for earlier transmission over other, less time-sensitive packets. The values possible are:

111 — Network control

110 — Internetwork control

101 — CRITIC/ECP

100 — Flash override

011 — Flash

010 — Immediate

001 — Priority

000 — Routine

The low-order bit (bit 7) of the "type of service" field has been reserved. That field is rarely used or implemented.

- *Total Length:* 16 bits. The total length of the IP datagram. This includes the header and the data.

- *Identification:* 16 bits. A unique number used to identify the IP datagram.

- *Flags:* 3 bits. The two low-order bits control fragmentation of an IP datagram. Bit 1 is the "don't fragment" bit. Bit 2 is the "more fragments" bit.

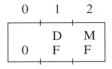

- *Fragment Offset:* 13 bits. Controls the reassembly of the IP datagram.

- *Time to Live:* 8 bits. Controls the number of hops that an IP datagram is permitted to traverse before it is purged. A datagram with a TTL of 0 must be discarded.

- *Protocol:* 8 bits. Defines the next higher protocol found in the data portion of the IP datagram. Table 1-4 is an excerpt from the Assigned Numbers RFC as an example of the values that might be found in the protocol field of an IP header. Make sure that you take a moment to locate ICMP, IGMP, TCP, and UDP in this partial list.

Decimal	Keyword	Protocol
0	Reserved	
1	ICMP	Internet Control Message
2	IGMP	Internet Group Management
3	GGP	Gateway-to-Gateway
4	IP	IP in IP (encapsulation)
5	ST	Stream
6	TCP	Transmission Control
7	UCL	UCL
8	EGP	Exterior Gateway
9	IGP	Any private interior gateway
10	BBN-RCC-MON	BBN RCC Monitoring
17	UDP	User Datagram
18	MUX	Multiplexing
27	RDP	Reliable Data
29	ISO-TP4	ISO Transport Class 4
46	RSVP	Reservation

88	IGRP	IGRP
89	OSPFIGP	OSPFIGP
101-254		Unassigned
255		Reserved

Table I-4 Sample IP Protocol Values

- *Header Checksum:* 16 bits. This is computed only on the IP header and is used as an indicator of the integrity of the IP datagram's header.

- *Source Address:* 32 bits. The IP address of the originator of the IP datagram. This will be discussed in much greater detail in Chapter 3.

- *Destination Address:* 32 bits. The IP address of the intended recipient of the IP datagram.

- *Options:* Variable length. The options that might be found include:

  security

  stream identifier (obsolete)

  source route

  record route

  timestamp

- *Data:* Variable length. The payload of the IP datagram.

The addresses in the IP header are the subject of the next chapter. For now consider a directed transfer of data from one computer to another. In this case the source address and the destination address are referred to as unicast addresses. More specifically the addresses refer to one and only one interface. The latest iteration of the communications model is redrawn in Illustration 1-6.

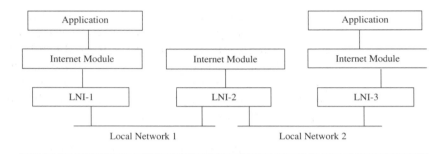

Illustration 1-6 Three-Level Communications Model

The leftmost and rightmost Internet modules interface to application programs. When this was last discussed, it was vague as to what the applications programs were or what they did. Now that the fields of the IP header have been discussed, it is possible to revise the communications model to show a bit more detail (see Illustration 1-7).

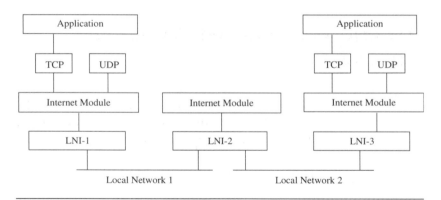

Illustration 1-7 Communications Model with Transport Layer

This revision was based on the presence of the protocol field in the IP header. I asked that you take note of the values 1, 2, 6, and 17, which indicate that the IP datagram's data field has information in it that should be interpreted as an ICMP, IGMP, TCP, or UDP frames, respectively. In the prior model the IP module was getting "application data" from a source and passing it to another vague source in another part of the network. The protocol field allows us to put names on those vague "application programs" of the prior model. The current communications model still has an "application program," but it is one layer higher than it was previously.

Note that only the leftmost and rightmost Internet modules have "TCP" and "UDP" modules connected to them. Both TCP and UDP will be discussed further, but suffice it to say now that TCP and UDP provide transport services to user applications. The Internet module, IP, provides transport services across an internetwork for specific protocol services but does not guarantee the integrity or delivery of the data. It does provide a pretty good indication that the IP header has not been corrupted. This is a function of the IP header checksum.

Reliable and Unreliable Transport Services

A transport service can be classified as reliable or unreliable. Several characteristics can be used to classify a transport service into one or the other category.

Reliable transport services typically:

- *Establish connections:* In the same manner that you would place a voice call through the "plain-old telephone service" (POTS) and establish that the person that you intended to call was on the other end before you began your conversation, a reliable transport service will establish a data connection context that the data transfer "conversation" will use for the duration of the "call." Because of this connection establishment there can be only two end points in a reliable transport service.

- *Acknowledge packets:* In a reliable transport conversation each packet that is sent must be acknowledged by the remote side. Timers are implemented that provide the sending side with an indication that an inordinate amount of time has elapsed since a packet was sent and there is a "good chance" that the packet was lost. The expiration of such a timer would trigger a retransmission of the suspected lost packet. In actuality the original packet might have been received and the acknowledgment packet gets lost.

- *Implement validation sequences:* This includes checksums, cyclic redundancy checks (CRC), and forward error correction (FEC) codes. These validation sequences have various capabilities to detect single or multiple errors or even to correct errors at the receiving end. The number of bits required, how they are implemented, where the codes are placed in the data, and the complexity of the calculation all depend on the amount of noise expected in the channel on which the data is being transmitted and the merits of not having to ask for a retransmission.

- *Implement flow control:* This is a mechanism by which a remote system can dictate the amount of data it is capable of receiving. This pacing keeps an optimal amount of data in buffers so that applications can keep a steady flow into their processes without having to wait for more data to be transmitted as a result of packet loss due to buffer overflows.

Unreliable transport services typically:

- *Do not establish connections:* Whenever a communications system uses an unreliable transport, it typically does not check to see whether the other site is available before it sends the data. The analogy of placing a phone call was used to illustrate a reliable connection-oriented service. A non-connection-oriented service can be illustrated with the postal system (nonregistered mail). A person who wishes to communicate via mail writes the letter (constructs the message), places it in an envelope, addresses it (encapsulates it in a header), affixes a stamp on it (pays the tariff), and posts it (transmits it). Then the postal system takes responsibility for the letter and makes its best effort to deliver it. The sender has no idea how long it will take to be delivered other than what past experience indicates. The sender does not know whether the addressee receives the letter or reads it. In the data communications industry a packet of data that is sent via an unreliable service is called a datagram. This is not the first time that the term has been used in this chapter. This would suggest that IP is an unreliable service, and it is. One further note: Since there is not an established connection, it is possible to send the same datagram to more than one location, as in multicasts and broadcasts.

- *Do not acknowledge packets:* A datagram "stands alone." It is sent with the understanding that the services that are charged with its delivery will attempt to deliver it, - using "best effort." The datagram may be discarded, or the destination application may not be capable of accepting it. No message will be sent to the sending application to indicate that it was received. Similarly the sending application will not start a timer whose expiration would indicate that the packet might be lost.

- *Validation sequences:* Checksums can be implemented in as little as 1 bit to indicate that the sum of all the bits in a packet is an odd value or an even value. The more bits that a checksum is implemented with the less chance that multiple errors would result in a valid checksum. With as few as 16 bits, a protocol can implement a pretty robust error detection mechanism. This is to say that for a small penalty it is prudent to implement some sort of integrity verification mechanism. Naturally it would follow that unreliable protocols are not likely to implement extremely complex algorithms for the forward correction of multiple errors.

- *Do not implement flow control:* Unreliable transport protocols typically do not have any pacing inherent in their design. If a packet is lost due to an overrun of buffers, too bad.

TCP/IP has two transport protocols. They are at extreme ends of the reliable–unreliable spectrum. The reasoning behind this is that if you want reliable communications, you can use TCP and pay the price of the overhead. All the services provided by TCP are well engineered and debugged. If you want to take your chances with an unreliable datagram service and understand the limitations, use UDP. UDP is a bare-bones transport service with little overhead. There is no "gray area" transport service that implements some feature set in between UDP and TCP. If the application requires a limited reliability feature, it must be implemented in the application itself, and UDP must be used.

Transmission Control Protocol (TCP)

The Transmission Control Protocol (TCP) is the transport protocol in the TCP/IP suite that handles reliable data transmission. The previous section discussed each of the features found in a reliable transport service, so it should be no surprise to find an implementation of some of them here. Illustration 1-8 shows the format of the TCP header.

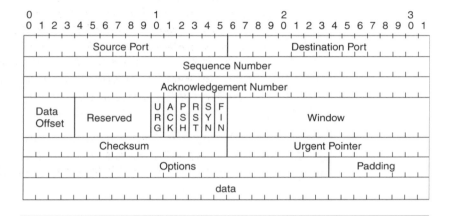

Illustration 1-8 TCP Header Format. (Note that one tick mark represents one bit position.)

The header contains, in addition to other fields, an acknowledgment, a sequence number, and a checksum that account for the acknowledged communications and validation sequence service commonly found in a reliable protocol. Not so obvious, because it is more of a procedural aspect of the protocol than a function of the header, TCP also implements connection-oriented communications and flow control. Evidence of this is the sequence number and acknowledgment number fields. Certain fields in the header are used in the procedure, such as the SYN flag, which synchronizes the communications session during connection establishment. For additional information, please refer to a specialized TCP/IP protocol text.

The point I want to make with regard to TCP is that all the fields in the header are there for the purposes of establishing the identification of the applications that are using the TCP transport services and providing reliable, connection-oriented services to those applications. Take note of the two fields *Source Port* and *Destination Port*. These fields identify the applications using the TCP service. The port fields are 16 bits in length and thus can handle a value from 0 to 65,535. The values of 0, 1023, and 1024 are reserved. The values in the range 1 to 1023 are called "well-known ports." These ports are administered by the Internet Assigned Numbers Authority (IANA), and the values of these ports, along with their use, can be found in the Assigned Numbers RFC. Table 1-5 is an excerpt of the well-known ports for TCP from the Assigned Numbers RFC.

Service	Port #	Description
tcpmux	1/tcp	TCP port service multiplexer
echo	7/tcp	Echo
systat	11/tcp	Active users
daytime	13/tcp	Daytime
qotd	17/tcp	Quote of the day
chargen	19/tcp	Character generator
ftp-data	20/tcp	File transfer [default data]
ftp	21/tcp	File transfer [control]
telnet	23/tcp	Telnet
smtp	25/tcp	Simple mail transfer
time	37/tcp	Time
nameserver	42/tcp	Host name server
nicname	43/tcp	Who is

Table 1-5 Selected TCP Ports

Telnetd is a daemon (a process) that acts as a server (in a client-server model) providing a simple remote terminal connection to the TCP/IP host that it is running on. Telnetd typically listens on the well-known port (23) for a connection request, although it is possible to configure it to listen on another port. If it is configured to listen on a port other than port 23, the user would have to know in advance what port the client should attempt a connection on. The standard port is 23; hence it is the well-known port. If the client is not instructed to attempt a connection on a specific port, it will attempt the connection on port 23, the default.

Ports in the range 1024 through 5000 are special-purpose ports known as "ephemeral ports." They are known as such because of their typically short usage. Ephemeral ports are the ones that the client uses when it initiates a connection with a server. Their "lives" span only the time during which the connection is made with the server. When the conversation ends and the service is no longer needed, the ports are released to an available pool.

Ports above 5000 are available for any use. Typically a user would make a specialized TCP/IP service available through one of these ports. For instance, if I had a piece of software that I wanted to make available for download but did not want to do it through the normal "anonymous" FTP site at my company, I could set up an FTPD daemon to listen to port 17000, and I would make the portion of the file system where the software resided accessible to that daemon. I would instruct the users to FTP to port 17000 in order to get my software. It does not have to be a common service that I make available through one of these ports it could be a home-grown service that does not warrant petitioning the IANA for a port allocation.

User Datagram Protocol (UDP)

The User Datagram Protocol (UDP) is the transport service that TCP/IP provides for connectionless, unreliable service. Illustration 1-9 shows the UDP header format.

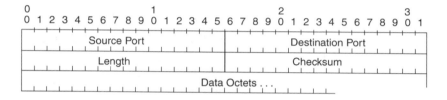

Illustration 1-9 User Datagram Header Format

No doubt you will note the significant lack of complexity in the UDP header as compared to the TCP header. Source Port and Destination Port serve the same functions as the ones in TCP, although they are different from those of TCP. True, some functions are provided in both TCP and UDP, and they have the same number. An example of this is the chargen service, which is available through both UDP and TCP on port 19. Table 1-6 is an excerpt from the Assigned Numbers RFC for the UDP well-known ports.

Service	Port #	Description
tcpmux	1/udp	TCP port service multiplexer
echo	7/udp	Echo
systat	11/udp	Active
daytime	13/udp	Daytime
qotd	17/udp	Quote of the day

chargen	19/udp	Character generator
smtp	25/udp	Simple mail transfer
bootps	67/udp	Bootstrap protocol server
bootpc	68/udp	Bootstrap protocol client
tftp	69/udp	Trivial file transfer
finger	79/udp	Finger
www-http	80/udp	World Wide Web HTTP
nntp	119/udp	Network News Transfer Protocol
snmp	161/udp	SNMP
snmptrap	162/udp	SNMPTRAP
bgp	179/udp	Border Gateway Protocol
ipx	213/udp	IPX
biff	512/udp	Used by mail system to notify users
who	513/udp	Maintains databases showing who's who
uucp	540/udp	UUCPD

Table 1-6 Selected UDP well-known Ports (RFC1700)

TCP/IP Connections

The communications model can now be revised one last time (Illustration 1-10). This model again replaces the vague "application program" with a specific example illustrating the source and destination of data. Now, just as an exercise, let's look at what it took to get to this point. Let's start with a user on the left side who wants to get a file off the host system on the right side. The user reviews the choices for getting the file and narrows the options down to two file transfer programs, FTP and TFTP. The File Transfer Protocol, FTP, is implemented to use TCP services that provide for a reliable, connection-oriented transfer. Trivial File Transfer Protocol, TFTP, uses services from UDP, the connectionless, unreliable service. Sounds scary to rely on UDP for a file transfer, but it really is not that bad, since some reliability features have been included in the TFTP application that were absent from its underlying transport mechanism. Our user chooses the reliable FTP. The user specifies the remote host's IP address to the FTP client application, which, through TCP and IP, crosses the Internet to the IP module on the rightmost side of the diagram. This IP module examines the IP header's protocol field and determines that the data contained in the datagram's data fields is a TCP segment. After a few checks, the header is stripped away and the data passed to the TCP process. The TCP process looks at the destination port, among a few other things, and sees that the data in the TCP segment should be passed in entirety to port 21. There is a process listening to port 21. In this case the process is FTPD, the File Transfer Protocol Daemon (server). Fortunately even though the headers were stripped off along the way, the source port and source IP address were passed along with the data to the FTPD daemon. Now the FTPD daemon knows how to return any data that the client on the far end of the connection requires.

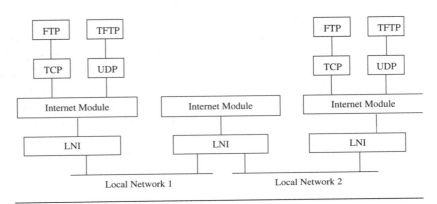

Illustration 1-10 Complete TCP/IP Communications Model

I glossed over some processes that are essential to the entire communications session. This was intentional. Throughout this chapter the discussion has moved from the physical network and the associated link layer protocols all the way up to the TCP/IP applications such as FTP, TFTP, and Telnet. These applications do not require the knowledge of the lower-layer details. All that is required in order for an application to communicate with another application across a TCP/IP internetwork is what is referred to as an *association*. Associations are of the form

{protocol, source IP address, source port, destination IP address, destination port}

This association uniquely identifies a connection throughout an entire internetwork. Half of the association, the IP address and port combination, is often referred to as a *socket*. A socket reference without an indication of protocol is not useful, because it is not unique. It is useful to be able to refer to the UDP socket of {destination IP address, destination port} to uniquely identify half of a TCP/IP conversation.

Summary

TCP/IP is a protocol suite that is implemented in layers. The following layers are found in the protocol architecture:

- application
- transport
- network
- link
- physical

The link layer is used to transport data between interfaces on the same network medium. Link layer protocols implement device driver functions and typically have knowledge only of devices that are physically attached to the medium and refer to them by their respective hardware addresses. Examples of link layer protocols include Ethernet, IEEE 802.5 Token Ring, Frame Relay, and PPP.

The network layer is responsible for the routing and relaying of datagrams in the internetwork. Examples of protocols at the network layer include the Internet Protocol (IP), ICMP, and IGMP. ICMP and IGMP rely on transport services provided by IP, but they cannot be logically removed from the network layer, because of the functions they provide.

The transport layer protocols provide end-to-end data delivery services to user applications. TCP, the Transmission Control Protocol, provides a reliable, connection-oriented transport service. UDP, the User Datagram Protocol, provides a bare-bones connectionless, unreliable transport service.

The application layer protocols provide functions for remote terminal login, file transfers, network management, mail transfer, file system sharing, and information retrieval. In general the applications provide the general utility to the network.

In a TCP/IP environment the application needs to know very little about the physical or logical architecture of the network. The architecture is transparent to the user processes. In many cases the user is required to know only the IP address of the remote system where the desired service is resident.

Two points are important to understand after reading this chapter. First, starting at the link layer protocols, it is possible to look at a certain field in each layer's encapsulating header to determine how to interpret the data portion of that layer. The reverse encapsulation process is often referred to with the analogy of "peeling away an onion." Second, a TCP/IP connection requires five pieces of information in order to be fully described. These pieces are the protocol, the source IP address, the source port, the destination IP address, and the destination port. Together these are known as an "association."

IP Address Fundamentals

In the prior chapter I presented an overview of the TCP/IP communication protocols in order to show how the protocols work together to provide a transport service to the user processes, or application layer. When I got to the point where I was supposed to cover the IP address in the discussion of the network layer, I pushed the details off to Chapter 2.

The Internet protocols have become widely known as TCP/IP. TCP/IP has become the moniker for the entire suite of protocols including, but not limited to, the Transmission Control Protocol, User Datagram Protocol, Internet Control Message Protocol, Address Resolution Protocol, and Internet Protocol. The addresses associated with these protocols have become commonly known as TCP/IP addresses. This, however, is not altogether accurate. These addresses apply only to the Internet Protocol, or IP, as it is most commonly referred to. When I say "IP address" throughout this text, I am referring to an address of the format defined and used in the Internet Protocol version 4.

On Names, Addresses, and Routes

I have not seen a coverage of IP addressing yet that does not lead with a summary of a paper published in the *Proceedings of COMPCON*, Fall 1978, by John Shoch. Far be it for me to break with tradition. This paper was titled "Internetwork Naming, Addressing, and Routing" and delineated the difference among a name, an address, and a route. Although it might seem intuitive to many of us at the present, the distinction, as Shoch pointed out, is that a name is an identifier for an object, an address is where the object can be found, and a route is the path taken to get to the address. In those days of dealing with PUP (PARC Universal Protocol) it was not altogether clear what the distinctions were until Shoch clarified the terms.

Radia Perlman in her book *Interconnections* provides a more in-depth perspective on the terms:

- *Name:* A name is location independent, with respect to both the source and the destination. If something is the name of a destination, it will remain unchanged even if the destination moves, and it is valid regardless of which source is attempting to reach the destination. An example of a name is a Social Security number, which remains unchanged even if the number's owner moves. Sometimes fields that are names are referred to as *identifiers* or *IDs*.

- *Address:* An address is valid regardless of the location of the source station, but the addresses may change if the destination moves. An example of an address is a postal address. The same destination postal address works regardless of the location from which a letter is mailed. However, if the destination moves, it is assigned a new address.

- *Route:* A route is dependent on the location of both the source and the destination. In other words, if two sources specify a route to a given destination, the routes are likely to differ. And if the destination moves, all routes to it are likely to change. An example of a route is, "To get to my house, go west 3 miles and take a right turn at the first light. It's the last house on the left."

Given that she says a "route is dependent on the location of both the source and the destination," it would seem that the example she provides would be more technically accurate to start with "To get to my house *from your house*, go west 3 miles . . .." The point is that a route is not valid without a starting point of reference, even if it is implied or relative to your current position.

With regard to these terms, there is very little confusion over what a route is. There are numerous examples in the industry of places where the term "address" is used and the term "name" should have been. It will be seen, by the end of the chapter, that an IP address is really both a name and an address at the same time.

The IP Address

Recall from the previous chapter that the IP header has a format as shown in Illustration 2-1. We categorically call IP addresses the two fields named Source Address and Destination Address. The IP address is 32 bits in length. Although there are some special-case uses for this address, it is most generally used to simultaneously identify both the network to which a host is attached and the interface that connects the network and the host together.

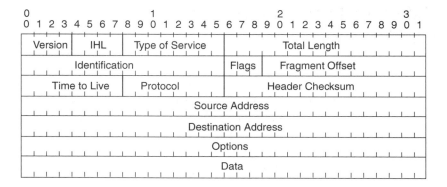

Illustration 2-1 Example of Internet Datagram Header

The address is able to identify the network and the interface through a division of the 32 available bits into two logical fields called the "network portion" and the "host portion." The host portion is also commonly referred to as the local address part of the address. The network portion can have as few as 8 bits and as many as 30 bits allocated to it. The host portion has whatever bits the network portion is not utilizing; therefore it can have as many as 24 bits and as few as 2 bits allocated to it. The allocation of bits between these two portions is facilitated by the use of two devices. The first is a prefix code that enables a host or a user to look only at the first few bits of an IP address to determine the classification of the IP address. The class of an IP address dictates the minimum number of bits allocated to the network portion. The second device used to determine a further split is called a network mask.

Address Terminology, Notation, and Numbering

Before going into the details of IP addressing, it is important to get introduced to the terminology that will be used throughout this book. You should become familiar with the following terms:

- *Bit* (binary digit): The smallest addressable unit of data on a computer. A bit has one of two possible states, often represented as a 1 and 0.

- *Byte:* Usually a unit of data that is 8 bits in length. In the past a byte was a unit of data in which a computer word could be divided. This definition resulted in bytes being other than 8 bits in length. I worked with a computer system in the mid 1970s that used an 18-bit computer word, the character set (XS-3) it used had bytes that were 6 bits in length.

- *Octet:* A unit of data that is *always* 8 bits in length. The 32-bit IP address is frequently referred to as 4 octets in length.

- *All ones:* "all 1s." The condition when the data unit, IP address, or address portion being referenced is filled entirely with bits with a value of 1.

- *All zeros:* "all 0s." The condition when the data unit, IP address, or address portion being referenced is filled entirely with bits with a value of 0.

- *High order:* This term is synonymous with "most significant," but throughout this text if it helps to remember that "high order" is the same as "leftmost," go with it.

- *Low order:* Same as "least significant." Rightmost.

- *Most significant:* Technically the bit or octet in a data unit that, if you were to take away or change the value from a 1 to a 0 (or all 1s to all 0s), would have the greatest impact on the data unit's value. This is best shown with an example. Assume an octet that has a value of "all 1s" as shown:

| 1 1 1 1 1 1 1 1 | This octet has a decimal value of 255.

Now change the rightmost bit to a 0:

| 1 1 1 1 1 1 1 0 | This octet has a decimal value of 254.

Now look at the original octet with the leftmost bit altered to be a 0:

| 0 1 1 1 1 1 1 1 | This octet has a decimal value of 127.

It is clear to see that changing the leftmost bit had the greatest impact on the value of the octet. The leftmost bit is the most significant bit in an octet. Similarly the leftmost octet is the most significant octet in an IP address:

| 1 1 1 1 1 1 1 1 1 1 1 1 1 1 1 1 1 1 1 1 1 1 1 1 1 1 1 1 1 1 1 1 |

(Value: 4,294,967,295)

Voiding the rightmost octet:

| 1 1 1 1 1 1 1 1 1 1 1 1 1 1 1 1 1 1 1 1 1 1 1 1 0 0 0 0 0 0 0 0 |

(Value: 4,294,967,040)

Voiding the leftmost octet:

00000000111111111111111111111111

(Value: 16,777,215)

- *Least significant:* The bit or octet that, if changed from a value of 1 (or all 1s) to a 0 (or all 0s), would have the least impact on the value of the entire data unit. In IP the rightmost bits are the least significant bits.

- *Dotted decimal notation:* The most common representation of a TCP/IP address. Take the 32-bit IP address and divide it into 4 octets. Convert each octet from binary into decimal. Put a "." (dot) between each of the 4 decimal numbers. Even though the numbers are now in decimal, each number is still referred to as an octet, since its value must be in the valid range of an 8-bit number (0 to 255). An example of this follows:

00001010000000011001110001011011

(Decimal Value: 167,877,723)

00001010 00000001 10011100 01011011

The first octet, the high-order octet, converts to 10.

The second octet converts to 1.

The third octet converts to 156.

The fourth octet, the low-order octet, converts to 91.

The dotted decimal notation for the IP address in this example is:

10.1.156.91

- *Hexadecimal notation:* Although much less common than dotted decimal, this notation still abounds. Start the same way as you would converting from a 32-bit IP address. Divide it into 4 octets and then divide each octet in half again such that you have eight 4-bit groups. Convert each group of 4 bits into their hexadecimal equivalents. Concatenate the resulting hexadecimal digits. It is common to prepend a hexadecimal number with "0x" to indicate that it is a base-16 (hexadecimal) number. For instance:

1 0 1 0 1 1 0 0 0 0 0 1 0 0 0 0 1 0 1 1 0 1 1 0 0 0 0 1 0 0 1 1

(Decimal Value: 2,886,776,339)

10101100	00010000	10110110	00010011
1010 1100	0001 0000	1011 0110	0001 0011
A C	1 0	B 6	1 3

The hexadecimal notation for the IP address in this example is:

0xAC10B613 (sometimes written as AC.10.B6.13)

Determining the Class of an IP Address

Every IP address, with the exception of a handful of special-purpose addresses, has a classification associated with it. To determine the class of an IP address, examine the four high-order bits of the address. Remember, these are the leftmost bits, also known as the four most significant bits of the IP address. Use the flowchart in Illustration 2-1 to determine the class.

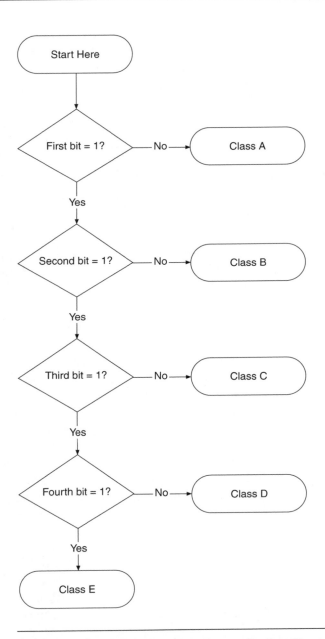

Illustration 2-2 IP Address Class Determination Chart

As previously discussed, the class of an IP address is one mechanism that is used to determine the split between the number of bits used for the network portion and the host portion of an IP address. The following sections discuss each of the IP address classes and the network/host split that each classification implies.

Class A

A Class A IP address has a 0 in the most significant bit position. If the high-order octet of the IP address has a 0 for its most significant bit, it is a Class A IP address no matter what the value of any other octet in the address is. This could be represented graphically as:

```
0 x x x x x x x x x x x x x x x x x x x x x x x x x x x x x x x
```

where x = "don't care."

If all the bits marked as "don't care" were set to 0 and the IP address were converted to dotted decimal notation, the IP address would be 0.0.0.0. If all the bits marked as "don't care" were set to 1 and converted to dotted decimal notation, the IP address would be 127.255.255.255. Without applying any special rules (which we eventually will), it can be seen that Class A IP addresses will invariably fall in the range 0.0.0.0 to 127.255.255.255, inclusive.

You were forewarned that the class of an IP address dictates a minimum number of bits allocated to the network portion. In fact a Class A IP address reserves the entire first octet for use as the network portion. Since any bits not used explicitly for the network portion are used for the host portion of the IP address, the three low-order octets of a Class A IP address are available as host addresses.

```
|<-Network->|<——————————— Host ———————————>|
| 0 x x x x x x x x x x x x x x x x x x x x x x x x x x x x x x x |
```

The implication is that there are 128 Class A networks (0 to 127). Each Class A network can have 16,777,216 (2^{24}) unique host identifiers! There will be special cases that restrict the total number of networks and hosts that are available. These will be discussed later; however, the objective for now is to form the foundation of understanding on which IP addresses are derived.

Class B

A Class B IP address has a "10" in the two most significant bit positions. This could be represented graphically as:

```
| 1 0 x x x x x x x x x x x x x x x x x x x x x x x x x x x x x x |
```

where x = "don't care."

If all the bits marked as "don't care" were set to 0 and the IP address were converted to dotted decimal notation, the IP address would be 128.0.0.0. If all the bits marked as "don't care" were set to 1 and converted to dotted decimal notation, the IP address would be 191.255.255.255. It can be seen that Class B IP addresses will fall in the range 128.0.0.0 to 191.255.255.255, inclusive.

A Class B IP address reserves the entire two high-order octets for use as the network portion. Since any bits not used explicitly for the network portion are used for the host portion of the IP address, the two low-order octets of a Class B IP address are available as host addresses.

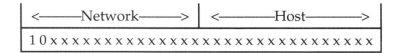

As a result, there are 16,384 Class B networks (128.0 to 191.255). Each Class B network can have a possible 65,536 (2^{16}) unique host identifiers, assuming that we are not applying any special rules yet.

Class C

A Class C IP address has a "110" in the three most significant bit positions. This could be represented graphically as:

```
1 1 0 x x x x x x x x x x x x x x x x x x x x x x x x x x x x x x
```

where x = "don't care."

If all the bits marked as "don't care" were set to 0 and the IP address were converted to dotted decimal notation, the IP address would be 192.0.0.0. If all the bits marked as "don't care" were set to 1 and converted to dotted decimal notation, the IP address would be 223.255.255.255. It can be seen that Class C IP addresses will fall in the range 192.0.0.0 to 223.255.255.255, inclusive.

A Class C IP address reserves the entire three high-order octets for use as the network portion. Since any bits not used explicitly for the network portion are used for the host portion of the IP address, only the low order octet of a Class C IP address is available as host addresses.

As a result, there are 2,097,152 Class C networks (192.0.0 to 223.255.255)! Each Class C network can have a possible 256 (2^8) unique host identifiers, assuming that we are not applying any special rules.

Class D

A Class D IP address has a "1110" in the four most significant bit positions. This could be represented graphically as:

```
1 1 1 0 x x x x x x x x x x x x x x x x x x x x x x x x x x x x x x
```

where x = "don't care."

If all the bits marked as "don't care" were set to 0 and the IP address were converted to dotted decimal notation, the IP address would be 224.0.0.0. If all the bits marked as "don't care" were set to 1 and converted to dotted decimal notation, the IP address would be 239.255.255.255. It can be seen that Class D IP addresses will fall in the range 224.0.0.0 to 239.255.255.255, inclusive.

Class D IP differ from Classes A, B, and C IP addresses. Class D addresses are reserved for multicast group usage. There is no relevance to network and host portions in multicast operations. Multicast will be discussed in more detail in a later chapter. For now let's simply state that one or more hosts can belong to a group, by assignment or by joining, and share data with all members of that group through the use of a single Class D IP address. There is a potential for having 268,435,456 unique multicast groups!

Class E

A Class E IP address has a "1111" in the four most significant bit positions. This could be represented graphically as:

```
1 1 1 1 x x x x x x x x x x x x x x x x x x x x x x x x x x x x x x
```

where x = "don't care."

If all the bits marked as "don't care" were set to 0 and the IP address were converted to dotted decimal notation, the IP address would be 240.0.0.0. If all the bits marked as "don't care" were set to 1 and converted to dotted decimal notation, the IP address would be 255.255.255.255. It can be seen that Class E IP addresses will fall in the range 240.0.0.0 to 255.255.255.255, inclusive.

Class E IP addresses are not available for general use. They have been reserved for future use.

Unicast Addresses

Classes A, B, and C, as defined previously, are used for unicast addresses. A unicast address is one that refers to a single source or destination. This is not to say that all destination addresses that you might find in an IP datagram are unicast addresses if they qualify as Class A, B, or C through examination of the first

3 bits. There are special-case addresses, as we will see, that would qualify as a Class A, B, or C address under the strict rules cited earlier; however, they would not be unicast addresses.

Subnetting

If there were no mechanism for being able to divide the IP address into network and host portions and there were not a separate and distinct field in the IP header for the two functions, the address architecture would be flat; there would be no means by which an administrator could develop a hierarchical network. In fact, this would be almost no different from the architecture that we would have at the link layer (hardware addresses), with the exception that we would be putting an additional layer of complexity into the protocol for the purpose of hiding the hardware implementations.

Luckily this is not the case; the three unicast classes of IP addresses provide some capability to develop hierarchical networks. We will see what is meant by a hierarchical topology in subsequent chapters. Unfortunately the granularity of network-to-host divisions is not conducive to efficient use of IP address space. That is, relying solely on the class of the IP address to define the network portion would lead to a tremendous waste. Take, for example, a fictitious midsized company with 400 computers (TCP/IP hosts) total. Three hundred of the hosts are at the company's central headquarters, and there are two satellite plants with 50 hosts apiece. Since we have determined to this point that a Class C network can have a possible 256 unique host numbers and this company's central site has 300 hosts, we have two options. We can use two Class C networks at the central site and deal with the technical problems of having two separate logical networks on the same physical network, or we can use a single Class B network for the central site. The Class B option was chosen by the network administrator because it would require less work to setup and maintain. The two remote sites are well served by having their own Class C network.

In this example a Class B and two Class C networks were used to internetwork three sites with a total of 400 sites among them.

	Available Space	Used Space
Class B	65,536 hosts	300 hosts
Class C	256 hosts	50 hosts
Class C	256 hosts	50 hosts
Total	66,048 hosts	400 hosts

Here is the math:

Utilization (%) = (used space/available space) × 100

Utilization (%) = (400 hosts/66,048 hosts) × 100 = .6%

Naturally I had the ability to define the numbers to suit my purpose. Six-tenths of a percent utilization of the available address space does seem like an awful waste. Even if the poor utilization is acceptable, the use of a Class B and two Class C networks would exaggerate the routing tables of the Internet if they were connected. The point, however contrived, is that without some other device to enable us to optimize the use of the available host portion, the IP address would be entirely too inefficient to be effective, and routing tables would become too large and cumbersome. That mechanism was formalized in 1985 by J. Mogul and J. Postel in RFC 950, "Internet Standard Subnetting Procedure."

This RFC discussed the potential difficulties that might be encountered when implementing a third level of hierarchy, subnets, and further defines the "strongly recommended" method for subnetting. There are several factors even beyond those of inefficiency and routing table growth that would motivate an organization to implement IP subnets. RFC 950 discusses these factors:

- Different technologies: Especially in a research environment, there may be more than one kind of LAN in use; e.g., an organization may have some equipment that supports Ethernet, and some that supports a ring network.

- Limits of technologies: Most LAN technologies impose limits, based on electrical parameters, on the number of hosts connected, and on the total length of the cable. It is easy to exceed these limits, especially those on cable length.

- Network congestion: It is possible for a small subset of the hosts on a LAN to monopolize most of the bandwidth. A common solution to this problem is to divide the hosts into cliques of high mutual communication, and put these cliques on separate cables.

- Point-to-Point links: Sometimes a "local area," such as a university campus, is split into two locations too far apart to connect using the preferred LAN technology. In this case, high-speed point-to-point links might connect several LANs.

Point-to-point links have traditionally been one of the most wasteful uses for IP addressing. With a point-to-point link there are exactly two hosts participating on the network. Even with the most restrictive subnet mask, there is 50 percent waste of address space on this type of network. This will be explained in detail later. Some fairly recent developments have enabled the use of "unnumbered IP interfaces" on point-to-point networks. This also will be explained in detail later.

The addition of another level of hierarchy to a network address, beyond the inherent class of the network, permits network administrators to more effectively utilize their address space. This additional structure is known as a subnet. A single IP network, such as the Class A network 10.0.0.0, can be chopped up into smaller networks through the use of a subnet mask that delineates the structure of the subnet addressing used within the control of the local network administrator.

Subnet Masks

IP subnets are implemented by borrowing a portion of the local part of the IP address and extending the concepts used in defining the network portion. This is done with a mask. Masks were in use in other areas long before they were applied to data communications. Photographers use masks in their darkroom laboratory work. Whenever photographers have an image that is especially well suited for their needs but the background is inappropriate, they use a mask to isolate the subject they want to keep from the rest of the picture. For instance, Illustration 2-3 is a photo of a little girl. A photographer would create a mask that would be placed between the negative and the photographic paper on the enlarger. The mask is opaque where the image's background should be filtered out and transparent where the foreground, the little girl, is allowed to pass through to the photographic paper. A mask for our example would look like Illustration 2-4. The result is an image of the little girl with the background removed. She has been effectively isolated from the other parts of the original photograph (Illustration 2-5).

Illustration 2-3 Original Photograph

Illustration 2-4 Image Mask

Illustration 2-5 Resulting Masked Photograph

Subnet masks work in essentially the same way. Let's start with the IP address 172.16.182.19:

1 0 1 0 1 1 0 0   0 0 0 1 0 0 0 0   1 0 1 1 0 1 1 0   0 0 0 1 0 0 1 1

Original IP Address

We can create a mask the same length as the address itself:

1 1 1 1 1 1 1 1   1 1 1 1 1 1 1 1   1 1 1 1 1 1 1 1   0 0 0 0 0 0 0 0

Network Mask

Wherever there is a 1 in the network mask, the original IP address can "project" through. Wherever there is a 0 in the network mask, the original IP address is "filtered out." The resulting masked address is:

1 0 1 0 1 1 0 0   0 0 0 1 0 0 0 0   1 0 1 1 0 1 1 0   0 0 0 0 0 0 0 0

Resulting Masked Address

Mask Mathematics

Now that the concept has been illustrated, let's dispose of the photographic analogy and look at it mathematically. Boolean algebra is the mathematical study of logic. It deals with "proofs" through the application of logic—algebraic operations on the values "true" and "false." The same mathematical principles used in Boolean algebra can be applied to binary numbers. In fact, these binary operations are the basis for all mathematics implemented in digital computing devices. Although that is way beyond the scope of this book, we should discuss a few operations to fully understand how masks are implemented.

The AND operator results in a TRUE if and only if the two operands (variables) are both TRUE. The following statements are correct:

TRUE	AND	TRUE	=	TRUE
TRUE	AND	FALSE	=	FALSE
FALSE	AND	TRUE	=	FALSE
FALSE	AND	FALSE	=	FALSE

Assuming that a binary 1 is TRUE and a binary 0 is FALSE, the table would look like:

1	AND	1	=	1
1	AND	0	=	0
0	AND	1	=	0
0	AND	0	=	0

This can be represented with the following logic tables:

AND	TRUE	FALSE
TRUE	TRUE	FALSE
FALSE	FALSE	FALSE

OR

AND	1	0
1	1	0
0	0	0

The NOT operator is a unary operator. This means that it has only a single operand. The NOT operator always results in the logical opposite of the operand. The following statements are correct:

NOT   TRUE   =   FALSE

NOT   FALSE   =   TRUE

Assuming that a binary 1 is TRUE and a binary 0 is FALSE, the table would look like:

NOT   1   =   0

NOT   0   =   1

This can be represented with the following logic tables:

NOT	
TRUE	FALSE
FALSE	TRUE

OR

NOT	
1	0
0	1

Those are the only two logical operators that you need to be acquainted with in order to understand the mask operation. The following is a piece of "metacode" that implements the mask operation:

For $n = 0$ to 31,

$$N_n = A_n \text{ AND } M_n$$
$$H_n = A_n \text{ AND (NOT } M_n)$$
next n

where
N_n is the n bit of the network identifier (network portion) after masking
H_n is the n bit of the host identifier (host portion) after masking
A_n is the n bit of the IP address before masking
M_n is the n bit of the network mask

Although the process is not normally performed in a loop, I have chosen to use a loop for ease of explanation. The metacode is explained as follows. A loop is executed 32 (0 to 31, inclusive) times, with the variable n being incremented at the completion of each iteration. The loop is executed 32 times, due to the number of bits in the IP address. The variable n is representative of the bit position:

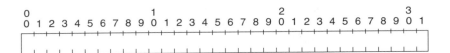

Each iteration of the loop sets a bit in both the network ID and the host ID. The network ID bit is set by performing a logical AND operation on the address bit (same position) and the mask bit. The host ID is a little more complicated. The mask bit must be inverted, since we are now interested in letting the host portion through and filtering out the network portion. To invert the bit, the NOT operation is performed on the mask bit. Then an AND operation is performed on the result of the NOT operation and the address bit. The result is the host ID bit for that iteration of the loop. At the completion of 32 iterations of the loop, both the network ID and the host ID are completely constructed.

Contiguous Mask Bits

RFC 950 specified that since subnets were described through the use of a mask, there was nothing to prevent anybody from setting up a specialized subnet procedure, such as the use of the low-order bits in the local portion of the address or every other bit of the local portion. It was recommended that the subnet mask be derived from the high-order bits of the local portion and that the bits be contiguous, but still it was only a recommendation.

Even though masks constructed from noncontiguous and non-high-order bits were allowed, I don't know of any hardware vendor that permitted its use. This is not because none of them allowed such a configuration—I am sure that some did—I just don't know who they are. It was common practice to subnet using the high-order bits of the host portion of the address. Subnetting in a manner other than that was foolish, and no serious networking professional that I know of would consider it. A more pragmatic reason for not doing it is that some vendors do not permit anything but contiguous, high-order bits in the subnet mask. I know of more than a few vendors that have this restriction. I used to hold it against them that they should be so brazen as to neglect the possibility of noncontiguous bits. Someplace along the way, I got a bit wiser and took the attitude of "so what? Why should they cater to the absurd?" I would be happy to rescind those thoughts if someone would give me a strong illustration of why anything other than contiguous, high-order subnet masks must be permitted.

Things have been revised with respect to this, anyway. It is now a requirement that if you are going to use subnets, the mask should be contiguous and occupy the high-order bits of the local address portion.

Subnet Terminology

There are some specific ways to refer to addresses and masks in use throughout the industry. Some are defined in RFCs, and others have become *de facto* standard terms. This section introduces you to some of what is used in the industry and in this text.

- Class A Mask—255.0.0.0: The mask that would be used to describe a Class A address without subnetting.

- Class B Mask—255.255.0.0.

- Class C Mask—255.255.255.0.

- *N*-bit network mask: The high-order *n* bits of the mask are set to 1. For instance, using a "24-bit network mask" means that the mask is 255.255.255.0.

- *N*-bit subnet mask: The mask uses the high-order *n* bits of the local address portion. You must know the class of the IP network in order for this statement to be meaningful: "I use a 10-bit subnet mask." Consider the following examples:

10.1.1.254 with a 16-bit subnet mask	Mask = 255.255.255.0
172.16.182.19 with a 10-bit subnet mask	Mask = 255.255.255.192
Class C with a 6-bit subnet mask	Mask = 255.255.255.252

- *N*-host bits: Only the low-order n bits are not used for the mask. For instance, someone who has 4 host bits is using a mask of 255.255.255.240.

- /N: A written notation with the same meaning as "*n*-bit network mask." For instance, the notation 172.18.250.3/24 means that the mask is 255.255.255.0.

- Network mask: All the bits used for masking the IP address.

- Subnet mask: Only the mask bits below the natural network mask. For instance, if I had a Class B address and a network mask of 255.255.255.192, the subnet mask would be the low-order 10-bits of the network mask, or 0.0.255.192.

- Natural, or inherent network, mask: The mask that would be used to describe an address without subnetting. The mask that is defined by the class of the address.

- Network ID: The result of an AND operation of the network mask with an IP address.

- Subnet ID: The result of an AND operation of the subnet mask with an IP address.

- Host ID: The result of a NOT operation of the network mask, then an AND operation of the prior result with an IP address. Please see the section "Mask Mathematics" and avoid this awkward explanation.

There are many ways to refer to subnets. The most accurate way is to specify how many bits are in the network mask. Many people use the "*n*-bit subnet mask" terminology, but this is falling out of favor. The force behind this change is CIDR (classless interdomain routing), which is a short-term strategy for the depletion of Internet address space. CIDR is discussed in Chapter 7.

Regardless of what the complete mask might be, a single octet within the mask might have from 0 to 8-bits used for a part of that entire mask. Table 2-1 should help you get acquainted with the octet numbering for cases in which only part of the octet is used for mask bits. Remember, only the high-order bits of the octet will be used for the mask.

Graphical Depiction	Number of Bits in Octet	Decimal Value
0 0 0 0 0 0 0 0	0	0
1 0 0 0 0 0 0 0	1	128
1 1 0 0 0 0 0 0	2	192
1 1 1 0 0 0 0 0	3	224
1 1 1 1 0 0 0 0	4	240
1 1 1 1 1 0 0 0	5	248
1 1 1 1 1 1 0 0	6	252
1 1 1 1 1 1 1 0	7	254
1 1 1 1 1 1 1 1	8	255

Table 2-1 Octet Numbering when Portion Used for Mask Bits

Special-Case Addresses

The previous discussions of individual classes of addresses commonly had some sort of disclaimer, such as "This is assuming that we are not applying any special rules yet that might restrict the total." I had to make a decision when I set out to write this book. I could be like all the rest of the people and tell you the final result—to jump to the bottom line—or I could show you. I chose to show you. The result of showing is that there are some intermediate steps where there are inaccuracies. When I said that a Class C address had address space to support 256 unique hosts, that was correct because an 8-bit number can have 256 unique values, and that particular 8-bit number is used for host IDs. It was also incorrect, due to some special cases that cannot be counted as available host IDs. I am now going to make it correct.

A 0 in any of the fields means that the field contains all 0 bits. A −1 in any field means that the field contains all 1 bits. The general meaning of all 1s is "all" and is used in broadcasts. Any IP address that has a field of all 1s can be used legally only as a destination IP address. The general meaning of all 0s is "this" and is often used when a host is uncertain of its IP address and needs to be informed of all or part of it. An IP address that has a field of all 0s can be used legally only as a source IP address.

The following are special-case IP addresses:

- {Network ID = 0, Host ID = 0} This host on this network. In the BOOTP process a host that does not yet know its IP address will send out a BOOTP request and use an IP address of all 0s for its source.

- {Network ID = 0, <Host-number>} Specified host on this network. Can be used only as a source address. Potentially used in the BOOTP process.

- {Network ID = –1, Host ID = –1} Limited broadcast. Can be used only as a destination address. The IP datagram that has a destination IP address of all 1s is sent as a broadcast to all hosts on the same physical medium as the originator of the limited broadcast datagram. The packet should not be forwarded by any host.

- {<Network-number>, Host ID = –1} Directed broadcast to specified network. Also used only as a destination address. The datagram that has this as a destination address should be forwarded to the specified network number and then broadcast to all hosts on that network.

- {<Network-number>, <Subnet-number>, Host ID = –1} Directed broadcast to specified subnet. Can be used only as a destination address. The datagram that has this as a destination address should be forwarded to the specified subnet and then broadcast to each host on that subnet.

- {<Network-number>, Subnet ID = –1, Host ID = –1} Directed broadcast to all subnets of a specified subnetted network. Can be used only as a destination address. The intent was to provide a mechanism for broadcasting on all subnets of the specified network. RFC 1812, "Requirements for IPv4 Routers," reports that this broadcast feature was "broken" and of limited utility. It is being recommended for future omission.

- {Network ID = 127, Host ID = <any>} Internal host loopback address. A packet with an IP address that has a 127 in its first octet should never be seen outside of the host (on the network). It is used primarily when a service resides on the same host that the client is on. In general the standard loopback address used on a host is 127.0.0.1.

IP Addressing Revisited

Now that the special-case IP addresses have been discussed, it is a good time to discuss the limitations that are imposed on the IP addressing as a result of the special cases.

- A Host ID of all 1s is a special case. This is used for broadcasts. It reduces the amount of available hosts by 1.

- A Host ID of all 0s is a special case. This is used for "this host." It also reduces the amount of available hosts by 1.

- A Network ID of all 1s is a special case. This is used by broadcasts. This reduces the address space available to the Class E addresses. Little current impact.

- A Network ID of all 0s is a special case. This is used for "this network." This reduces the number of Class A networks by 1.

- A Network ID of 127 is a special case. This is used for the loopback interface. This reduces the number of Class A networks by 1.

- A Subnet ID of all 1s is a special case. This is used for subnet broadcasts. This reduces the number of subnets by 1. Since it was broken and is being omitted in the future, there will be no impact to subnet numbering eventually. Some vendors still prevent a subnet with an ID of all 1s from being used as a valid network. Eventually this feature will converge, and everyone will permit the use of all subnets. Test the waters, but be wary of interoperability.

The Straight Skinny of IP Address Space— A Summary

Now that we have applied the special cases to our previously "perfect" world, what is the bottom line? How much host space do we really have?

- Class A addresses: There are 126 Class A addresses possible. Remember that 0 and 127 are taken away by the special-case addresses. In a Class A network there is room for a maximum of 16,777,214 hosts. We lost two hosts due to special-case addresses.

- Class B addresses: There are 16,384 Class B networks (128.0 to 191.255). No Class B addresses were lost due to special-case addresses. Each Class B network can have a possible 65,534 hosts. Two lost.

- Class C addresses: There are 2,097,152 Class C networks (192.0.0 to 223.255.255). No Class C networks were lost. Each Class C network can have a possible 254 unique host identifiers. Two lost.

- Subnets: Whenever subnetting is used, you may or may not lose one or two of the subnet IDs due to the all-1s case and the all-0s case. The all-0s case was not specified as a special case in the list just reviewed; however, RFC 950 extended the use of the all-0s "this" to the concept of subnets. I am not certain whether it was ever used but its relevance has since been dropped from the special-case addresses, if it ever was used. The point is that if you want to use the all-1s or all-0s subnet, you will have to verify the correct operation and interoperability of all equipment in the intranet. Further, the implication of all this is that the minimum number of subnet bits (other than 0) that can be used is either 1 or 2. You may use a 1-bit subnet mask (e.g., 172.16.0.0 255.255.128.0) if you verify that everything functions normally with an all-1s and all-0s subnet ID. You will have to use 2 bits in order to support two subnets otherwise, since the all-1s and 0s would not be available.

- Hosts: You will always lose two host IDs per subnet. The minimum number of host bits that you can use is two. You would lose the all-1s and all-0s host ID (11 and 00), and you would have two host IDs for use (10 and 01). The bottom line is that the smaller the number of host bits (the larger the subnet mask), the greater the impact a loss of two host IDs per network will have.

Network Devices

Chapters 3 and 4 cover a few topics that build an essential base of knowledge that will eventually assist in the process of designing an efficient IP address scheme. This chapter is an introduction to devices that you might find on a TCP/IP network. The devices are defined categorically by function, with a few references to manufacturers for illustrative purposes only. This book does not endorse any particular manufacturer.

Hosts

In TCP/IP a host is basically any device that has an IP address on the network. Traditionally a host is thought of as a central general-purpose computer; a mainframe like an IBM 3090 is a host. Put those notions aside. In TCP/IP almost *everything* is a host. If it has an IP address, it is a host. There are special types of hosts, such as a router or a TCP/IP to "something" gateway. These will be discussed in this chapter. Another type of host, called a multihomed host, has more than one IP address defined on it.

For the most part—in this book, anyway—a reference to a host is a reference to a general-purpose computer, such as a user's workstation. The next sections will define some other devices, most of them special-purpose computers, that can be found in TCP/IP networks.

A Reference Model

The ISO (International Organization for Standardization) defined an Open System Interconnection (OSI) reference model on which it would develop a set of protocols, commonly known as the OSI protocols. These protocols have not been generally well accepted or implemented, for reasons well beyond the scope of this book. The reference model has endured and is often used in discussions that deal with layered protocols. Illustration 3-1 shows what the OSI reference model looks like.

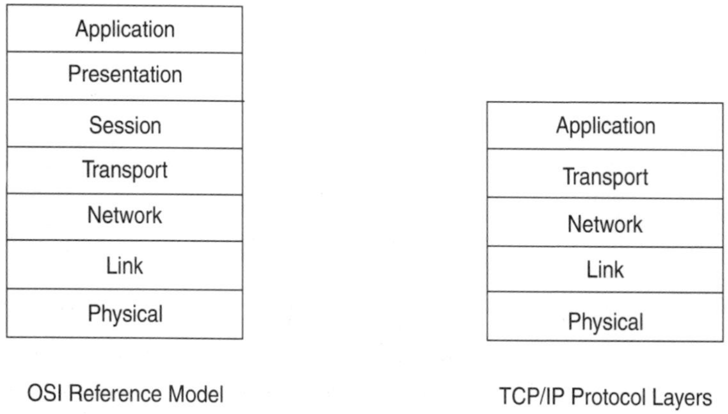

Application
Presentation
Session
Transport
Network
Link
Physical

OSI Reference Model

Application
Transport
Network
Link
Physical

TCP/IP Protocol Layers

Illustration 3-1 Comparison of OSI to TCP/IP Protocol Layers

Some layers function almost identically to the layers of TCP/IP. Throughout Chapter 2 and again in its summary, the TCP/IP model was discussed. Even though small differences exist in the functions provided by the layers, let us generalize that the physical layer (layer 1) through the transport layer (layer 4) are enough alike that we can say that we have discussed them already and do not warrant much further discussion at this time. For the sake of continuity, however, here is a summary:

- Physical layer (layer 1): The physical network medium. Unshielded twisted pair (UTP), coaxial cable, and radio frequency are examples.

- Link layer (layer 2): The protocol standards for interfacing with the physical network medium. Ethernet, IEEE 802.3, Token Ring, PPP, and Frame Relay are examples.

- Network layer (layer 3): The protocols for establishing end-to-end routing. IP, ICMP, and IGMP are examples.

- Transport layer (layer 4): The protocols for end-to-end transport of data with a given level of service (reliable or unreliable). TCP and UDP are examples.

- Session layer (layer 5): The protocols for maintenance of end-to-end sessions.

- Presentation (layer 6): The protocols used for conversion of data from one format to another, such as from ASCII to EBCDIC.

- Application layer OSI (layer 7): The user applications.

Of course, the big difference is that TCP/IP stops at the transport layer. Anything above the transport layer in TCP/IP is considered to be the application layer (TCP/IP). The session and presentation layer functions are built into the applications if they require the use of the function. An example of this is the

TN3270 (Telnet-3270) application, which allows a user of a TCP/IP workstation to establish a terminal session with an IBM 3270–based system. On the surface that does not sound too bad, but the TN3270 application has to be able to convert from ASCII, which the TCP/IP workstation uses, to EBCDIC, which the 3270 terminal requires. In the OSI protocol the application would be oblivious to the two different character sets, since the conversion would be handled at the OSI presentation layer.

Repeaters

The physical networks typically have some sort of electrical limitation associated with them. This electrical limitation will translate into distance limitation. A station on one end of a co-axial cable would be able to communicate effectively with a station on the remote end under normal conditions only if the cable were a certain length or less. Ethernets and Token Rings are subject to limitations like this. To overcome some of these limitations, we use a special type of amplifier, known as a *repeater*, to boost the signal and to get additional distance on the physical medium. See Illustration 3-2.

In the reference models a repeater works only at layer 1, the physical layer. There is no concern for hardware addresses; in fact, a repeater has no hardware address. The signal may simply be amplified or, if it is a digital signal, regenerated. A repeater can be used only to a join two networks with the same physical characteristics, i.e., both are 10base2 CSMA/CD networks.

Illustration 3-2 Network with Repeater

Bridges

Sometimes the network will not need to be made to handle greater distances, but additional devices cannot be added, because the maximum number of devices that the specification limits it to is on the verge of being exceeded. This is where a *bridge* can be useful. Bridges operate at layer 2, the link layer, of the reference model. As a layer 2 device a bridge receives a frame, checks for the hardware address in the "forwarding database" to determine whether the destination of the frame is on the physical network that the bridge received it from or whether it has knowledge of an interface that it should send it out of. Bridges typically are used to join two networks of the same type; however, there are bridges that can join an Ethernet and a Token Ring at the link layer. These bridges are known as *translational bridges,* since they have the ability to convert the byte ordering of the Token Ring hardware address to that of Ethernet, and vice versa.

Bridges are also useful in applications other than when the physical network is on the verge of exceeding its connection capacity. Bridges are useful for segmenting "high talkers and listeners"—transmit and receive station pairs—into cliques. The traffic would be passed to the other network only if the bridge detected that the destination was not local. Bridges are also one of the few networking choices for traffic that cannot be routed. Examples of nonroutable traffic are Netbios, Netbeui, and DEC LAT. There are tricks, such as tunneling of the traffic in a routable protocol, but these protocols are more often bridged.

Bridges may have an IP address associated with them. This would typically be for management purposes. The Simple Network Management Protocol (SNMP) requires a device to have an IP address in order to be able to poll it for status or, at the least, "alive" status through PING (Packet Internet Groper) functionality.

TCP/IP traffic can be bridged. It does not have to be routed. If TCP/IP is being bridged throughout an organization, the IP addressing would be set up as if it were a single IP network (no need to subnet), with all hosts in the enterprise being homed to that one network. Bridges would have only a single IP address associated with them, since its only purpose would be as an address for management.

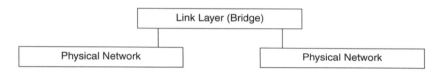

Illustration 3-3 Network with Local Bridge

Bridges may be implemented so that they span a wide area network (WAN) link. The bridge in Illustration 3-3 is termed a "local" bridge. A bridge that is used to interconnect two networks over a WAN link is called a "remote" bridge and must be implemented in pairs. See Illustration 3-4.

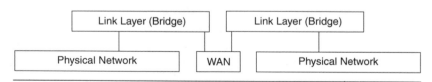

Illustration 3-4 Network with Remote Bridges

Routers

Bridges have shortcomings.

- The forwarding decisions are not very sophisticated. In the absence of an entry in its forwarding database for the destination hardware address of the packet it has received a bridge will forward the packet onto all connected interfaces except the one it received the packet from.

- Loops cannot exist in a bridged network. A protocol called Spanning Tree must be run on the bridges if there is any possibility that loops exist. The Spanning Tree Protocol does not require much background traffic to support it, but it can take more than just a few seconds before the network can converge after a link failure.

- Broadcast traffic is sent throughout the network. Any time a link layer broadcast is sent from a station, it must traverse the entire network. In a large network broadcast traffic can be significant.

- Bridges normally are used only to join networks that are of the same type. The exception is the translational bridge.

If a protocol has an address at the network layer (layer 3), it is a candidate for routing. Some of the protocols that can be routed include TCP/IP, Novell IPX, DECnet, and AppleTalk. Routers, although they have their own inherent shortcomings, have some advantages over bridges.

- The forwarding decisions that a router makes can be extremely sophisticated or fairly simplistic. The decision belongs to the network designers and implementers. The basis for the decisions will be covered in the next chapter.

- In a routed network loops are not only permitted but also encouraged. In a bridged network loops have to be "broken" so that traffic is not passed over redundant links. In a routed network the routing protocol determines how traffic should be forwarded. Routing loops can occur, and they can be detrimental to the health of the network; however there are safeguards, such as split horizon and "count to infinity," that reduce the likelihood that routing loops will occur and lessen their impact should they occur.

- Link layer broadcast traffic is not forwarded across a router. Most broadcasts at the network layer are also not forwarded. The "all-1s" destination IP address is known as a limited broadcast. This broadcast is kept local to the network on which it is originated. In a bridged IP network these broadcasts would be forwarded across the bridge.

- Disparate network types can be joined using routers. Any network on which TCP/IP can be run can be joined with another network running TCP/IP through the use of bridges. Typical examples would be Token Ring, Ethernet, and serial networks.

Illustration 3-5 shows a routed network. Unlike bridges, which would typically have only one IP address per physical device for administration purposes only, a router by definition must have at least two IP addresses. This makes a router a special instance of a multihomed host. In fact, a router must have an IP address for each logical TCP/IP network that it wishes to participate in and route data between. There are cases in which a router would have many IP addresses on a single physical port. More on that in Chapters 7 and 8. Illustration 3-5 would require at least two IP addresses to be defined on the router: one for the network on the left and one for the network on the right.

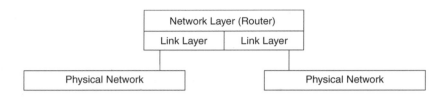

Illustration 3-5 Network with Local Router

Routers can also span a wide area network, as shown in Illustration 3-6, which depicts two routers, each with a local network, being spanned with a wide area network link. Although sometimes the wide area network link between the two routers does not require an IP address on the routers' ports, a worse case is that there are three TCP/IP networks being shown. The local network on the far left is being joined to the local network on the far right over a WAN link that is also running TCP/IP. The general case is that both routers would have different host numbers but would have identical network/subnet numbers on the link that joins them (the WAN). Therefore there are three IP networks being shown; only the wide area network is common to both routers.

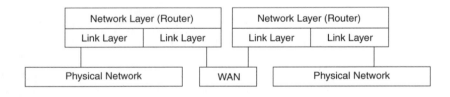

Illustration 3-6 Network with WAN Routers

Gateways

Repeaters, bridges, and routers have an increasing level of sophistication and provide a higher degree of network packet-forwarding sophistication with each jump. Repeaters work at layer 1, the physical layer. Bridges work at layer 2, the link layer. Routers work at layer 3, the network layer. Another type of device that might be found in a network is known as a *gateway*. This is not to be confused with the somewhat obsolete usage. Routers used to be called gateways in the earlier days of the Internet. Nowadays a gateway has come to be known as a device that operates at layers above the network layer, layers 4 through 7 in the OSI reference model. Gateways perform some level of translation, usually protocol translation, such as TCP/IP to IBM SNA. There is no need for a discussion of gateways in this book beyond this cursory clarification of the term.

Network Management Systems

Most networks have a computer system that serves a special purpose. This network management system (NMS) monitors the health of the connected network devices. Network management systems can be implemented on any operating system but are commonly found on UNIX. DOS, Windows, OS/2, and Apple Macintosh versions can be found as well. Network management functions can be implemented in custom-developed software or in off-the-shelf software. Prices range from a few hundred dollars to a hundred thousand dollars.

In a TCP/IP environment network management is most often implemented through the Simple Network Management Protocol, or SNMP. TCP/IP network devices that support SNMP include an SNMP agent in the software. This SNMP agent "listens" for requests on UDP port 161. These requests ask for information about the network device. The device answers with an SNMP reply and includes information about the requested piece of information. SNMP devices may also be able to send SNMP traps to the network management station. Traps provide the NMS with unsolicited status about the device, such as "link down, interface 1."

SNMP network management systems are very useful in the monitoring of a network and the determination that a network problem exists. They have the ability to plot trends, such as packets or octets, through an interface over time. They are also useful for providing a graphical view of the network and connectivity.

Network Analyzers

Network management systems aid in the determination that a problem exists in a network. They work well to identify that a hardware component or a network circuit has failed. They often do little to isolate protocol problems. This is the domain of the network analyzers, also called protocol analyzers. Like network management systems, these analyzers are implemented on a variety of platforms under a variety of operating systems. They are commonly stand-alone devices, usually portable, but can be simple software that can make a normal PC listen passively to a network and record the packets. Network analyzers can provide information on all layers of all protocols or can be used exclusively for certain layers and specific protocols.

Once the packets have been captured, and sometimes during the capture, they can be decoded to provide a human-readable interpretation of the contents of the packets. Some analyzers have the ability to "suggest" the nature of network problems through software called an "inference engine." This is a rule-based system that suggests, or infers, a condition, based on the satisfaction of rules in a knowledge database.

A special type of network analyzer is used in conjunction with a network management system. An RMON (remote monitor) can be a stand-alone piece of equipment typically placed at strategic points in a network and generally left there. It can also be implemented in network devices, such as routers. An RMON is specifically designed to allow an NMS to set up packet captures and decodes, as well as some other network analyzer functions.

A point of clarification: Network analyzers generally do not actively participate, protocolwise, in any way on the network that is being monitored. There are exceptions to this, such as the Distributed Sniffer System by Network General, which uses TCP/IP to transport testing information to a central control console. RMON devices must use TCP/IP, typically on the same network as is being monitored, for the transport of the testing information to a network management system. I was careful to say that network analyzers do not generally participate in the protocols of the network; they *do* participate in the network electrically. I have seen cases in which network WAN problems have cleared up as a result of the insertion of the analyzer in the circuit!

Summary

This chapter provided a brief introduction to the layered protocols of the OSI reference model and correlated the layers of TCP/IP to the model. This chapter also introduced the network devices that can be found in a network and illustrated the utility of each of the devices through the OSI reference model.

An important definition discussed in this chapter is the TCP/IP host. From TCP/IP's perspective a host is any device that has a IP address assigned to it. A special type of host that has more than one IP address associated with it is known as a multi-homed host.

The most important device, as far as the contents of this book are concerned, is the router. It makes packet-forwarding decisions, based on the destination IP address found in a TCP/IP packet or specifically the IP datagram. The router is said to work at layer 3, the network layer. A router must have at least two IP addresses defined on it. A physical port on a router may have more than one IP address bound to it.

Other device types, such as the repeater, bridge, and gateway, were discussed. The intent was to provide a better understanding of the router with a discussion of the other devices and the function within the reference model.

Other types of devices can be found in a TCP/IP network. Some are used specifically for the transmission of the data at the physical layer. These include modems, CSU/DSUs, transceivers, and line drivers. These mostly relate only to local networking media and do not directly affect IP internetworking. Others are specific implementations of repeaters and bridges, such as wiring hubs, Token Ring media access units (MAUs), and Ethernet switches. These devices are for the most part commonplace. New variations are being introduced continually. To get more information on the wealth of network devices that are available, contact a reputable networking reseller.

Routing

Chapter 3 discussed network devices commonly found in a TCP/IP network. Although other devices were discussed, focus was given to bridges and routers. With a bridged TCP/IP network all hosts are found on a single IP network, with each host having a unique host address on that network, as in Illustration 4-1. This works fine for small networks with only a few sites, but since it is nonhierarchical, it presents serious scalability consequences. The optimal choice for all networks, big or small, is to route the TCP/IP traffic. This requires the network to be partitioned into multiple TCP/IP networks, with each host interface common to each TCP/IP network having a unique host address. See Illustration 4-2.

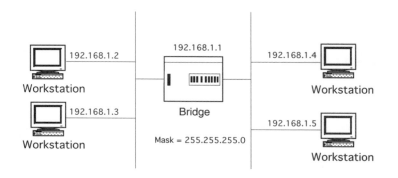

Illustration 4-1 Example of a Bridged Network

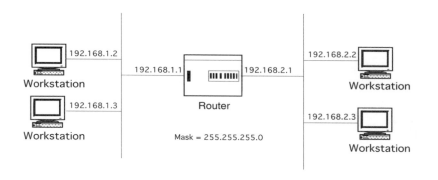

Illustration 4-2 Example of a Routed Network

In the routed network two Class C networks are being used. The router is multihomed, since it is connected to both of the networks. The router has the ability to take traffic off the network on the left and to forward it to the network on the right (and vice versa), based on the destination address found in the IP datagram. The router makes this decision with the aid of a *routing table,* also called a *forwarding information base (FIB).*

This chapter deals with the router's process of determining how a datagram should be forwarded. It is critical to understand this in order to develop an optimal address scheme.

The Routing Table

The format for a routing table varies with each manufacturer; however, the content is almost universal. I have included excerpts from two IP routers and one UNIX workstation in Tables 4-1, 4-2, and 4-3.

Destination	Route Mask	Next Hop	Port	Metr	Typ	Src	Age
0.0.0.0	0.0.0.0	172.16.3.65	J3.1	1	REM	MGMT	0
172.16.3.0	255.255.255.192	172.16.3.1	J5	0	DIR	LOC	72177
172.16.3.64	255.255.255.192	172.16.3.126	J3.1	0	DIR	LOC	68994
172.16.3.128	255.255.255.192	172.16.3.190	J1	0	DIR	LOC	72184
172.16.3.192	255.255.255.192	172.16.3.254	J1	0	DIR	LOC	72184
172.16.4.0	255.255.255.192	172.16.3.4	J5	115	REM	OSPF	29766
172.16.4.64	255.255.255.192	172.16.3.4	J5	90	REM	OSPF	13662
172.16.4.128	255.255.255.192	172.16.3.4	J5	100	REM	OSPF	29766
172.16.6.64	255.255.255.192	172.16.3.65	J3.1	576	REM	OSPF	17268
172.16.8.0	255.255.255.192	172.16.3.65	J3.1	90	REM	OSPF	68985
172.16.8.64	255.255.255.192	172.16.3.65	J3.1	130	REM	OSPF	13662
172.16.8.128	255.255.255.192	172.16.3.65	J3.1	75	REM	OSPF	68985

172.16.25.0	255.255.255.192	172.16.3.62	J5	50	REM	OSPF	71289
172.16.25.128	255.255.255.192	172.16.3.62	J5	35	REM	OSPF	71294
172.16.25.192	255.255.255.192	172.16.3.62	J5	35	REM	OSPF	71294

Table 4-1 Advanced Computer Communications Route Table

O	E2	172.16.3.0	255.255.255.0
		[110/2] via 172.17.253.30, 01:27:31, TokenRing0	
O		172.16.67.64	255.255.255.192
		[110/548] via 172.17.253.30, 01:27:31, TokenRing0	
O		172.16.65.64	255.255.255.192
		[110/548] via 172.17.253.30, 01:27:31, TokenRing0	
O	IA	172.16.71.64	255.255.255.192
		[110/142] via 172.17.253.30, 01:27:31, TokenRing0	
O	IA	172.16.4.0	255.255.255.192
		[110/257] via 172.17.253.30, 01:27:31, TokenRing0	
O	E2	172.16.8.0	255.255.255.0
		[110/2] via 172.17.253.30, 01:27:31, TokenRing0	
O	IA	172.16.8.0	255.255.255.192
		[110/102] via 172.17.253.30, 01:27:31, TokenRing0	

Table 4-2 Cisco Systems Route Table

Destination	Gateway	Genmask	Flags	Metric	Ref	Use	Iface
172.16.8.0	0.0.0.0	255.255.255.192	U	0	0	246846	eth0
127.0.0.0	0.0.0.0	255.0.0.0	U	0	0	163840	lo
0.0.0.0	172.16.8.1	0.0.0.0	UG	0	0	224692	eth0

Table 4-3 UNIX Route Table

Each of the route tables shown has a destination, a route mask, a next hop (gateway), a metric, and an interface (port) field. The routers also indicate the routing protocol that is the source of the routing entry and the age of the route. The UNIX routing table provides some statistics on the number of packets that have traversed the route, as well as whether the route is direct (the destination IP network is directly defined on that workstation's interface) or indirect (the destination IP network must be reached through a router). Workstations may or may not have a routemask field. For the remainder of the book I will illustrate my examples with route tables from Advanced Computer Communications (ACC) routers unless otherwise stated. The issue being illustrated will apply almost universally to all routers and most workstations.

Four general type of routes can be found in a route table:

- Host routes: A route to a specific host system. This type of route is most easily identified by a route mask of all 1s (255.255.255.255).

- Hierarchical network prefix routes: A route to a specific network. This type of route has a route mask with a length greater than or equal to 1 bit and less than or equal to 30 bits.

- Default route: A route to be used for any destination when a more specific route does not exist. This type of route has a destination and a route mask of all 0s (0.0.0.0). A route table may have multiple instances of a default route with different next hops or metrics.

- Loopback route: On a UNIX workstation this is the route defined and used by the loopback interface. A loopback route has a destination of 127.0.0.0 in the route table.

Let's revisit the ACC route table (Table 4-1) and discuss some of the specifics of it. The following is an explanation of each of the fields:

- Destination: The IP address of the destination network or host;

- Route mask: The mask that defines which bits of the destination field are significant in the route decision;

- Next hop: The IP address of a router that is the next hop to the destination network;

- Port: The physical port that the TCP/IP packet must be sent out of in order to reach the next hop router;

- Metric: A value assigned to the route to assist in determining the routing preferences;

- Type: A value that refers to the type of route: DIR = direct (the router is directly connected to the destination network) or REM = remote (the destination is reachable through another router);

- Source: The routing protocol that caused the route to be created: MGMT = management (static routes), LOC = Local (direct routes), ICMP (dynamic route created by ICMP), RIP (dynamic route created by RIP), OSPF (dynamic route created by OSPF);

- Age: The amount of time in seconds since the route was last updated.

The Forwarding Process

On receiving a packet, a router verifies that the IP header was not corrupted, performing a checksum of the IP header and comparing it to the value in the datagram checksum field. Provided that the checksum is determined to be valid, the destination IP address is examined. If the packet is not destined for the router, i.e., the destination address is not equal to one of the router's IP interfaces, the packet is queued for forwarding.

Assuming that the packet must be forwarded, three possibilities exist:

- The destination address is a unicast address. The address is a Class A, B, or C address and is not a special-case broadcast address.
- The destination address is a broadcast address.
- The destination address is a multicast address. The address is a Class D address.

If the destination address falls into the first category (unicast address), the router determines which interface the datagram should be sent out of and what the IP address is for the next-hop router (if any). The time-to-live (TTL) field is decremented and verified that it is not equal to 0. The packet is discarded if TTL equals 0. The datagram is fragmented if necessary, and the hardware address of the link layer destination is determined and a link layer header built to encapsulate the IP datagram for transmission on the physical medium.

If the destination address falls within the second category (broadcast address), the router must determine whether the broadcast is a limited broadcast or is a directed broadcast. If it is a limited broadcast (255.255.255.255), the packet cannot be forwarded out to another interface, but it might be used by the router itself. It is queued for local delivery to the router. If the datagram is a directed broadcast, it is treated as a unicast address for forwarding to the network, where it will be broadcast to all stations. That is, the router determines, through examination of the destination's network prefix and the routing table, which interface the datagram should be forwarded out of and the IP address of the next-hop router (if any). The TTL field is decremented and checked for packet discard eligibility. The datagram is fragmented if necessary, and the hardware address of the link layer destination (possibly link layer broadcast) is determined. The link layer header is constructed to encapsulate the IP datagram on the physical medium.

The case in which the destination address is a Class D address (multicast address) will be discussed in a later chapter.

Determining the Optimal Route

Once a packet has arrived at a router and is determined to be a unicast or a directed broadcast that must be forwarded, it is necessary to determine the interface it should be sent out of and the next-hop router's IP address. There may not be a next-hop router in all instances. When a packet is destined for a network that is directly defined on one of the router's interfaces, the packet is sent from the router directly to the destination IP address without traversing an additional router.

In many cases, as in the ACC routers and as illustrated previously, the "direct versus remote" decision has been incorporated into the route table, and the interface and next-hop decisions are made in the same way as all other forwarded packets are. In instances when the decisions are separated, the router's IP interfaces must be examined and compared to the destination address of the datagram to be forwarded. For each

IP interface defined on the router, the network mask must be applied to the router's IP address and the packet's destination IP address. If the network portion of each address is identical, the destination network of the datagram is considered local, and the router does not need to forward the packet to another router for delivery. The router must, in that case, cross-reference the IP address to the hardware address of the destination and forward the packet out of the identified port.

In cases when the route table implements these decisions or when the IP datagram must be sent to a next-hop router, a procedure is defined to find the most appropriate port and next-hop address. These procedures reduce the entire set of route table entries to a subset of routes consisting of zero, one, or more than one viable route alternatives for the datagram. These procedures are generally known as *pruning rules*.

- *Rule 1—Basic Match:* Prior to the application of this rule, the working set of route entries is equal to the entire route table. For each entry in the route table, the route mask is applied to both the destination IP address of the datagram and the corresponding destination field in the route table. All route entries except the ones in which the masked portion of the destination address and the destination route are identical are removed from the working set of route entries. Default routes are the exception. They are always included in the working set of route entries.

  Consider Table 4-4. Before the Basic Match pruning rule is applied, this routing table is the working set of route entries. Assuming that an IP datagram arrives destined for 172.16.8.66, the working set of route entries after the Basic Match pruning rule is applied as shown in Table 4-5.

Destination	Route Mask	Next Hop	Port	Metr	Typ	Src	Age
0.0.0.0	0.0.0.0	172.16.3.65	J3.1	1	REM	MGMT	0
172.16.0.0	255.255.0.0	172.16.3.65	J3.1	1	REM	MGMT	0
172.16.3.0	255.255.255.192	172.16.3.1	J5	0	DIR	LOC	72177
172.16.3.64	255.255.255.192	172.16.3.126	J3.1	0	DIR	LOC	68994
172.16.3.128	255.255.255.192	172.16.3.190	J1	0	DIR	LOC	72184
172.16.3.192	255.255.255.192	172.16.3.254	J1	0	DIR	LOC	72184
172.16.4.0	255.255.255.192	172.16.3.4	J5	115	REM	OSPF	29766
172.16.4.64	255.255.255.192	172.16.3.4	J5	90	REM	OSPF	13662
172.16.4.128	255.255.255.192	172.16.3.4	J5	100	REM	OSPF	29766
172.16.6.64	255.255.255.192	172.16.3.65	J3.1	576	REM	OSPF	17268
172.16.8.0	255.255.255.0	172.16.3.65	J3.1	621	REM	OSPF	29766
172.16.8.0	255.255.255.192	172.16.3.65	J3.1	90	REM	OSPF	68985
172.16.8.64	255.255.255.192	172.16.3.65	J3.1	130	REM	OSPF	13662
172.16.8.64	255.255.255.192	172.16.3.62	J5	720	REM	OSPF	52002
172.16.8.128	255.255.255.192	172.16.3.65	J3.1	75	REM	OSPF	68985
172.16.25.0	255.255.255.192	172.16.3.62	J5	50	REM	OSPF	71289
172.16.25.128	255.255.255.192	172.16.3.62	J5	35	REM	OSPF	71294
172.16.25.192	255.255.255.192	172.16.3.62	J5	35	REM	OSPF	71294

Table 4-4 Route Table to Search

Destination	Route Mask	Next Hop	Port	Metr	Typ	Src	Age
0.0.0.0	0.0.0.0	172.16.3.65	J3.1	1	REM	MGMT	0
172.16.0.0	255.255.0.0	172.16.3.65	J3.1	1	REM	MGMT	0
172.16.8.0	255.255.255.0	172.16.3.65	J3.1	621	REM	OSPF	29766
172.16.8.64	255.255.255.192	172.16.3.65	J3.1	130	REM	OSPF	13662
172.16.8.64	255.255.255.192	172.16.3.62	J5	720	REM	OSPF	52002

Table 4-5 Route Table after Basic Match

- *Rule 2—Longest Match:* After the Basic Match pruning rule has been applied, the working set of route entries is examined to see which entry (entries) has the longest (most specific) route mask. All routes in the working set that have a shorter (more general) route mask are discarded. Even though the default route has a zero-length route mask, the Longest Match pruning rule applies to it as well. Should the working set of route entries prior to the application of the Longest Match pruning rule have contained only a default route, the working set of route entries afterward would have just the default route in it. The previous example would be reduced to the working set of route entries after the application of the Longest Match pruning rule, as shown in Table 4-6.

Destination	Route Mask	Next Hop	Port	Metr	Typ	Src	Age
172.16.8.64	255.255.255.192	172.16.3.65	J3.1	130	REM	OSPF	13662
172.16.8.64	255.255.255.192	172.16.3.62	J5	720	REM	OSPF	52002

Table 4-6 Route Table after Longest Match

- *Rule 3—Weak Type of Service:* Most routers do not support this function, even though some modern routing protocols have the capability to support Type of Service routing. OSPF is an example of a routing protocol that can support Type of Service routing. The IP header has a field identified as "Type of Service (TOS)" that spans the second octet of the header and supports two distinct functions, precedence and type of service. The high-order 3 bits of the field are the "precedence" field, and the next 4 bits are the "type of service" flags. These TOS flags can influence how routing decisions are made for the packet being examined. The flags are:

D—Delay

T—Throughput

R—Reliability

C—Cost

They are set in order to bias a potential routing decision in favor of their respective factor.

The three bits that represent the "precedence" field influence the treatment of the packet while it is in queue in a router. Congestion in routers results in a growth of queues and delays associated with traversing the queues. The precedence field permits the router to select certain packets for earlier transmission over other, less time-sensitive packets. Since the precedence affects only queueing, it should not be used to influence the routing decision.

Each route in the routing table may have a Type of Service field associated with it. The way the Weak TOS pruning rule is applied, the TOS flags (bits 3–6 of the TOS field) of the datagram are compared to the TOS field of all the candidate routes in the working set. If a match is made, all routes except those that match are discarded from the working set. If no match is made, all routes except the ones that have a Type of Service equal to 0000 are discarded from the working set of route entries.

Routers and routing protocols that do not support Type of Service routing will set the Type of Service flags in the route table to 0000. The pruning rule still applies.

- *Rule 4—Best Metric:* Each route in the working set of route entries is ordered according to the metric field. The route(s) with the best metric are retained, and the other routes are discarded from the working set of candidate routes. The earlier example would be reduced down to the working set of route entries shown in Table 4-7 after the application of the Best Metric pruning rule.

Destination	Route Mask	Next Hop	Port	Metr	Typ	Src	Age
172.16.8.64	255.255.255.192	172.16.3.65	J3.1	130	REM	OSPF	13662

Table 4-7 Route Table after Best Metric

- *Rule 5—Vendor Policy:* In many cases the working set of route entries would have been reduced down to a single candidate route by this point; however, it is possible to end up with a set of candidate routes all with equal metrics. The Vendor Policy pruning rule leaves the choice to the router vendor as to how to handle this condition. Possibilities are selection of the route that was less recently used (load splitting), administrative preference, or first in list (discard others). The Vendor Policy pruning rule can be very sophisticated or extremely simplistic.

After the application of the pruning rules, there should be either no routes in the working set of route entries or one route. If the working set is empty, the packet should be discarded and an appropriate ICMP error generated. Otherwise the packet should be wrapped in a link layer protocol, using the hardware address of the next hop and queued for forwarding.

Even though guidelines on interpreting a route table exist, sometimes a device on the network does not "play by the [pruning] rules," so to say. I ran into a host system not long ago that needed to be statically routed. After its tables were built, it became obvious that nonoptimal routes were being taken by the workstation when it sent packets out but that the packets were returning by an optimal path. It turned out that the way the workstation interpreted its routing table was incorrect. It was using the first route from the top that satisfied the Basic Match pruning rule. The first route in the table was the default route. Make sure that you understand the algorithms that each device that makes a routing decision uses to choose the next hop for the packet.

Dynamic Routing Protocols

A couple of classifications can be used with routing protocols: interior routing protocols and exterior routing protocols, and link-state protocols and distance-vector protocols. The first, interior versus exterior, is a distinction based on an "autonomous system." An autonomous system is an area of routing that is under a common administrative control. Network administrators have the ability to define the address scheme and routing protocols within an autonomous system. The routing protocols that are designed for optimal operation within an autonomous system fall into the category of interior routing protocols. Those protocols that are designed to route between autonomous systems are called exterior routing protocols. Exterior Gateway Protocol (EGP) and Border Gateway Protocol (BGP) are examples of exterior routing protocols.

Exterior routing protocols are used to route packets within the Internet. In the recent past they provided routing only between classes of networks. No capabilities were provided to discriminate between subnets. Since you or I can do very little to affect the efficiency of the routing tables in the Internet, this book deals primarily with interior routing protocols. Remember, within an autonomous system the network administrator has control over subnetting and routing architectures.

Routing protocols can also be divided into another category that defines its underlying routing architecture: distance vector and link state. A distance-vector routing protocol keeps track of distances (hop count or cost) to each network and the physical interface to use to get to the network. A link-state protocol keeps track of direct neighbors and sends updates of its neighbor information to each of its neighbors. Eventually a router has all the information required to depict the network. The routing table is computed using this topology data.

Several interior routing protocols are in use today in a TCP/IP network. They include RIPv1 (RIP), RIPv2, OSPF, IGRP, and E-IGRP. RIP and OSPF are the most common standard routing protocols. They are opposites in many regards. RIP is a distance-vector routing protocol, whereas OSPF is a link-state routing protocol. RIP does not include subnet information;

OSPF does include subnet mask information. These and other features of the routing protocols greatly affect the addressing scheme chosen within an autonomous system.

RIP (RIP Version 1)

RIP stands for Routing Information Protocol. The first version of the protocol was formally defined in RFC 1058 (June 1988). It is by far the most widely used interior routing protocol. This comes as a result of the following factors:

- *Ease of use and implementation:* There are generally three steps to running RIP in a network. First, set the route broadcast update interval. Second, specify the neighboring routers. Third, turn on RIP routing. There is not much else that can be done or configured. It just starts working.

- *Age:* RIP was in use in TCP/IP networks even before RFC 1058 was written. RIP was the most popular, if not the only, interior routing protocol for a long time.

It is easiest to understand the operation of RIP through an illustration. Consider the network in Illustration 4-3. This TCP/IP network has three Class C networks in use. The mask of 255.255.255.0 is being used throughout. The networks are 192.168.1.0, 192.168.2.0, and 192.168.3.0.

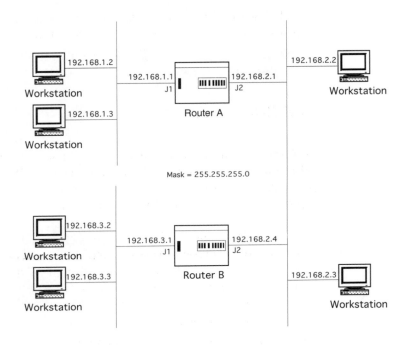

Illustration 4-3 Mechanics of RIP

To configure RIP routing, Router A would need to be told to listen to updates from Router B. This would enable RIP updates on the network in common between Router A and Router B (192.168.2.3), as well as define the "trusted neighbor." Router B would need to be told that Router A is a trusted neighbor. The RIP update interval has a default value of 30 seconds, but in most routers this can be set to a different value. Assuming the default update interval is all right, RIP can be enabled.

Henceforth at the expiration of each update interval, Router A will send a limited broadcast (UDP port 520) on port J2, telling the network and any routers running RIP about network 192.168.1.0. Router B, trusting a RIP update from Router A, installs the route in its route table if it does not already have the entry in it. If Router B does already have a route entry for 192.168.1.0, it will check to see whether the metric for the newly arrived route is better than the current route entry's metric. If it is better, the old route entry is replaced with the new route. If the newly received update exactly describes a route that is in the route table, the age of the existing route entry is reset to 0.

Router B also broadcasts route updates on its port J2 to tell all the RIP routers about network 192.168.3.0. Router A receives the update and installs the route entry or updates the timer for the route. The following is Router A's route table during normal operation in the network shown in Illustration 4-3.

Destination	Route Mask	Next Hop	Port	Metr	Typ	Src	Age
192.168.1.0	255.255.255.0	192.168.1.1	J1	0	DIR	LOC	3569
192.168.2.0	255.255.255.0	192.168.2.1	J2	0	DIR	LOC	3569
192.168.3.0	255.255.255.0	192.168.2.4	J2	1	REM	RIP	25

RIP is notorious for its slow network convergence (how long it takes for all routing in the network to stabilize on a correct routing table after a network change). This is greatly affected by the update interval. If Router A stops hearing a route update from Router B, the route for network 192.168.3.0 will start to age. After six update intervals, the route is marked as unusable, with a metric of 16. The route is purged shortly thereafter. Using the default values, the route would not be marked as invalid in Router A's route table for 180 seconds following the "failure" of Router B. Certain mechanisms help to speed things up under the right circumstances. Route poisoning is one way to halt the use of a route in a remote router.

The major thing to know about RIP is its handling of network mask information. The bottom line is that RIP does not pass information about the network masks in its route update. So long as you are aware of this and its effects, you can avoid the pitfalls and possibly even take advantage of some side effects. RIP infers a route mask for a network route entry, based on the inherent class of the IP address, unless the router receiving the update has an interface configured for a subnet of the same IP network, in which case the subnet mask in effect on the router will be used.

RIP Example 1: Consider Illustration 4-4. The route mask has changed from the previous example. The mask now being used (255.255.255.240) would allow each Class C network to be divided into 14 or 16 subnetworks, each with 14 hosts per subnet. The illustration does not try to explain what on earth the network administrator was thinking in devising this scheme; it serves only to make a point. Instead of explaining the mechanics up front, let's look at Router A's route table and take note of a peculiarity.

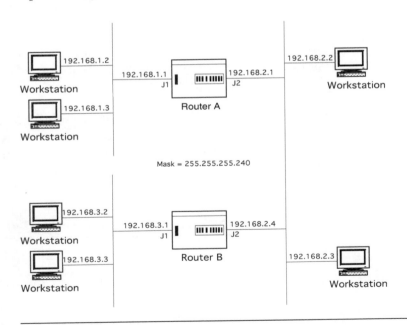

Illustration 4-4 RIP Example I

Destination	Route Mask	Next Hop	Port	Metr	Typ	Src	Age
192.168.1.0	255.255.255.240	192.168.1.1	J1	0	DIR	LOC	3569
192.168.2.0	255.255.255.240	192.168.2.1	J2	0	DIR	LOC	3569
192.168.3.0	255.255.255.0	192.168.2.4	J2	1	REM	RIP	13

Why does entry 192.168.3.0 have a route mask that is different from the others? Router A does not have network 192.168.3.0 defined on any of its interfaces. Therefore, if Router A receives an update with a route 192.168.3.0, it can assume only that the route mask is the inherent class of the network. In this case it is assumed that the mask should be the normal Class C mask of 255.255.255.0. As far as this example is concerned, the mis-masked route entry is "no big deal." Since the only place that any subnets of the Class C network 192.168.3.0 can be reached from is through Router B, Router A can send any IP datagram with a destination address having 192.168.3 as the first three oc-tets to Router B, and it will know how to deliver them. Certainly it would be nice if Router A knew that it could route only pack-ets destined for the first subnet of that Class C address, but that's not the way RIP works.

RIP Example 2: What would the routing table on Router A, in the previous example, look like if the same subnet mask (255.255.255.240) were used but the first and second octet of all the IP addresses were changed from "192.168" to "172.16"? An-swer:

Destination	Route Mask	Next Hop	Port	Metr	Typ	Src	Age
172.16.1.0	255.255.255.240	172.16.1.1	J1	0	DIR	LOC	3569
172.16.2.0	255.255.255.240	172.16.2.1	J2	0	DIR	LOC	3569
172.16.3.0	255.255.255.240	172.16.2.4	J2	1	REM	RIP	13

The route mask for entry 172.16.3.0 is 255.255.255.240 because the network has changed from being based on subnetting of three Class C networks to subnetting of a single Class B network. As such, all routers have a subnet of that one Class B network defined on them. It inferred the mask, based on its local interfaces IP addresses and masks.

RIP Example 3: When the mask was incorrectly identified in RIP Example 1, it worked out that everything would function despite the mistake. See if you can figure out what's going to happen to routing between Router A and Router C. Can Router A ping Router B? What about routing between Host A and Host C? Can they ping each other? See Illustration 4-5.

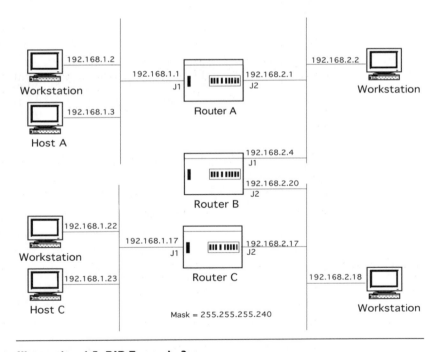

Illustration 4-5 RIP Example 3

Here is a hint. This is Router B's routing table:

Destination	Route Mask	Next Hop	Port	Metr	Typ	Src	Age
192.168.2.0	255.255.255.240	192.168.2.4	J1	0	DIR	LOC	3569
192.168.2.16	255.255.255.240	192.168.2.20	J2	0	DIR	LOC	3569
192.168.1.0	255.255.255.0	192.168.2.1	J1	1	REM	RIP	13
192.168.1.0	255.255.255.0	192.168.2.17	J2	1	REM	RIP	4

Router A (192.168.2.1) can ping Router C (192.168.2.17). Host A (192.168.1.3) cannot ping Host C (192.168.1.23).

Routers A and C can ping each other because all the routers, including Router B, have IP subnets from the Class C network 192.168.2.0 defined on them. So long as Router A uses a destination IP address of 192.168.2.17 and a source address of 192.168.2.1 for the ping packet, there can be no confusion regarding the routing. Remember, with the mask that is being used, the addresses 192.168.2.1 and 192.168.2.17 reflect the same host ID (1) on different IP networks.

A problem occurs when Router B receives an RIP update from Router A. Router B sees the IP network 192.168.1.0 in the update. Not having an interface with that Class C defined on it, Router B infers that the route mask to be used is the inherent mask of the network. In this case a Class C mask is used, and the route is installed in the routing table. Router C sends an update to Router B for network 192.168.1.16 (the all 0-s host portion for the second subnet), but because Router B still has no way of knowing what the actual mask should be, it assumes the inherent Class C mask. The routes have different next hops, so the route is installed.

Router B sends an update to Router A. In that update Router B includes the route to network 192.168.1.0 with the next hop of

192.168.2.17. Router A rejects the route because it already has a 192.168.1.0 entry in its routing table. Further, the network is a local route, indicating that it is directly defined on Router A. There can be no better route than the one it already has.

Assume that Host A sends a ping packet to Host C. As soon as the ping packet arrives at Router A, it is discarded because Router A has no route to that particular subnet in its routing table. The ping fails.

There is also a desirable side effect of the mismasking of route entries. This will be discussed in Chapter 7, "Addressing to Achieve Route Table Efficiency."

Open Shortest Path First (OSPF)

OSPF is a much more complicated routing protocol than RIP. Configuration of RIP is brief and simple; only a few parameters can be changed. OSPF offers a virtual plethora of configuration options. These include:

- OSPF areas
- area route summarization
- enabling OSPF on a router or on specific interfaces
- virtual links
- metrics
- importation of routing information from other routing protocols
- exportation of routing information to other routing protocols

- OSPF interface timers, such as the hello interval and the dead interval

- authentication

OSPF is a complicated, yet extremely powerful and efficient routing protocol. This section will not cover OSPF in depth; please refer to one of the many excellent references, including RFC 1583 "OSPF Version 2," that discuss the details of the protocol. It is necessary, however, to cover portions of the OSPF protocol in order to point out the aspects that have to do with IP addressing. So here's a quick overview of OSPF.

OSPF is a link-state routing protocol. Whenever a new router joins with a network running OSPF, the router will exchange a database with another router on the network. This database represents the network topology to the router. From the information in this link-state database, the router is able to compute an optimal routing table. The new router is now capable of effective routing. From this point on the router must maintain contact with each of its neighbors. If it loses contact, the neighbor will imminently sense that it has lost contact and floods an advertisement out to all OSPF routers that the connection has been lost. All routers update their respective link-state databases with the information from the recent link-state advertisement and force a recomputation of the routing table. One huge advantage over RIP is that the link-state database contains information on all the subnets that the routes use. Let's look at the same network that gave RIP trouble:

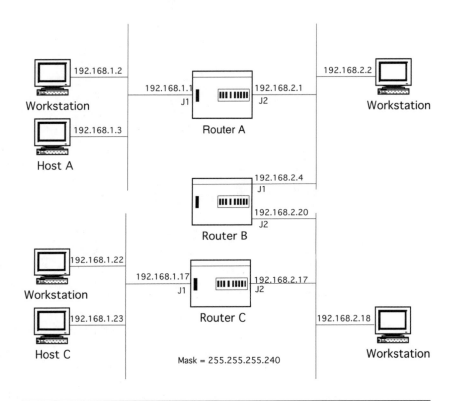

Illustration 4-6 OSPF Example I

OSPF Example 1: Because RIP could not pass subnet mask information in the route update, Router B assumed that the route
update for network 192.168.1.0 used a mask of 255.255.255.0,
which prevents packets from passing correctly between the
192.168.1.0/28 network and the 192.168.1.16/28 network. (See
Illustration 4-6.) OSPF would construct a routing table on Router
B that looks like this:

Destination	Route Mask	Next Hop	Port	Metr	Typ	Src	Age
192.168.2.0	255.255.255.240	192.168.2.4	J1	0	DIR	LOC	3569
192.168.2.16	255.255.255.240	192.168.2.20	J2	0	DIR	LOC	3569
192.168.1.0	255.255.255.240	192.168.2.1	J1	1795	REM	OSPF	2184
192.168.1.16	255.255.255.240	192.168.2.17	J2	1795	REM	OSPF	2662

On Router C the routing table would look like this:

Destination	Route Mask	Next Hop	Port	Metr	Typ	Src	Age
192.168.1.16	255.255.255.240	192.168.1.17	J1	0	DIR	LOC	3002
192.168.2.16	255.255.255.240	192.168.2.17	J2	0	DIR	LOC	3569
192.168.1.0	255.255.255.240	192.168.2.20	J2	3590	REM	OSPF	72184
192.168.2.0	255.255.255.240	192.168.2.20	J2	1795	REM	OSPF	3569

It is clear from the routing tables that all four networks in the illustration are represented. There can be no problem determining the next hop of a packet at any point in the network.

In an error-free OSPF network very little overhead traffic is required to maintain the routing. Each router sends an OSPF hello packet to its neighbors at the expiration of the hello interval (usually 10 seconds). If the dead interval (usually 40 seconds) expires before receipt of the next hello, the link is marked down. This represents the worst case on the amount of time that OSPF requires to determine link failure. If a router determines that one of the physical ports that an OSPF interface is defined on fails, the router can advertise that the link is down. This triggers a flurry of routing table recalculation on each router that receives the link-state advertisement (LSA). This LSA is small.

It takes only about 40 octets for the largest link-state advertisement above the IP layer. (OSPF is implemented on top of IP.) When an OSPF router rejoins, the process starts over again, with an exchange of OSPF link-state information.

It is easy to see that in a stable network little overhead is associated with OSPF. A bouncing link, a tentative interface that continues to cycle between operable and inoperable, can cause the greatest impact to an OSPF network. In fact, not only is the link-state advertisement being flooded to all routers with each transition, but also the routers are forced to recalculate the routing table. This calculation is not an insignificant computation, and it tends to cascade within each set of routers in a series.

To minimize the impact of the flooding and recalculation, the concept of *areas* was developed. An area is the boundary for flooding of link-state advertisements. An OSPF router within an area will have a complete map of the topology only within the area to which it belongs, plus some summary information about the OSPF topology beyond its borders. This information is summarized by a special-purpose router called an *area border router*. This router serves as a gateway between the backbone area (area 0.0.0.0, commonly called area 0) and another, non-backbone area. The backbone area must be contiguous in an OSPF network, and all areas must connect to the backbone area via an area border router.

The area border router has the ability to summarize link-state advertisements received from one area and to send only a summary link advertisement into the adjoining area. The advantage to this can be significant or minimal, depending on how well that addressing scheme was laid out. See where I was going? It all boils down to addressing in the long run. Consider Illustration 4-7.

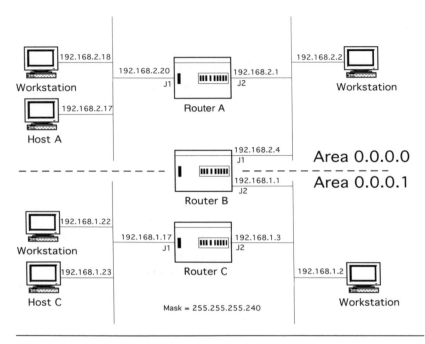

Illustration 4-7 OSPF with Areas

The illustrated network consists of three routers in two different areas, area 0 and area 1. All of Router A and the 192.168.2.4
IP interface of Router B are in the backbone area, area 0. The
192.168.1.1 IP interface of Router B and all of Router C are in
area 1. If the J1 port on Router A fails, Router A will detect that
the link is down and will flood a link-state advertisement to all
routers in the area. Router B receives the LSA, applies any summarization rules, and creates a summary link-state advertisement, if necessary, to be flooded into area 0.0.0.1.

Route summarization can also occur at an area border router.
All the networks in each of the areas that it adjoins can be summarized into only a few route entries if the addressing scheme
permits. Summarization will be discussed in a subsequent
chapter.

Static Routing

RIP and OSPF are examples of dynamic routing protocols. Information must be exchanged between the routers. This information exchange is the basis for route table construction. A static route is configured by the network administrator and, once installed, will not change except through manual intervention. A static architecture might be worth consideration for a number of reasons:

- *No traffic overhead due to static routing.* The routing update in an RIP network can get rather large. Even though the running average might suggest a small percentage of total bandwidth over the course of a day, keep in mind that the update is sent out at 30-second intervals (default). At the expiration of the update interval, the route update will be transmitted. For some amount of time, depending on the link speed and the size of the update, the link may be saturated.

- *Dial media (ISDN).* Routers have the ability to evaluate the destination address of a packet, determine which remote site needs to have a connection established, and place "the call" in order to pass the traffic. This could be a local call and might be subject to a usage fee, based on the connect time. The call could be across the country and would be subject to the long-distance carrier's tariffs. In either case you wouldn't want a call to be placed every time a route update is sent.

- *Import into OSPF.* Static routes can be imported into OSPF routing. This means that you can statically define a portion of your network and import those routes into a dynamic portion of the network.

- *Route efficiency.* Static routing can lead to some sophisticated route schemes. The network administrator has the ability to design a routing strategy that considers many different factors when biasing a route decision. The administrator also has the ability to set up route aggregation schemes.

There are also a few reasons not to do static routing:

- *Static is static.* In the event of a failure, static routing cannot recover well by shifting traffic loads to compensate. Those are capabilities of a dynamic routing protocol.

- *Configuration is a pain.* All the initial configuration, the maintenance and updates, and the continuous redesign are manual operations.

ICMP Routing

Many people in this industry do not consider ICMP to be a routing protocol. Well, in a lot of ways, it is. ICMP, the Internet Control Message Protocol, has a message type that redirects routing from a nonoptimal route to one that is more optimal. This message is known as an ICMP Redirect. The format for an ICMP Redirect is shown in Illustration 4-8 and has the following values:

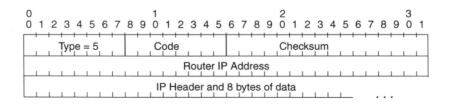

Illustration 4-8 ICMP Redirect

- *Type:* Value is 5 for a Redirect message.

- *Code:* 0 for Network Redirect, 1 for Host Redirect, 2 for TOS (Type of Service) and Network Redirect, and 3 for TOS and Host Redirect.

- *Checksum:* Self-explanatory.

- *Router IP address:* The IP address of the router having a better route to the destination than was originally used.

Illustration 4-9 shows the classic example of when a redirect occurs. Workstation C has the following route table:

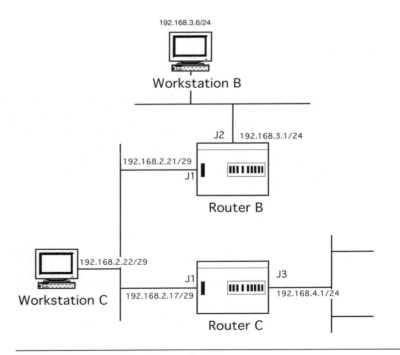

Illustration 4-9 Classic ICMP Redirect Scenario

Destination	Gateway	Genmask	Flags	Metric	Ref	Use	Iface
192.168.2.22	0.0.0.0	255.255.255.248	U	0	0	246846	eth0
127.0.0.0	0.0.0.0	255.0.0.0	U	0	0	163840	lo
0.0.0.0	198.168.2.17	0.0.0.0	UG	0	0	224692	eth0

Router C's route table is:

Destination	Route Mask	Next Hop	Port	Metr	Typ	Src	Age
192.168.2.16	255.255.255.248	192.168.2.17	J1	0	DIR	LOC	540
192.168.3.0	255.255.255.0	192.168.2.21	J1	75	REM	OSPF	245
192.168.4.0	255.255.255.0	192.168.4.1	J3	0	DIR	LOC	540

Workstation C has a default route to Router C. When Workstation C wishes to communicate with Workstation B, it sends its packets to Router C. Router C sees that the next hop for getting to the 192.168.3.0/24 network is 192.168.2.21 and is reachable through the same interface that the original packet was received on. This triggers an ICMP Redirect from Router C to Workstation C, telling of the more optimal path. In the future when Workstation C sends data to Workstation B, it should send the packets directly to 192.168.2.21 (Router B).

There are many other types of messages and functions for ICMP. RFC 792 defines ICMP.

Direct Routing

Whenever a router or a workstation sends a packet to a device on an IP network that has been defined locally on the router or workstation, it must translate the IP address of the destination to the destination's hardware address. On a physical network that permits multiple access (Ethernet, Token Ring, Frame Relay are examples), there must be some mechanism for cross-referencing the IP address to the hardware address or vice versa. On an Ethernet the protocols for maintaining the cross-reference are Address Resolution Protocol (ARP) and Reverse ARP (RARP). Other types of networks may have similar functionality or may require a manual mapping of the address resolution.

IP routers forward packets based on information about IP networks in their routing tables. Once a router determines that a packet must be forwarded to another router (next hop), the router must encapsulate the IP datagram into an appropriate link layer header and use the hardware address of the next hop as the link layer destination. This is also true if a router has the destination network locally defined and the packet is to be delivered to a host on that network. The router must find out the hardware address of the host for the link layer header.

The mechanics of ARP and RARP are beyond the scope of this book. RFC 826 defines ARP. RFC 903 defines RARP. RFC 1293 defines Inverse ARP. RFC 1735 defines NBMA (nonbroadcast, multiple access) ARP used on Frame Relay and X.25 networks.

Hand Tracing a Route

When routing does not seem to be working correctly, one of the best ways to diagnose a problem is to hand trace the routing from source to destination and back. Starting at the source of the IP datagram, use the pruning rules that are applicable for the platform, determine the next hop, and follow the path all the way to the destination. Do this for the reverse also. Just because you have routing to get to an address does not mean that you could get back. Illustration 4-10 is an example of hand tracing.

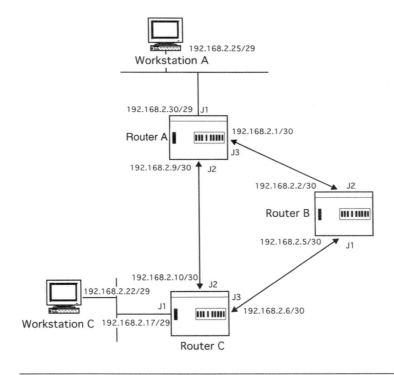

Illustration 4-10 Example Network for Hand Tracing a Route

Assume the following route tables in each of the workstations and routers:

- *Workstation A:*

Destination	Gateway	Genmask	Flags	Metric	Ref	Use	Iface
192.168.2.25	0.0.0.0	255.255.255.248	U	0	0	246846	eth0
127.0.0.0	0.0.0.0	255.0.0.0	U	0	0	163840	lo
0.0.0.0	192.168.2.30	0.0.0.0	UG	0	0	224692	eth0

- *Workstation C:*

Destination	Gateway	Genmask	Flags	Metric	Ref	Use	Iface
192.168.2.22	0.0.0.0	255.255.255.248	U	0	0	246846	eth0
127.0.0.0	0.0.0.0	255.0.0.0	U	0	0	163840	lo
0.0.0.0	198.168.2.17	0.0.0.0	UG	0	0	224692	eth0

- *Router A:*

Destination	Route Mask	Next Hop	Port	Metr	Typ	Src	Age
192.168.2.0	255.255.255.252	192.168.2.1	J3	0	DIR	LOC	467
192.168.2.4	255.255.255.252	192.168.2.10	J2	75	REM	OSPF	452
192.168.2.8	255.255.255.252	192.168.2.9	J2	0	DIR	LOC	492
192.168.2.16	255.255.255.248	192.168.2.10	J2	20	REM	OSPF	452
192.168.2.24	255.255.255.248	192.168.2.30	J1	0	DIR	LOC	492

• *Router B:*

Destination	Route Mask	Next Hop	Port	Metr	Typ	Src	Age
192.168.2.0	255.255.255.252	192.168.2.2	J2	0	DIR	LOC	455
192.168.2.4	255.255.255.252	192.168.2.5	J1	0	DIR	LOC	456
192.168.2.8	255.255.255.252	192.168.2.1	J2	75	REM	OSPF	441
192.168.2.8	255.255.255.252	192.168.2.6	J1	75	REM	OSPF	441
192.168.2.16	255.255.255.248	192.168.2.6	J1	75	REM	OSPF	450
192.168.2.24	255.255.255.248	192.168.2.1	J2	75	REM	OSPF	449

• *Router C:*

Destination	Route Mask	Next Hop	Port	Metr	Typ	Src	Age
192.168.2.0	255.255.255.252	192.168.2.9	J2	75	REM	OSPF	245
192.168.2.4	255.255.255.252	192.168.2.6	J3	0	DIR	LOC	478
192.168.2.8	255.255.255.252	192.168.2.10	J2	0	DIR	LOC	540
192.168.2.16	255.255.255.248	192.168.2.17	J1	0	DIR	LOC	540
192.168.2.24	255.255.255.248	192.168.2.9	J2	20	REM	OSPF	463
192.168.2.25	255.255.255.255	192.168.2.5	J3	2	REM	MGMT	0

In this example the workstations can reach one another, but the response time is off from what is expected, and the physical port statistics on the routers indicate nonoptimal routing. To start with, look at the routing table on Workstation A and verify that the default gateway and the IP interfaces were configured with the correct mask. Everything looks fine; the default gateway is 192.168.2.30. Telnet to Router A (192.168.2.30). If Workstation A were sending packets to Workstation C, the destination IP address would be 192.168.2.22, and the source address would be 192.168.2.25. The route in Router A's routing table that would provide the next hop is the fourth one down; 192.168.2.22 falls into a six-host network, 192.168.2.16/29. The next hop is 192.168.2.10, the J2 port on Router C. Telnet to Router C. Examining its route table revealed that the 192.168.2.16/29 network is locally attached. The packet can be routed directly to Workstation C from Router C, since they share an Ethernet connection.

Now we have to do the same thing for the reverse direction, since Workstation C must respond to Workstation A's packet. Look at Workstation C's routing table. The default gateway is 192.168.2.17, and the IP interfaces are configured correctly. Telnet to 192.168.2.17. Now the destination IP address that we are looking for is 192.168.2.25. The routing table reveals a host route (denoted by the route mask 255.255.255.255) to the host 192.168.2.25, and the next hop is configured for 192.168.2.5! Now I remember! I had installed a bunch of static routes a few weeks ago, trying to troubleshoot a different problem. I must have left one in. I'll bet that if I remove it, everything will be fine again.

Hand tracing a route from source to destination and back can take some time but will invariably reveal flaws in a routing architecture. Luckily some tools help to make this a little faster. Traceroute is common among these tools. Traceroute's function is to show you the hops taken to get from a source to a destination. It does this through the use of both ICMP and UDP. The following is the result of a traceroute from Router C to Router A:

```
hop  1:192.168.2.17
hop  2:192.168.2.5
hop  3:192.168.2.9
Target (192.168.2.25) reached on hop 4, round-trip time 280 ms.
```

It is easy to see that the second hop was not as expected. The packet should have been routed from 192.168.2.17 to 192.168.2.9

on the second hop. Traceroute does not indicate the reason for this, so it's back to the hand tracing of the routing. This time, however, I can start at 192.167.2.17 on the return path. Traceroute can save time in the debugging process, but it won't do the complete analysis for you.

Summary

This chapter dealt with the fundamentals of routing. Foremost, a person must have an understanding of the routing table elements and how next hops are selected for the packet being routed. The route table pruning rules, which a router uses to select the packet's next-hop destination, are:

- Rule 1—Basic Match
- Rule 2—Longest Match
- Rule 3—Weak Type of Service
- Rule 4—Best Metric
- Rule 5—Vendor Policy

Not all devices choose a next hop in the same manner that IP version 4 routers do. Make sure that you understand the algorithms used in your network for choosing next-hop destinations.

Routing protocols can be broken down into several categories. They can be interior or exterior. Interior routing protocols handle routing within an autonomous system (a system under a single administrative control) that is capable of making decisions about subnetting and routing policies. Two examples of interior routing protocols are RIP and OSPF. Exterior routing protocols handle routing between autonomous systems. EGP and BGP are exterior routing protocols.

Routing protocols can be link state or distance vector. OSPF is an example of a link-state protocol. OSPF permits the use of variable subnet masks by including the route mask information in the link-state database. OSPF converges rapidly after a network change. If a link fails in the network, it is possible to converge to a stable state in only a few seconds. OSPF also introduces the concept of areas. An area is the boundary for flooding of link-state advertisements and for summarizing routing information. It can be complicated getting OSPF operational.

RIP is an example of a distance-vector routing protocol. RIP does not convey information about route masks in its route update broadcasts. As such, it must infer the route mask to use from the inherent class of the address and whether that network has a subnet defined on one of the router's interfaces. The route mask chosen is sometimes wrong and can lead to unexpected routing results. RIP relies on the receipt of routing updates at a regular interval (usually every 30 seconds). If it fails to get a route update for a previously known route, the route will eventually get marked as unusable and shortly afterward be flushed from the route table. A route could be marked as up for a long time after an outage. RIP is known for slow network convergence but is simple to implement.

Other routing protocols, such as IGRP, EIGRP, and RIPv2, were not discussed. There are similarities and differences among these routing protocols and RIP or OSPF. I chose RIP because of its widespread use and OSPF because it is a strong, modern, standards-based protocol.

IP Address Layout

Everything up to this point has been to provide you with background and motivation that support the discussion on the design or redesign of IP addressing schemes. This is where the rubber meets the road. Indeed, sometimes you have to redesign the addressing architecture. This happens as a result of inappropriate planning or address administration. It can also be necessary as a result of changes in infrastructure. Address redesign is healthy, and so is a visit to the dentist.

Address-Needs Assessment

Renovation of an addressing scheme might be a painful process. The first time you do it to a network will be brutal. The second time you do it, you should be only slightly uncomfortable. The reason for this is that when a network is started, it is typically within a single workgroup, and then the company or office takes notice and says, "I want that, too." And they get added, and so on.

The birth of a network is seldom planned. It just happens, and it propagates. Eventually people start to see performance decline, and then things start to happen that make people take notice. The network administrator answers with more bandwidth here and there, and the problem goes away. And the network expands some more. Performance declines. The network administrator adds more bandwidth and another router. Several subnets lose their routing within the network, and the network administrator adds a few host routes to fix the problem.

That is how an address scheme develops. Nowhere during the evolution did anyone say, "What if we needed to change the addressing? How difficult would that be?"

At this point a redesign looks pretty much like an initial design. (To be honest, any large-scale network change makes me pucker. IP readdressing is no different.) There may be a few extra considerations, such as saving pools of addresses to avoid complete readdressing, network outages, interim steps, and project management.

With the playing field leveled between design and redesign, let's look at the points that should be considered when (re)designing an IP address scheme.

- *Infrastructure Topolgy:* Different network topologies, such as Ethernet, point to point, and frame relay networks, require different IP addressing architectures. *Chapter 5.*

- *Internet connection:* This is one of the biggest issues when determining the address scheme. How many hosts are going to require an address directly on the Internet? None, just a few, or all? Is there ever going to be a desire to connect to the Internet? How will that be done? Legal IP address or not? How many networks were you allocated? *Chapter 6.*

- *Size of routing tables:* Routing efficiency is improved with the reduction of entries in the route table. In Chapter 4 we discussed the pruning rules a router uses to select a next-hop destination. If the working set of routes at the start of the pruning process is all routes in the routing table, it only follows that the Basic Match pruning process would be improved if the table were smaller and fewer routes had to be examined to determine whether a basic match existed. *Chapter 7.*

- *Address efficiency:* Registered Internet addresses seem to be at a premium these days. The InterNIC evaluates all requests for an address allocation carefully to determine whether the applicant really needs "that many addresses." The motto of the day is "Do more with what you have." Efficiency of address utilization is important in cases like this. *Chapter 8.*

- *Ease of administration:* One of the goals in designing an address scheme should always be to make the address scheme easy to use and understand and to make future changes easier. *Chapter 9.*

- *Anticipated growth and unanticipated change:* An addressing scheme should permit growth and change within the constraints of desired address efficiency. Growth that is anticipated should always be a major consideration of an address design. *Chapter 10.*

Common Topology Addressing

This chapter provides an overview of general IP addressing issues associated with common network topologies. The topologies presented here include Ethernet and Token Ring, point-to-point connections, dial-in pooled access, and Frame Relay. Others are in use, such as FDDI and X.25, and ATM is emerging. The general addressing issues discussed with respect to the subset presented in this chapter are universal.

Introduction to the IP Address Worksheet

I have developed a system that I use when designing an address plan. This and subsequent chapters will all use this system to explain concepts as they are introduced. Illustration 5-1 shows a portion of the IP address worksheet. The entire worksheet is contained in Appendix C. Please feel free to copy the worksheets out of the appendix and to cut and paste (real scissors, real glue) them together for use in this and subsequent chapters.

.0/24	.128/25	.192/26	.224/27	.240/28	.248/29	.252/30
0	0	0	0	0	0	0
1	1	1	1	1	1	1
2	2	2	2	2	2	2
3	3	3	3	3	3	3
4	4	4	4	4	4	4
5	5	5	5	5	5	5
6	6	6	6	6	6	6
7	7	7	7	7	7	7
8	8	8	8	8	8	8
9	9	9	9	9	9	9
10	10	10	10	10	10	10
11	11	11	11	11	11	11
12	12	12	12	12	12	12
13	13	13	13	13	13	13
14	14	14	14	14	14	14
15	15	15	15	15	15	15
16	16	16	16	16	16	16
17	17	17	17	17	17	17
18	18	18	18	18	18	18
19	19	19	19	19	19	19
20	20	20	20	20	20	20
21	21	21	21	21	21	21
22	22	22	22	22	22	22
23	23	23	23	23	23	23
24	24	24	24	24	24	24
25	25	25	25	25	25	25
26	26	26	26	26	26	26
27	27	27	27	27	27	27
28	28	28	28	28	28	28
29	29	29	29	29	29	29
30	30	30	30	30	30	30
31	31	31	31	31	31	31

Illustration 5-1 Portion of IP Address Worksheet

The worksheet represents the subnetting that is possible with an 8-bit host partition as in the case of a Class C address. The concepts can all be extended to Class A or Class B addresses. The worksheet just gets bigger, that's all. For a Class C address the worksheet has 256 rows, not including the header. The rows are numbered consecutively, starting at 0 and ending at 255. The rows represent all the possible addresses for a Class C network. The columns represent the subnet mask.

.0/24	.128/25	.192/26	.224/27	.240/28	.248/29	.252/30

For a Class C network 192.168.1.0, the network mask 255.255.255.0 would be represented by the leftmost column. This could be represented in this text more easily through the use of the alternative "/n" method. The representation 192.168.10.5/28 would indicate that the Class C address specified is subnetted with a mask of 255.255.255.240.

Note the two types of shading on the IP address worksheet. Boxes shaded as in the first row and in the rightmost column of rows 4 and 8, for example, indicate that the address is not available to be used as a host address. Addresses that have an all-0s host portion are special-case addresses. Boxes shaded as in the last row of the full worksheet and in the rightmost column of rows 3 and 7 indicate that the address is not available to be used as a host address. Addresses that have an all-1s host portion are special-case addresses.

Look at the rightmost column of the worksheet. The header indicates that this column applies to a mask of 255.255.255.252. For the Class C network 192.168.1.0, the addresses in the range 192.168.1.0 to 192.168.1.31 can be subdivided, using a mask of 255.255.255.252, into eight separate networks:

192.168.1.0

192.168.1.4

192.168.1.8

192.168.1.12

192.168.1.16

192.168.1.20

192.168.1.24

192.168.1.28

Note that these eight addresses are shaded in the worksheet to reflect the fact that this address is the special-case "all-0s" address.

The broadcast address for each of these networks is:

192.168.1.3

192.168.1.7

192.168.1.11

192.168.1.15

192.168.1.19

192.168.1.23

192.168.1.27

192.168.1.31

These addresses are shaded to reflect the fact that they are the all-1s address on the network. All columns have a number of consecutively grouped unshaded cells. These represent all of the potential valid host addresses for a given subnet. There are only two hosts available per subnet when using a mask of 255.255.255.252.

Addresses in the range 192.168.1.0 to 192.168.1.31 can be sub-divided into any of the following:

- 8 networks using a mask of 255.255.255.252

- 4 networks using a mask of 255.255.255.248

- 2 networks using a mask of 255.255.255.240

- 1 network using a mask of 255.255.255.224

The entire Class C network 192.168.1.0 can be subdivided into any of the following (or any combination thereof):

- 64 networks of 2 hosts using a mask of 255.255.255.252

- 32 networks of 6 hosts using a mask of 255.255.255.248

- 16 networks of 14 hosts using a mask of 255.255.255.240

- 8 networks of 30 hosts using a mask of 255.255.255.224

- 4 networks of 62 hosts using a mask of 255.255.255.192

- 2 networks of 126 hosts using a mask of 255.255.255.128

- 1 network of 254 hosts using a mask of 255.255.255.0

Consider the two-router network in Illustration 5-2. Assume that we can use only IP addresses from 192.168.1.0 to 192.168.1.31. Also assume that we must use numbered IP inter-faces on the routers, which would require a two-host network for connecting Router A to Router C on the point-to-point link. We need 5 IP addresses for the Ethernet at the remote branch office and 13 IP addresses for the Ethernet at the corporate of-fice, or three networks with a total of 20 IP addresses. Should be doable. If you use fixed-length subnet masks, you could divide the address space in half, by using a 28-bit network mask (255.255.255.240), with each half having 14 hosts (Illustration 5-3).

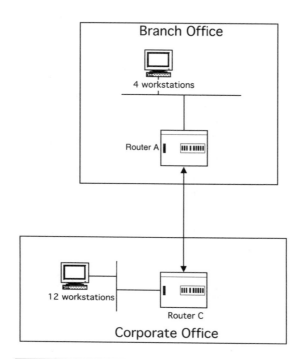

Illustration 5-2 Example Network

.0/24	.128/25	.192/26	.224/27	.240/28	.248/29	.252/30
0	0	0	0	0	0	0
1	1	1	1	1	1	1
2	2	2	2	2	2	2
3	3	3	3	3	3	3
4	4	4	4	4	4	4
5	5	5	5	5	5	5
6	6	6	6	6	6	6
7	7	7	7	7	7	7
8	8	8	8	8	8	8
9	9	9	9	9	9	9
10	10	10	10	10	10	10

Illustration 5-3 Networks with 14 Hosts per Network

11	11	11	11	11	11	11
12	12	12	12	12	12	12
13	13	13	13	13	13	13
14	14	14	14	14	14	14
15	15	15	15	15	15	15
16	16	16	16	16	16	16
17	17	17	17	17	17	17
18	18	18	18	18	18	18
19	19	19	19	19	19	19
20	20	20	20	20	20	20
21	21	21	21	21	21	21
22	22	22	22	22	22	22
23	23	23	23	23	23	23
24	24	24	24	24	24	24
25	25	25	25	25	25	25
26	26	26	26	26	26	26
27	27	27	27	27	27	27
28	28	28	28	28	28	28
29	29	29	29	29	29	29
30	30	30	30	30	30	30
31	31	31	31	31	31	31

Illustration 5-3 (Continued)

This is not viable, because we need at least three networks, due
to the point-to-point link having to use numbered interfaces. If
you used a 29-bit network mask, we could divide the host space
into four equal-sized networks with six hosts per network (Illustration 5-4).

.0/24	.128/25	.192/26	.224/27	.240/28	.248/29	.252/30
0	0	0	0	0	0	0
1	1	1	1	1	1	1
2	2	2	2	2	2	2

Illustration 5-4 Four Networks with Six Hosts per Network

3	3	3	3	3	3	3
4	4	4	4	4	4	4
5	5	5	5	5	5	5
6	6	6	6	6	6	6
7	7	7	7	7	7	7
8	8	8	8	8	8	8
9	9	9	9	9	9	9
10	10	10	10	10	10	10
11	11	11	11	11	11	11
12	12	12	12	12	12	12
13	13	13	13	13	13	13
14	14	14	14	14	14	14
15	15	15	15	15	15	15
16	16	16	16	16	16	16
17	17	17	17	17	17	17
18	18	18	18	18	18	18
19	19	19	19	19	19	19
20	20	20	20	20	20	20
21	21	21	21	21	21	21
22	22	22	22	22	22	22
23	23	23	23	23	23	23
24	24	24	24	24	24	24
25	25	25	25	25	25	25
26	26	26	26	26	26	26
27	27	27	27	27	27	27
28	28	28	28	28	28	28
29	29	29	29	29	29	29
30	30	30	30	30	30	30
31	31	31	31	31	31	31

Illustration 5-4 (Continued)

The problem is that we have a requirement for one network to
have 13 IP addresses, and this subnet permits a maximum of

only six hosts per network. Even using two of these six host networks would fall short of the total hosts required. It appears that there is no solution if we use fixed-length masks. We could use variable-length masks, but that would require extreme caution if we wanted to use RIP routing. Remember, RIP routing does not include route masks in the routing updates. We could use OSPF, though. Let's look at how the network might be divided up using variable-length masks (Illustration 5-5).

.0/24	.128/25	.192/26	.224/27	.240/28	.248/29	.252/30
0	0	0	0	0	0	0
1	1	1	1	1	1	RTR A 1
2	2	2	2	2	2	RTR C 2
3	3	3	3	3	3	3
4	4	4	4	4	4	4
5	5	5	5	5	5	5
6	6	6	6	6	6	6
7	7	7	7	7	7	7
8	8	8	8	8	8	8
9	9	9	9	9	RTR A 9	9
10	10	10	10	10	10	10
11	11	11	11	11	WS A 11	11
12	12	12	12	12	WS B 12	12
13	13	13	13	13	WS C 13	13
14	14	14	14	14	WS D 14	14
15	15	15	15	15	15	15
16	16	16	16	16	16	16
17	17	17	17	RTR C 17	17	17
18	18	18	18	18	18	18
19	19	19	19	WS A 19	19	19
20	20	20	20	WS B 20	20	20
21	21	21	21	WS C 21	21	21
22	22	22	22	WS D 22	22	22
23	23	23	23	WS E 23	23	23
24	24	24	24	WS F 24	24	24

Illustration 5-5 Variable-Mask Solution

25	25	25	25	WS G 25	25	25
26	26	26	26	WS H 26	26	26
27	27	27	27	WS I 27	27	27
28	28	28	28	WS J 28	28	28
29	29	29	29	WS K 29	29	29
30	30	30	30	WS L 30	30	30
31	31	31	31	31	31	31

Illustration 5-5 (Continued)

The first network, 192.168.1.0/30, has two available hosts. This network will be used for the point-to-point network between Router A and Router C. The second network, 192.168.1.8/29, can have six hosts in it. The branch office requires four workstations and one router address (five total host addresses). This network would fit the requirement, with one host address to spare. The third network, 192.168.1.16/28, can have 14 hosts. Since the corporate office requires only 13 host addresses, this network will fit the requirement and also have one host address to spare. Overall there isn't too much left over. There was one network, 192.168.1.4/30, left over as "room to grow" (nothing is ever *wasted*).

Illustration 5-6 shows what the network looks like with addresses assigned. Since we restricted ourselves to use only the first 32 addresses in the 192.168.1.0 Class C address, seven-eighths of all the address space in that one Class C network is still available. In fact, we could install another seven networks just like it, using the remainder of the 192.168.1.0 Class C address!

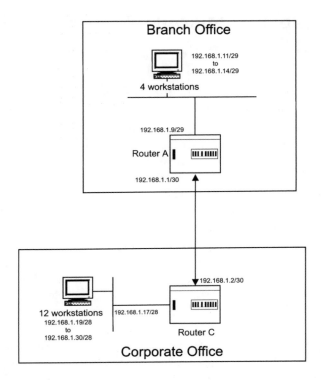

Illustration 5-6 Example Network with Addresses

Additional examples of how to design an appropriate address scheme taking efficiency of routing and address utilization, administrative ease of use, and management, growth, and Internet connectivity will be provided. The IP addressing worksheet in Appendix C divides the host portion of a Class C address into subnets and lets you see clearly where each network begins and ends when a specific mask is used.

Broadcast-Capable, Multiple-Access Networks: Ethernet and Token Ring

There are a few options for addressing on an Ethernet or a To-ken Ring. One strategy is to have a single IP network sufficient in size to be able to provide address space for the hosts that need connectivity through that medium. The address space should include some reserved IP addresses that will be allo-cated as the network grows. Illustration 5-7 depicts a single Ethernet using only a portion of the address space for a Class C network.

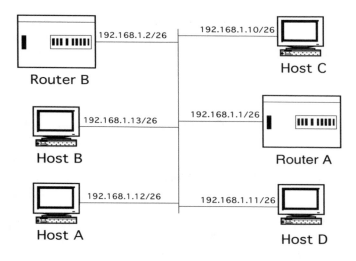

Illustration 5-7 IP Addressing on a LAN (Single Network)

The Class C network, 192.168.1.0, is subnetted with a mask of 255.255.255.192. This network is capable of supporting 62 hosts, so there is plenty of room for expansion. The most popular net-work sizes for an Ethernet or a Token Ring permit from 14 to 126 hosts.

Another addressing scheme involves the division of an Ethernet into workgroups, or cliques. Each workgroup should have the majority of its needed resources internal (including disk space, printers) to the workgroup. Illustration 5-8 shows a Token Ring with two workgroups. A 29-bit network mask (255.255.255.248) permits a maximum of six hosts per network.

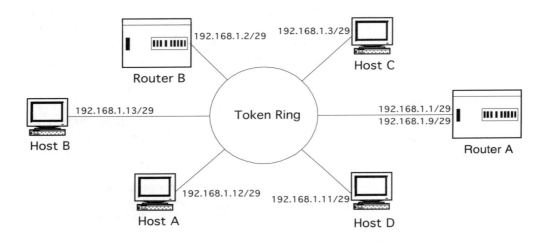

Illustration 5-8 IP Addressing in a LAN (Multiple Networks)

The first workgroup—Router B, Host C, and Router A—is using the 192.168.1.0/29 network. Host B, Host A, Host D, and Router A all participate on the 192.168.1.8/29 network. When Host C wishes to exchange a file with Host A, a router must forward the traffic between the two networks. Router A is multihomed; it has IP interfaces on both workgroup networks. Router A will forward the traffic from 192.168.1.3/29 to 192.168.1.12/29.

Occasionally members of working groups change in their traffic patterns and use the router too much to facilitate their communications. There are essentially three options:

- Move one of the hosts into the other host's workgroup;

- Multihome the hosts in both workgroups; or

- Abolish hopes of achieving a workgroup addressing scheme.

LAN Transit Networks

I was amazed to find that a bastion of networks out there are still predominantly non-TCP/IP networks. I was at a site recently where they were routing IPX (heavily) and bridging IP for management (Telnet console access, or SNMP). Administration was divided into the Novell group, which supported LAN applications, and the WAN group, which managed interconnections. I have seen cases in which a LAN group resisted having TCP/IP on its network. In one case that I know of, the LAN group permitted a network of only two TCP/IP hosts to participate on its IPX LAN. I thought it was worth showing Illustration 5-9.

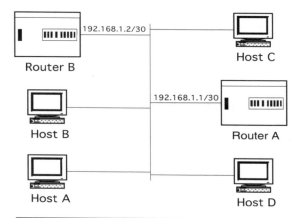

Illustration 5-9 IP LAN Transit Network

Router A and Router B share the same IP network, 192.168.1.0/30. That network can have only two hosts, so it looks very much like a point-to-point link, which is what it logically is. The LAN is used only for TCP/IP connectivity across some distance, although its main purpose is to service IPX workstations and servers.

Point to Point (Numbered)

Some router manufacturers do not offer an option for an unnumbered IP interface. If this is the case each end of a point-to-point link must have an IP address. Since there can be only two hosts on a point-to-point link, it would be a waste to use a network that could support more than two hosts. In Illustration 5-10 the routers have a point-to-point link between them. They are configured to use network 192.168.2.0/30, one of the subnets that supports only two hosts total. In an RIP environment the damage can be much more severe. Whenever you are restricted to using a fixed-length subnet mask, the number of hosts allocated to a point-to-point link would be the same as what is allocated to an Ethernet, or vice versa.

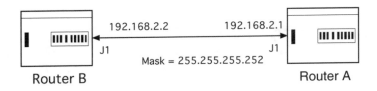

Illustration 5-10 Point to Point (Numbered)

Point to Point (Unnumbered)

The good news is that many routers do support unnumbered IP on point-to-point links. This is not as big a boon to OSPF as it is to RIP, since OSPF can support variable-length subnet masks, but it is savings and has some big rewards. For instance, you don't need to be configured for every network that could possibly be at the other end of the link. This is especially nice for the dial-backup application, as well as ISDN remote dial-in applications. The routers are able to support unnumbered interfaces because they use an identifier for each end point, the router ID. Illustration 5-11 shows an unnumbered IP network between Router A and Router B.

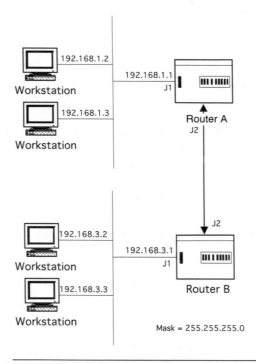

Illustration 5-11 Point-to-Point Network (Unnumbered)

As mentioned, ISDN (and other dial-up services) is a special type of point-to-point connection. When it is up, it looks and behaves just like a digital leased line. Routers typically run PPP across the ISDN link. What makes an ISDN line different is that it also behaves like a telephone. Through the use of the D-channel signaling, a router can place a call with ISDN as simply as a computer can dial and connect with a modem. It is a very powerful feature that allows a router to "place a call" over ISDN and to begin routing, based on the destination IP address within a packet. After a period of inactivity the router can tear down the call and be ready to place the next one. Unnumbered IP interfaces work nicely on any point-to-point dial connection, since it would be cumbersome to configure the interfaces to be able to use the same network as all the remotes use. The alternative is to multihome the router with an address from each one of the remote location's IP networks.

Pooled Dial-In Access

Pooled dial-in access links should be treated as individual point-to-point links that are mass terminated on a single device or multiple devices. The links could be most efficiently addressed using a 2-bit host ID. For instance, in Illustration 5-12, each of the four remote hosts could be running SLIP (Serial Line IP) or PPP (Point to Point Protocol), using addresses dynamically assigned by the terminal server (something most terminal servers can do) with a 30-bit network mask that provides only two host addresses. The router could be configured in a similar manner, but it would be presumed that there is a network (perhaps an Ethernet) local to Router C that would require address space.

ISDN Primary and Basic Rate interfaces can be viewed in a similar manner. A Primary Rate interface has the ability to terminate up to 23 B-channel calls, whereas a Basic Rate interface can terminate only up to two B-channel calls. These can be unnumbered or numbered IP interfaces, depending on the design and the capabilities of the routers/terminal adapters that are used. In any case the topology is very similar to "pooled access." See Illustration 5-12.

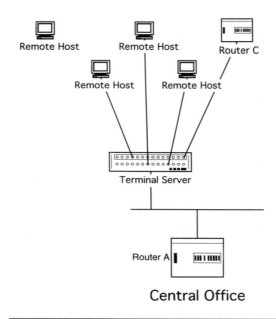

Illustration 5-12 Pooled Dial-in Access

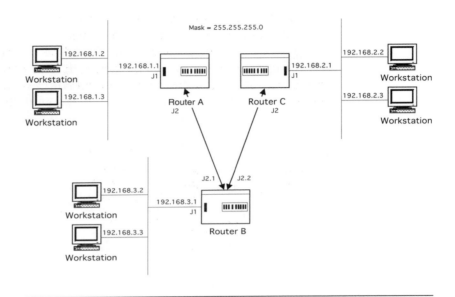

Illustration 5-13 ISDN Basic-Rate Interface Pooled Access

Nonbroadcast Multiple-Access Networks: Frame Relay

Frame Relay and X.25 are examples of networks that permit multiple devices (more than two) to connect and communicate but do not have the capability to support broadcast. To avoid a clamor of calls and e-mail, let me say that I do understand that Frame Relay was designed to look just like a local area network and to support broadcast capability. I have never seen a carrier offer any kind of broadcast or multicast capability, but I am sure that some must support it. In this text, which should be fairly close to "real world," I will discuss Frame Relay as if there were no broadcast capability. See Illustration 5-14.

A typical Frame Relay network would have a number of routers, each with a single physical interface into the Frame Relay
network, or "cloud." To the Frame Relay subscriber it would
appear that they are the only devices on the network—a virtual
private network. Each site that needs to communicate directly
with another site would require a permanent virtual circuit
(PVC). The end points of the PVC are identified with a data link
connection identifier (DLCI). Even though a router may have
more than one PVC that is terminated on it to allow direct access to multiple sites, it still may require only one physical connection to the carrier.

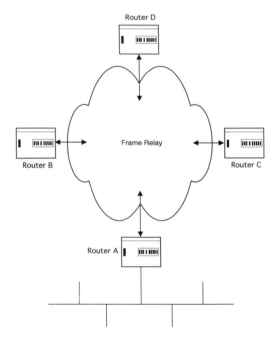

Illustration 5-14 Logical Frame Relay View

It is important to note that Frame Relay is based on the premise
that modern digital networks are nearly error free. As such

some of the functions that were essential in X.25 have been removed, their functions handled by the higher-layer protocols. Another interesting distinction is the way in which bandwidth is sold and allocated. A subscriber will pay for a guaranteed data rate, called the committed information rate (CIR). As long as the subscriber keeps the data flowing into the cloud at a rate equal to or less than the CIR, the carrier agrees not to discard any packets. The subscriber may burst above the CIR and all the data may be allowed through; however, under conditions of congestion the Frame Relay service provider may discard any packets that make up the excess above the CIR.

Frame Relay (Full Mesh)

One way to configure a Frame Relay network is to provision each site with a PVC to every other site. This is known as a full-mesh configuration (Illustration 5-15). Carriers typically charge for the presence of the PVC and for the CIR the PVC is provisioned to use. As a result, the full-mesh Frame Relay configuration is going to typically be the more expensive configuration. Sometimes it is not cost-prohibitive, though, so it pays to ask the carrier's account manager.

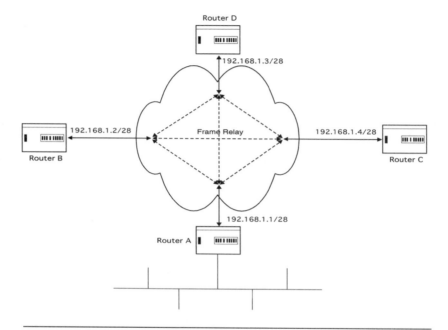

Illustration 5-15 Full-Mesh Frame Relay (View 1)

Router B knows that in order to pass traffic to Router D, it must use the link layer address, the DLCI, that corresponds to Router D. The Frame Relay switch will use the path specified by the permanent virtual circuit to deliver the frame to Router D. IP addressing is simple in a full-mesh network. Pick a network size sufficient to accommodate the number of devices internetworked, using the Frame Relay service plus some growth, and assign a host ID from the chosen subnet to each router's Frame Relay interface, as shown in Illustration 5-15. An address scheme that uses only a single IP network for addressing all of the devices on the Frame Relay network is known as a "cloud model." All hosts are in the single IP network cloud.

The number of PVCs required to provision a network in a full-mesh configuration is equal to $N*(N-1)/2$, where N is the number of nodes in the Frame Relay network. A network with four sites would require six PVCs to interconnect them. This is shown in Illustration 5-16. Imagine what a 20-site full-mesh network would look like if it were drawn out similar to the 4-site network in the illustration.

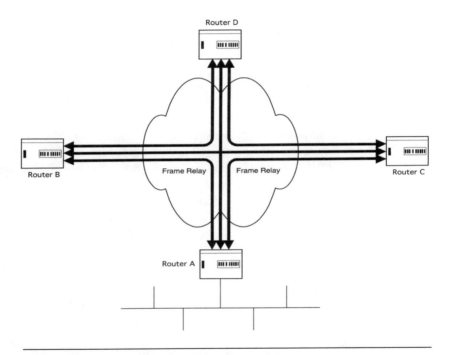

Illustration 5-16 Full-Mesh Frame Relay (View 2)

Both RIP and OSPF work well in a full-mesh Frame Relay network using the cloud model for IP addressing. In fact, OSPF works best when implemented in this way. OSPF relies on a constant contact with its neighbors and since each router in a full-mesh Frame Relay network has a PVC between itself and any other router in the Frame Relay network, these adjacencies are easily maintained. In actuality, only one router per network needs to maintain these neighbor relationships with all the other routers in the network. This router is known as the *designated router* (DR). In a full-mesh Frame Relay network it may not matter which of the routers on the IP network becomes the designated router.

Frame Relay (Hub and Spoke)

A Frame Relay configuration that is far more popular than the full-mesh configuration is a topology commonly called "*hub and spoke*." One central Frame Relay hub router has a PVC to each of the remote sites. Each remote site has a PVC to only one location, the Frame Relay hub router. There will be exactly (N–1) PVCs used in a hub-and-spoke Frame Relay network. One reason to configure this type of network is that the nonhub routers are truly remote offices that need some resources that are centrally located (at the same site where the hub router is located) and the remote sites seldom communicate with one another. The remote sites can communicate with one another but they must, in all cases, do this through the hub router.

One of two different IP addressing models may be used for a hub-and-spoke Frame Relay network, the cloud model, which we have already discussed, and the point-to-point model. Again, the cloud model would have a single IP network. Each router's Frame Relay interface would be assigned a host address from that network. This is in contrast to the point-to-point model, which allocates an IP network for each PVC, and each end point has a host address in that network assigned to it. Illustration 5-17 depicts a point-to-point addressing model in a hub-and-spoke Frame Relay network.

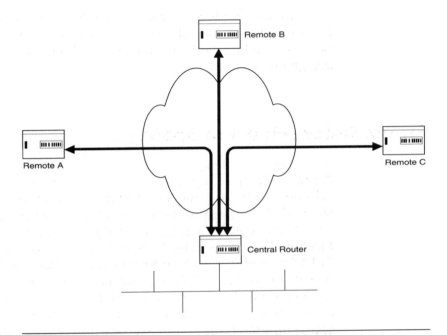

Illustration 5-17 Hub-and-Spoke Frame Relay

RIP typically does not have any issues with being able to operate in either IP addressing model in a hub-and-spoke Frame Relay network. OSPF, because of the way it needs to maintain adjacencies, requires a point-to-point addressing model. The designated router on a given IP network can always maintain its adjacencies, since there are always at most two routers on a Frame Relay point-to-point IP network. If you use a cloud model on a hub-and-spoke Frame Relay network and run RIP, it is possible to convert over to OSPF without having to change the IP addressing. It is kind of a cheat, but I have done it effectively. The key is that the hub router must be forced into being the designated router. Another router will become the backup designated router, and it won't be able to maintain its adjacencies, but that has never been a problem. If the hub router fails, there will be bigger problems than worrying about what the backup designated router is. Use this approach with caution, since there are no guarantees how another router would handle the situation or even if it would allow a router to be ineligible to become the designated router. The best policy for Frame Relay addressing is to use the point-to-point address model for OSPF routing.

Frame Relay (Partial Mesh)

Sometimes a company starts with either a full-mesh Frame Relay network and cuts back on its meshing, based on usage or a hub and spoke, and adds PVCs because certain sites seem to "collaborate" with each other. The result is something less than a full-mesh network and more than a hub-and-spoke network. This is known as a *partial-mesh Frame Relay network.*

For RIP routing the cloud or point-to-point address model will work. For OSPF the cloud model cannot be counted on to work. Generally there are no guarantees as to whether a single router will have a PVC to each of the other routers. In Illustration 5-18 Router E does not have a PVC to Router A. It is necessary to define a network for each PVC and to allocate addresses accordingly.

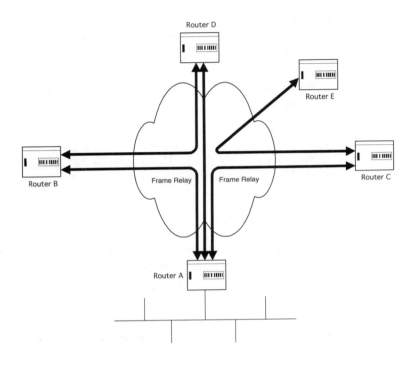

Illustration 5-18 Partial-Mesh Frame Relay

Summary

Many different topologies can be found in a modern TCP/IP network. This chapter summarized some of the more common topologies and discussed the addressing schemes that could be used with each. The following were discussed in the chapter:

- *Ethernet and Token Ring:* Examples of broadcast-capable multiple-access networks. It is typical to use a single IP network on each segment or ring and to allocate addresses for hosts out of that network.

- *Point-to-point links:* There are exactly two hosts per point-to-point link "this" end and "that" end. Therefore, the IP interfaces for those hosts can be configured to use unnumbered IP interfaces or numbered IP interfaces. If an IP address must be assigned to the hosts, it is common to use a network defined with a 30-bit network mask. These networks have enough host addresses to support only two hosts.

- *Pooled dial-in access:* These are treated in the same manner as point-to-point links except that the pooling device will often serve as a point of route aggregation (discussed later).

- *Frame Relay:* This is an example of a nonbroadcast multiple-access network. Frame Relay topologies are commonly configured as hub-and-spoke. Other possibilities are full mesh and partial mesh. Depending on the Frame Relay topology and the routing protocol used in the intranet, the addressing scheme can be in the format of the cloud model (one network, many hosts) or the point-to-point model (many networks, two hosts per net).

Addressing for Internet Connections

The addresses that are used within an autonomous system are greatly dependent on whether the hosts within that system must have direct connections to the Internet. The reason for this is that if the hosts are to have direct Internet connections, the addresses must be unique among all the hosts that are connected to the Internet. To ensure this uniqueness, address-assignment agencies screen requests for addresses and make allocations. There are also guidelines for choosing an addressing scheme if an entity wishes to use TCP/IP for data transport but has no intention of connecting to the Internet. These topics are discussed in this chapter.

The Internet Connection

The Internet has become explosively popular in the past couple of years. More and more companies are opting to give their employees access to the resources of the Internet and offering access to information about their company or its products to the people using the Internet. It is easy to find a way to get your information published on the Internet and available to the masses. Typically a phone call to the local Internet service provider (ISP) is all that it takes to get the ball rolling. The ISP can get a domain name, such as JQZ.COM, allocated to you and set up a Web server with your content on it.

The decision about how to get all of a company's employees access to the Internet can be a bit more daunting. The details for making the decision are well beyond the scope of this book. Let's assume for the moment that the decision is black or white. That is, we will assume that if a company wants to make all the Internet's resources available to all the people and systems in the organization, it must get a "legal" Internet address allocation. This is really not the case, but we'll discuss the gray areas at the end of the chapter.

What is a "legal" address? A "legal" address is one for which a company has, at one time or another, petitioned a legitimate Internet address-allocation authority for a network number and the authority was obliged to grant the request (or at least offer a partial allocation). The petitioning entity is provided with an IP network number (or more than one) that is registered exclusively for its use. No other entity may connect to the Internet and advertise routing to those addresses except for the organization to which it is registered. In short, a "legal" address is an address for which the user is the registered owner.

In the earlier days of the Internet it was not so difficult to get an IP network allocated to an organization that had much more addressing space than the organization could possibly require. If a company could justify a requirement for more than the number of hosts that a Class C address could provide, it could (almost) easily request and receive a Class B network number. It was unheard of that multiple Class C networks would be allocated to an entity if a single Class C were insufficient. This was in part due to the fact that if two Class C networks were allocated, the Internet backbone's routing table would increase by two routes, whereas a Class B allocation would increase it by only one route. Further, it was beyond expectation that the Internet, which linked universities, government agencies, and research firms, would ever become a consumer product and reach into the homes of millions of people.

Class B networks are not nearly as easy to get today. Quite a few are still available, but they are difficult to get. I have seen a few appeals for the return of unused Class B networks to the allocation pool. To be sure, you must be able to justify a significant efficiency of address space utilization if there is to be any hope of getting a Class B network allocation, assuming that there are some networks that have yet to be divvied out. Today, if you petition for a network allocation, you are much more likely to get more than one Class C address if the petition justifies more than one Class C network's address space. Even so, chances are good that the address requirement will be scrutinized and the request reduced to a more "realistic" allocation. Don't let the possibility of having part of your petition rejected deter you from requesting the "realistic" amount of addresses that you think you will need now and in the foreseeable future. Class C allocations of more than one network number are being made in such a way that the routing tables will no longer grow by the number of networks that are allocated to a single entity. Attempts are being made to allocate networks in such a way that Internet routing tables increase by only one route with the addition. This is known as *supernetting* and will be discussed in Chapter 7.

Petitioning for a registered IP network number is not very difficult. The easiest way is to contact your local ISP. Many have reasonable fees for doing the paperwork for you and will work with you to get the requisite information and to file the documents. Appendix B provides the current template from:

ftp://rs.internic.net/templates/internet-number-template.txt

To register with the InterNIC for a network number, you merely fill out the information in the template and file the request. All the information for how to do this can be found in the template document. There are recurring fees for ownership of IP network numbers, as well as domain names! When the IP network number allocation is made, you will be notified of the IP network that has been registered for your exclusive use. The success of CIDR (explained later) depends, however, on getting network allocations directly from your Internet service provider, except in extenuating circumstances. Check with your local ISP for a network allocation.

Private IP Network Allocation

An entity that does not have any intention of providing Internet access to the desktops of its employees yet wishes to use TCP/IP on its networks has several choices. It can use a registered IP network number, any valid IP network number(s) even though they may be registered under another organization, or network numbers specifically allocated for use by private IP networks.

Using a registered IP network number is not a bad choice, especially if there is a glimmer of a hope that someday (within the next year) Internet service will be offered to the desktop. There are some drawbacks, though. First, the IP address-allocation authority will not happily grant a frivolous request. There is a shortage of address space as it is; if every company using TCP/IP required unique addressing, the shortage would be even greater. Second, the address space allocated to the entity would be "tight." That is to say, the addresses would have to be used efficiently, with little room for administrative amenities (discussed in Chapter 9). If the Internet will not be offered to the desktop, there are better choices than the use of a "legal" IP network for addressing.

TCP/IP is a suite of protocols. IP addresses can have a first octet that ranges from 1 to 255. The value of the first octet determines that class of the network, which in turn determines the address space that can be used. All this was covered in Chapter 2. The point is that TCP/IP does not define the Internet or the global usage of the addresses. It does require that in a TCP/IP inter-network all addresses be unique. Many first- or even second-time TCP/IP network implementers will decide on the quantity of hosts that a network will have in it and will choose one of the many IP network numbers that will fulfill the host require-ments. More often than not, the network number is chosen for its appearance on paper or for its euphonic qualities (how it sounds rolling off the tip of the tongue). In a pure sense this is not an incorrect way of choosing the network number for an or-ganization; however, it has some problems. Mistakes happen. Everyone knows that. I am here to tell you that if you are the ad-ministrator of a network that uses someone else's registered IP network and—somehow—that network is advertised on the Internet and its traffic is rerouted to you, you will definitely hear about it.

The best option is to use a set of IP networks that have been set aside specifically for use in private IP networks. RFC 1597, "Ad-dress Allocation for Private Subnets," delineates a group of net-works that, if they were to get inadvertently advertised on the Internet, would not harm anybody's routing. The private IP network allocations include one Class A network, 10.0.0.0; 16 Class B networks, 172.16.0.0–172.31.0.0; and 256 Class C net-works, 192.168.0.0–192.168.255.0. This RFC set aside quite a bit of host space. All of the examples in this book are illustrated us-ing these private IP networks.

Although you can combine all of the networks set aside in RFC 1597, depending on your requirement, it is more common to choose the Class A network, the Class B networks, or the Class C networks and to use just that one set of allocations through-out your network. Which one should you choose? It depends

on the objective you set for your addressing scheme. After you
have read the next chapter, you will see that there are ways of
using RIP routing and achieving route aggregation if you can
take advantage of the assumptions that a router makes with regard to network masks in the route updates. This would typically require the use of the Class B or Class C allocations. If the
goal is to design a scheme that is easy to administer and that
uses OSPF, the Class A allocation would work extremely well.

Firewalls and Network Address Translators

You might address with private IP networks and then, whether
planned or not, still need to provide Internet access to internal
resources. In fact, this is a strategy that has relieved some of the
stress on the IP network allocation demand. The concept is
fairly simple. Get an allocation of registered addresses that are
globally unique. Use private IP networks as defined in RFC
1597 for addressing within the autonomous system. Use a fire-
wall, a router, or a dedicated piece of hardware that implements a function called a network address translator at the
boundary between the Internet and the autonomous system.
This device will map an address in one domain to another, statically or dynamically.

One of the benefits is that this will save globally unique addresses. The only devices that need to be mapped are the ones
that need access to or by the Internet. Devices such as routers
would not need to be mapped at all. Further, those devices in
the autonomous system that would be initiating connections to
Internet resources would be able to share a pool of globally
unique addresses instead of being allocated a constant globally
unique address.

Most firewalls implement this feature. A few routers are starting to emerge that implement a network address translator.

Some hardware devices are even dedicated to the function. These hardware devices and the routers that implement NAT are capable of maintaining a large translation table servicing thousands of simultaneous connections. One popular device is the Private Internet Exchange (PIX), which was introduced in 1994 by Address Translation, Inc.

Summary

The biggest decision to be dealt with when determining what the addressing plan will be for an enterprise is whether Internet service will be offered to the desktop. In the past a company that required Internet access typically used registered IP network numbers in the autonomous system. This is still a popular choice, as evidenced by the number of network number requests that the InterNIC processes on a monthly basis.

Companies that are implementing TCP/IP networks with no intention of connecting to the Internet may be able to get and implement the addressing using registered IP network numbers, but this is becoming more and more uncommon with the requirements that the InterNIC is placing on address-utilization efficiency. Instead it is good practice to design the addressing within an autonomous system that will not connect to the Internet around the private IP address allocations set aside in RFC 1597. They are:

Class A: 10.0.0.0 through 10.255.255.255

Class B: 172.16.0.0 through 172.31.255.255

Class C: 192.168.0.0 through 192.168.255.255

If addressing is designed to use an unregistered IP network number or one or more of the private IP network numbers, it is still possible to provide Internet access to hosts within the autonomous system. The technology known as NAT, or network address translation, makes this possible by mapping registered, globally unique addresses to the private or unregistered addresses in use within the autonomous system.

Addressing to Achieve Route Table Efficiency

A routing table can be judged on its precision for delivering packets in the shortest period of time, with the least number of hops, or for the least amount of money. Whatever the metric is that determines the routing decisions, the route table has to be searched in its entirety in order to perform the Basic Match pruning rule. Each unicast packet received by a router must have a next hop identified for it. The larger the initial working set of routes, the more time it takes to search for the next hop. The smaller the initial working set of routes, the better.

There are two aspects to achieving route table efficiency. First, you have to plan for route reduction in the IP addressing scheme. It does not happen naturally, even if you do everything else right. Second, the routing architecture must be able to summarize routes.

The concepts of route aggregation have recently been extended to the Internet backbone itself. This is discussed later in this chapter.

Addressing for Route Aggregation— An Example

Route summarization, aggregation, reduction, and collapsing mean about the same thing. It is the representation of more than one route with a single route, sometimes even hundreds or thousands of routes with a single route entry. The classic example is a workstation that has the following route table:

Destination	Gateway	Genmask	Flags	Metric	Ref	Use	Iface
172.16.8.0	0.0.0.0	255.255.255.192	U	0	0	246846	eth0
127.0.0.0	0.0.0.0	255.0.0.0	U	0	0	163840	lo
0.0.0.0	172.16.8.1	0.0.0.0	UG	0	0	224692	eth0

This workstation has a route entry for its locally defined IP interface and for the loopback address, and it has a default gateway. The default route stands for all routes not explicitly defined in the routing table. This one route entry can represent an entire intranet or the entire Internet.

Remember the example used to illustrate the utility of the IP address worksheet? Let's add a third router to the mix (Illustration 7-1). To continue this history, the small company that was used in our examples was purchased by a large regional corporation that wanted to take its success to a national level and so bought some smaller companies that were prominent in other regions. Our example company was one of these purchased companies. The new corporate office wants to be connected to each of the new regional offices. Illustration 7-1 depicts the corporate office router's connection to the regional office.

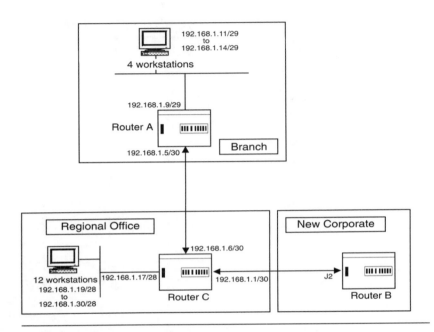

Illustration 7-1 Example Corporate Network

Illustration 7-2 shows how the IP address worksheet looks with the addition of Router B. Note that we have done a pretty good job of packing all the IP addresses to the left of Router B into a small area in the IP address worksheet. In fact, it is within the boundary of the 192.168.1.0/27 network, as denoted by the thick black lines bracketing it. This network can support a maximum of only 30 hosts. From Router B's perspective, you can get to any host in the 192.168.1.0/27 network by going out the J2 interface on Router B. The routing table for Router B is small:

Destination	Route Mask	Next Hop	Port	Metr	Typ	Src	Age
192.168.1.0	255.255.255.252	192.168.1.2	J2	0	DIR	LOC	3569
192.168.1.0	255.255.255.224	192.168.1.1	J2	1	REM	MGMT	0

and anything else . . .

.0/24	.128/25	.192/26	.224/27	.240/28	.248/29	.252/30
0	0	0	0	0	0	0
1	1	1	1	1	1	RTR C 1
2	2	2	2	2	2	RTR B 2
3	3	3	3	3	3	3
4	4	4	4	4	4	4
5	5	5	5	5	5	RTR A 5
6	6	6	6	6	6	RTR C 6
7	7	7	7	7	7	7
8	8	8	8	8	8	8
9	9	9	9	9	RTR A 9	9
10	10	10	10	10	10	10
11	11	11	11	11	WS A 11	11
12	12	12	12	12	WS B 12	12
13	13	13	13	13	WS C 13	13
14	14	14	14	14	WS D 14	14
15	15	15	15	15	15	15
16	16	16	16	16	16	16
17	17	17	17	RTR C 17	17	17
18	18	18	18	18	18	18
19	19	19	19	WS A 19	19	19
20	20	20	20	WS B 20	20	20
21	21	21	21	WS C 21	21	21
22	22	22	22	WS D 22	22	22
23	23	23	23	WS E 23	23	23
24	24	24	24	WS F 24	24	24
25	25	25	25	WS G 25	25	25
26	26	26	26	WS H 26	26	26
27	27	27	27	WS I 27	27	27
28	28	28	28	WS J 28	28	28
29	29	29	29	WS K 29	29	29
30	30	30	30	WS L 30	30	30
31	31	31	31	31	31	31

Illustration 7-2 Example Route Aggregation

The route entry on the second line of the route table summarizes all four network routes. The first entry in the route table is there because the IP address of 192.168.1.2 is defined on the J2 interface of Router B.

Had there been other devices out to the right of Router B, they would need to know only that to get to anything in 192.1.68.1.0/27, send it to Router B. The network to Router B is shown in Illustration 7-3.

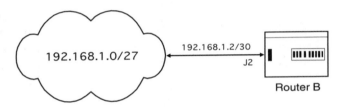

Illustration 7-3 Network Route to Router B

The company that purchased our little example company also bought seven other regional companies. The CIO liked the job that the network administrator did on the IP addressing at our example company, adopting the IP addressing architecture and using it on the other sites. Since the network administrator was so frugal in the use of IP addresses, there was room left over in the 192.168.1.0 class C network, enough for seven more regional offices. What a coincidence. Now the network might look like the one in Illustration 7-4.

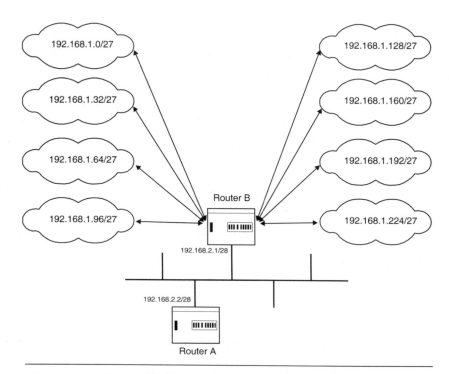

Illustration 7-4 Example Network with Route Aggregation 2

Router B's routing table could look like this:

Destination	Route Mask	Next Hop	Port	Metr	Typ	Src	Age
192.168.2.0	255.255.255.240	192.168.2.2	J1	0	DIR	LOC	3569
192.168.1.0	255.255.255.252	192.168.1.2	J2	0	DIR	LOC	3569
192.168.1.0	255.255.255.224	192.168.1.1	J2	1	REM	MGMT	0
192.168.1.32	255.255.255.252	192.168.1.34	J3	0	DIR	LOC	3569
192.168.1.32	255.255.255.224	192.168.1.33	J3	1	REM	MGMT	0
192.168.1.64	255.255.255.252	192.168.1.66	J4	0	DIR	LOC	3569
192.168.1.64	255.255.255.224	192.168.1.65	J4	1	REM	MGMT	0

192.168.1.96	255.255.255.252	192.168.1.98	J5	0	DIR	LOC	3569
192.168.1.96	255.255.255.224	192.168.1.97	J5	1	REM	MGMT	0
192.168.1.128	255.255.255.252	192.168.1.130	J6	0	DIR	LOC	3569
192.168.1.128	255.255.255.224	192.168.1.129	J6	1	REM	MGMT	0
192.168.1.160	255.255.255.252	192.168.1.162	J7	0	DIR	LOC	3569
192.168.1.160	255.255.255.224	192.168.1.161	J7	1	REM	MGMT	0
192.168.1.192	255.255.255.252	192.168.1.194	J8	0	DIR	LOC	3569
192.168.1.192	255.255.255.224	192.168.1.193	J8	1	REM	MGMT	0
192.168.1.224	255.255.255.252	192.168.1.226	J9	0	DIR	LOC	3569
192.168.1.224	255.255.255.224	192.168.1.225	J9	1	REM	MGMT	0

and anything else . . .

If Router B had a specific route to each network, it would have more than 30 routes in its routing table. Since the routes were designed to collapse into a fewer number of routes, Router B needs to know about only 17 routes (9 specific routes and 8 general routes). This is about half of what would have been required if all networks were represented by a specific route.

Router A's routing table could look like this:

Destination	Route Mask	Next Hop	Port	Metr	Typ	Src	Age
192.168.2.0	255.255.255.240	192.168.2.2	J2	0	DIR	LOC	3569
192.168.1.0	255.255.255.0	192.168.2.1	J2	1	REM	MGMT	0

and anything else . . .

This table has two routes; 32 routes were collapsed into a single route entry! Router A needs to know only that any packet with a destination whose first three octets (determined by route mask) are 192.168.1 should be forwarded to Router B as the next hop.

Planning for Aggregation

Now that you have seen an example of route aggregation, let's go back to the excerpt from the IP addressing worksheet. Look at network 192.168.1.16/30 in Illustration 7-5. This is a specific network in a hypothetical address plan. This network, along with 192.168.1.20/30, can be aggregated by a general route of 192.168.1.16/29. This route and up to two additional routes also can be subsumed (another term for aggregated) by a more general route, 192.168.1.16/28. Route 192.168.1.0/27 can subsume any route with more than 27 bits of network mask in the range 192.168.1.0 to 192.168.1.31. Route 192.168.1.0/24 can subsume any route to any network in the 192.168.1.0 Class C network.

.0/24	.128/25	.192/26	.224/27	.240/28	.248/29	.252/30
0	0	0	0	0	0	0
1	1	1	1	1	1	1
2	2	2	2	2	2	2
3	3	3	3	3	3	3
4	4	4	4	4	4	4
5	5	5	5	5	5	5
6	6	6	6	6	6	6
7	7	7	7	7	7	7
8	8	8	8	8	8	8
9	9	9	9	9	9	9
10	10	10	10	10	10	10
11	11	11	11	11	11	11
12	12	12	12	12	12	12
13	13	13	13	13	13	13
14	14	14	14	14	14	14
15	15	15	15	15	15	15
16	16	16	16	16	16	16
17	17	17	17	17	17	Start 17

Illustration 7-5 Example IP Address Worksheet showing Route Aggregation

18	18	18	18	18	18	Here 18
19	19	19	19	19	19	19
20	20	20	20	20	20	20
21	21	21	21	21	21	21
22	22	22	22	22	22	22
23	23	23	23	23	23	23
24	24	24	24	24	24	24
25	25	25	25	25	25	25
26	26	26	26	26	26	26
27	27	27	27	27	27	27
28	28	28	28	28	28	28
29	29	29	29	29	29	29
30	30	30	30	30	30	30
31	31	31	31	31	31	31

Illustration 7-5 (Continued)

If it were just that simple, there would be no problem. Network topologies must have the right "shape" to allow for route aggregation. Typically the network should have funnels, or bottlenecks, to be able to take advantage of aggregation. If there are other paths for the routing, the specific network routes might have a chance to get into the routing tables. In addition, with alternative paths it becomes difficult to use RIP and let the networks aggregate naturally. This is discussed later in this chapter. In our example Router B is the funnel. Everything at the top of the illustration was part of network 192.168.1.0/24, and everything to the bottom was part of 192.168.2.0/24, two distinct Class C networks.

Funnels appear throughout the modern intranet. Frame Relay lends itself to route aggregation when used in the popular hub-and-spoke topology. Dial-in remote-access modem pools are excellent points for route aggregation, as is an ISDN Primary Rate interface.

RIP and Route Aggregation

Some interesting side effects can be achieved by using RIP rout-ing. Due to the fact that RIP does not pass subnet information in its route updates, RIP must make assumptions about the net-work masks. This was presented in Chapter 4. If a router re-ceives an RIP route update and the router does not have an interface configured for the class of that network, it will use the natural mask for the route. If it does have a network defined on one of the router's interfaces, it will use the mask defined for that interface. The following network route update is sent out:

Destination = 192.168.1.0 Metric = 1

A router that has the following addresses defined directly on its interfaces receives the route update:

Address	Subnet
192.168.2.1	255.255.255.192
192.168.4.129	255.255.255.192

The router will have a route table entry installed:

Destination	Route Mask	Next Hop	Port	Metr	Typ	Src	Age
192.168.2.0	255.255.255.192	192.168.2.1	J2	0	DIR	LOC	3569
192.168.4.128	255.255.255.192	192.168.4.129	J3	0	DIR	LOC	3569
192.168.1.0	255.255.255.0	192.16 8.2.23	J2	1	REM	RIP	0

However, suppose that the same route were received by a router with the following interfaces defined on it:

Address	Subnet
192.168.2.1	255.255.255.192
192.168.1.129	255.255.255.192

Then the route table would look like this:

Destination	Route Mask	Next Hop	Port	Metr	Typ	Src	Age
192.168.2.0	255.255.255.192	192.168.2.1	J2	0	DIR	LOC	3569
192.168.1.128	255.255.255.192	192.168.1.129	J3	0	DIR	LOC	3569
192.168.1.0	255.255.255.192	192.168.2.23	J2	1	REM	RIP	0

The only difference between the two routers in this example is that the second router has a subnet of the Class C network 192.168.1.0 on one of its interfaces. This forces the router to use the same subnet mask as is used for the 192.168.1.128/26 network. In some cases this would cause incorrect routing choices to be made by the router. Look at the example in Illustration 7-6, where this is not the case.

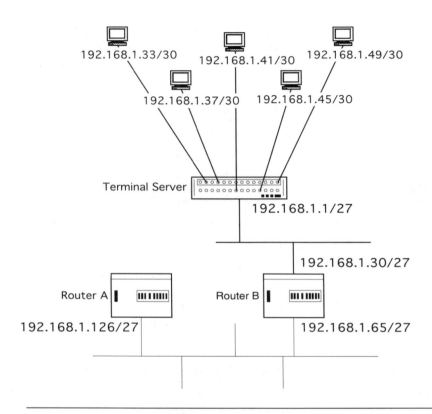

Illustration 7-6 Example Network with RIP Aggregation

At the top of the illustration are five hosts connected to a terminal server. Each host is assigned an address in one of the point-to-point IP networks. The terminal server also has a host ID in each of the point-to-point IP networks, although these addresses are not shown in the illustration. For instance, for the point-to-point IP network 192.168.1.32/30, the workstation is the 192.168.1.33/30 address, and the terminal server is the 192.168.1.34/30 address. In addition to the IP addresses required for the five point-to-point IP networks, the terminal server has an IP address assigned to its Ethernet port, but it is in a network defined by a smaller mask (permits more hosts). Terminal servers often have the ability to run RIP routing. Turn RIP routing on for both Router A and Router B and for the terminal server. The terminal server would have a routing table like this:

Destination	Route Mask	Next Hop	Port	Metr	Typ	Src	Age
192.168.1.64	255.255.255.224	192.168.1.30	J2	1	REM	RIP	17
192.168.1.32	255.255.255.252	192.168.1.34	J1.1	0	DIR	LOC	812
192.168.1.36	255.255.255.252	192.168.1.38	J1.2	0	DIR	LOC	812
192.168.1.40	255.255.255.252	192.168.1.42	J1.3	0	DIR	LOC	812
192.168.1.44	255.255.255.252	192.168.1.46	J1.4	0	DIR	LOC	812
192.168.1.48	255.255.255.252	192.168.1.50	J1.5	0	DIR	LOC	812
192.168.1.0	255.255.255.224	192.168.1.1	J2	1	DIR	LOC	812

This is expected. We get a pleasant surprise when we examine the routing table for Router B:

Destination	Route Mask	Next Hop	Port	Metr	Typ	Src	Age
192.168.1.64	255.255.255.224	192.168.1.65	J2	0	DIR	LOC	358
192.168.1.32	255.255.255.224	192.168.1.1	J1	1	REM	RIP	18
192.168.1.0	255.255.255.224	192.168.1.30	J1	0	DIR	LOC	359

The five point-to-point networks on the terminal server have been subsumed by a single IP route entry of 192.168.1.32/27! This is an example in which the assumptions that a router makes regarding the network mask can work in your favor. There are times, however, when the assumptions can just as easily be wrong.

For instance, look at Illustration 7-7. It is very much like the one we just discussed, except that the Ethernet between Router A and Router B has been readdressed.

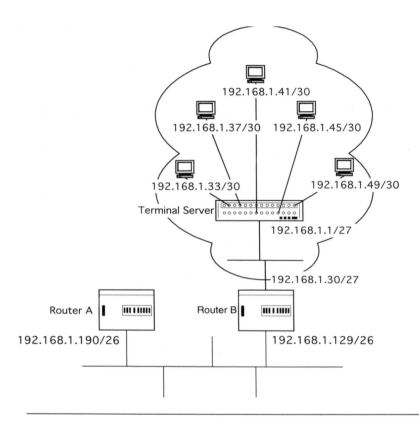

192.168.1.41/30

192.168.1.37/30   192.168.1.45/30

192.168.1.33/30   192.168.1.49/30

Terminal Server

192.168.1.1/27

192.168.1.30/27

Router A   Router B

192.168.1.190/26   192.168.1.129/26

Illustration 7-7 Example Network with RIP Aggregation 2

The routing table for Router A is:

Destination	Route Mask	Next Hop	Port	Metr	Typ	Src	Age
192.168.1.128	255.255.255.192	192.168.1.190	J1	0	DIR	LOC	358
192.168.1.0	255.255.255.192	192.168.1.129	J1	1	REM	RIP	18

There is a route entry for the locally defined IP address, as well as an RIP route to the network 192.168.1.0/26. This route has also subsumed all the other routes on Router B. The routing table on

Router A couldn't be better. Now let's look at the routing table on the terminal server:

Destination	Route Mask	Next Hop	Port	Metr	Typ	Src	Age
192.168.1.32	255.255.255.252	192.168.1.34	J1.1	0	DIR	LOC	812
192.168.1.36	255.255.255.252	192.168.1.38	J1.2	0	DIR	LOC	812
192.168.1.40	255.255.255.252	192.168.1.42	J1.3	0	DIR	LOC	812
192.168.1.44	255.255.255.252	192.168.1.46	J1.4	0	DIR	LOC	812
192.168.1.48	255.255.255.252	192.168.1.50	J1.5	0	DIR	LOC	812
192.168.1.128	255.255.255.224	192.168.1.30	J2	2	REM	RIP	24
192.168.1.0	255.255.255.224	192.168.1.1	J2	0	DIR	LOC	812

The terminal server has a route entry for 192.168.1.128, but look at the route mask; it is wrong. The mask should have been 255.255.255.192. Any addresses from 192.168.1.159 to 192.168.1.190 would not be reachable from the terminal server, as a result of the wrong mask being assumed for the route. The terminal server should issue an ICMP Destination Unreachable notification.

Here is an alternative. Use a different Class B or Class C network for each grouping of networks, as is shown in Illustration 7-8.

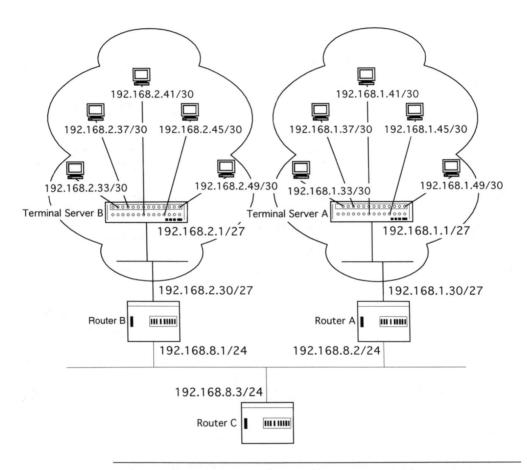

Illustration 7-8 Example Network with RIP Aggregation 3

Three Class C networks are being used in this example. Network 192.168.1.0/24 is being used in the rightmost terminal server cloud. Network 192.168.2.0/24 is being used in the leftmost terminal server cloud. Network 192.168.8.0/24 is being used on the Ethernet shared by Routers A, B, and C. The routing tables for the three routers are as follows:

Router A

Destination	Route Mask	Next Hop	Port	Metr	Typ	Src	Age
192.168.1.32	255.255.255.224	192.168.1.1	J1	1	REM	RIP	18
192.168.1.0	255.255.255.224	192.168.1.30	J1	0	DIR	LOC	359
192.168.2.0	255.255.255.0	192.168.8.1	J2	1	REM	RIP	5
192.168.8.0	255.255.255.0	192.168.8.2	J2	0	DIR	LOC	358

Router B

Destination	Route Mask	Next Hop	Port	Metr	Typ	Src	Age
192.168.1.0	255.255.255.0	192.168.8.2	J2	1	REM	RIP	6
192.168.2.0	255.255.255.224	192.168.2.30	J1	0	DIR	LOC	359
192.168.2.32	255.255.255.224	192.168.2.1	J1	1	REM	RIP	19
192.168.8.0	255.255.255.0	192.168.8.1	J2	0	DIR	LOC	358

Router C

Destination	Route Mask	Next Hop	Port	Metr	Typ	Src	Age
192.168.1.0	255.255.255.0	192.168.8.2	J2	1	REM	RIP	6
192.168.2.0	255.255.255.0	192.168.8.1	J2	1	REM	RIP	24
192.168.8.0	255.255.255.0	192.168.8.3	J2	0	DIR	LOC	358

Router C has no IP interface defined with any subnet of the Class C networks 192.168.1.0/24 or 192.168.2.0/24; therefore the best assumption that Router C can make is that the mask should be the inherent mask for the Class C networks (255.255.255.0). This would indicate that the entire Class C network can be reached via the "next hop" specified in the routing table. In this case it is true.

Using the quirks of RIP routing to lead to a smaller, more compact routing table can be rewarding. It can reduce the size of the routing tables throughout the intranet significantly. It does require planning and it can leave you scratching your head about why routing works to "these sites" but not to "those sites."

OSPF and Route Aggregation

Unlike RIP, OSPF includes the route mask information in its route updates (link-state advertisements). The manner in which we were able to get some route summarization with RIP is not available for use with OSPF. There is, however, a way to summarize routes in OSPF. In Chapter 4, OSPF was discussed and the concept of areas introduced.

In OSPF an area is a group of IP networks in which the routers share the same link-state databases. The OSPF backbone area (area 0.0.0.0) is required in every autonomous system running OSPF. This may be the only area in the domain, or it may be one of many. Area 0.0.0.0 is always used to join any other areas. For that reason area 0 must always be contiguous. In places where it is not possible to be physically contiguous, virtual links are used to join the two or more portions of the backbone area into a logically contiguous area.

Area border routers serve as the conduit between different areas, usually the backbone area and any other area. The area border router maintains a link-state database for each area that it participates in. All routing in or out of an area passes through the area border router(s). The area border router is a funnel for traffic into and out of the areas. Funnels are excellent places to get route aggregation. Area border routers are capable of summarizing routes into and out of areas. Illustration 7-9 depicts route summarization.

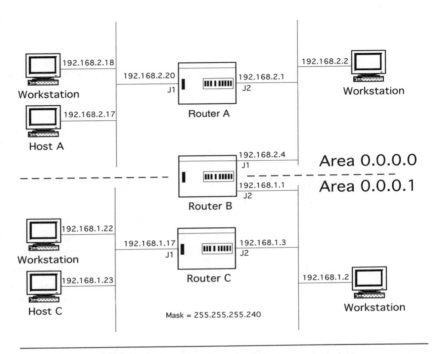

Illustration 7-9   Example Network with OSPF Aggregation

Router B is the area border router between the backbone area and area 0.0.0.1. If route summarization is configured for Router B, it will collapse the routes it receives from the backbone area and will send a summary of the routes to Router C in area 0.0.0.1. Likewise, it can collapse the routes it receives from area 0.0.0.1 and summarize them into the backbone area. The summarization rules are usually defined on the area border router. These rules will define the summary address and mask to be applied to incoming route information, and the summary route information will be sent instead of the specific route information.

If Router B were configured to collapse the routes to the inherent network mask, Router C's route table would look like this:

Destination	Route Mask	Next Hop	Port	Metr	Typ	Src	Age
192.168.1.0	255.255.255.240	192.168.1.3	J2	0	DIR	LOC	358
192.168.1.16	255.255.255.240	192.168.1.17	J1	0	DIR	LOC	358
192.168.2.0	255.255.255.0	192.168.1.1	J2	258	REM	OSPF	24

Using the summarization capability of the area border router can be powerful, but the addressing plan must have been developed to support it. If the addressing scheme does not collapse into a compact representation at the border router, network perturbations on the other side of the area border router will probably trigger route table recalculations. Calculating a route table in a large OSPF network can be CPU intensive.

Static Routing and Route Aggregation

Setting up a network as completely static has its advantages and disadvantages. One advantage is that the network architect can get the most efficient routing tables possible. The disadvantage is that the network does not react well to changes in topology; rerouting must be manually effected. Many people believe that static routing is an administrative nightmare that should not be considered. I am not among them. This is not to say that I would architect a completely static network. I would certainly consider a hybrid routing network such as OSPF and static routing. OSPF (and some implementations of RIP) permit static routes to be imported into the dynamic routing system. In the next example static routing will be mixed with OSPF to illustrate several points. Illustration 7-10 shows the network under normal conditions.

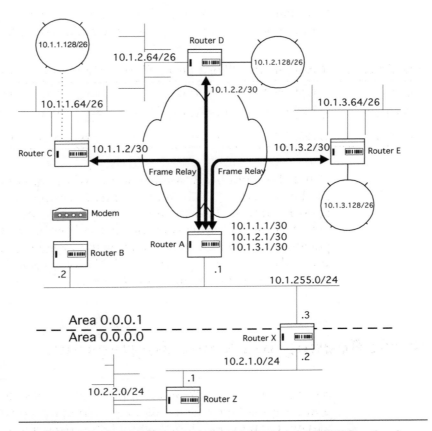

Illustration 7-10 Example Network with Static and OSPF Routing I

Following are the routing tables for several of the routers:

Router A

Destination	Route Mask	Next Hop	Port	Metr	Typ	Src	Age
10.1.1.0	255.255.255.0	10.1.1.2	J2	1	REM	MGMT	0
10.1.1.0	255.255.255.252	10.1.1.1	J2	0	DIR	LOC	358
10.1.2.0	255.255.255.0	10.1.2.2	J2	1	REM	MGMT	0

10.1.2.0	255.255.255.252	10.1.2.1	J2	0	DIR	LOC	358
10.1.3.0	255.255.255.0	10.1.3.2	J2	1	REM	MGMT	0
10.1.3.0	255.255.255.252	10.1.3.1	J2	0	DIR	LOC	358
10.1.255.0	255.255.255.0	10.1.255.1	J1	0	DIR	LOC	420
10.2.0.0	255.255.0.0	10.1.255.3	J1	62	REM	OSPF	24

Router B

Destination	Route Mask	Next Hop	Port	Metr	Typ	Src	Age
10.1.1.0	255.255.255.0	10.1.255.1	J1	1	REM	OSPF	32
10.1.2.0	255.255.255.0	10.1.255.1	J1	1	REM	OSPF	34
10.1.3.0	255.255.255.0	10.1.255.1	J1	1	REM	OSPF	31
10.1.255.0	255.255.255.0	10.1.255.2	J1	0	DIR	LOC	420
10.2.0.0	255.255.0.0	10.1.255.3	J1	62	REM	OSPF	24

Router C

Destination	Route Mask	Next Hop	Port	Metr	Typ	Src	Age
0.0.0.0	0.0.0.0	10.1.1.1	J1	1	REM	MGMT	0
10.1.1.0	255.255.255.252	10.1.1.1	J1	0	DIR	LOC	358
10.1.1.64	255.255.255.192	10.1.1.65	J2	0	DIR	LOC	358
10.1.1.128	255.255.255.192	10.1.1.129	J3	0	DIR	LOC	358

Router X

Destination	Route Mask	Next Hop	Port	Metr	Typ	Src	Age
10.1.1.0	255.255.255.0	10.1.255.1	J2	1	REM	OSPF	523
10.1.2.0	255.255.255.0	10.1.255.1	J2	1	REM	OSPF	126
10.1.3.0	255.255.255.0	10.1.255.1	J2	1	REM	OSPF	442
10.1.255.0	255.255.255.0	10.1.255.3	J2	0	DIR	LOC	1420

10.2.1.0	255.255.255.0	10.2.1.2	J1	0	DIR	LOC	1420
10.2.2.0	255.255.255.0	10.2.1.1	J1	63	REM	OSPF	352

Router Z

Destination	Route Mask	Next Hop	Port	Metr	Typ	Src	Age
10.1.0.0	255.255.0.0	10.2.1.2	J1	0	REM	OSPF	128
10.2.1.0	255.255.255.0	10.2.1.1	J1	0	DIR	LOC	1421
10.2.2.0	255.255.255.0	10.2.2.1	J2	0	DIR	LOC	1421

Router A serves as the Frame Relay hub router. The Frame Relay network is using a point-to-point addressing model, as denoted by the fact that the Frame Relay connection uses a network with a mask of 255.255.255.252, which has room for only two unique host identifiers. Static routing has been used between the Frame Relay hub router and the remote sites. Each remote site has two networks (10.1.x.64/26 and 10.1.x.128/26), plus the point-to-point IP network. If dynamic routing were used on this link, the Frame Relay hub router would have two dynamic route entries for each of the remote local area networks for each static route that subsumes them (10.1.x.0/24). The Frame Relay hub router imports these static routes into OSPF so the other routers, such as Router B and Router X, can route to the remote sites.

Router B is the dial-backup hub router. Whenever a network outage occurs that requires a remote site to establish an alternative connection, such as loss of Frame Relay service, the remote site will connect to Router B with a dial-up link. Router B has an adequate amount of interfaces that use unnumbered IP for the connection. Router B is running OSPF on all interfaces.

Router C is an example of one of the remote sites. It has three networks configured on it (10.1.1.0/30, 10.1.1.64/26, and

10.1.1.128/26) and one unnumbered interface (J4), which is used for dial backup. The unnumbered interface is the only interface configured for OSPF, although it is operational only when the primary port is inoperative. Router C has a default route (0.0.0.0) configured to send any traffic that it does not have a more specific route for to the Frame Relay hub router.

Router X, an area border router, is configured to summarize 10.1.x.x routes from area 0.0.0.1 as a route entry of 10.1.0.0 255.255.0.0 into area 0.0.0.0. Similarly Router X is configured to summarize 10.2.x.x routes from area 0.0.0.0 as a route entry of 10.2.0.0 255.255.0.0 into area 0.0.0.1.

Router Z is a backbone router because it is internal to area 0.0.0.0 and has no other areas defined on its interfaces. Router Z has only one dynamic route in its routing table (10.1.0.0 255.255.0.0), which is the route that was created by the summarization at Router X.

Now let's look at what happens when the Frame Relay connection to Router C is lost. See Illustration 7-11.

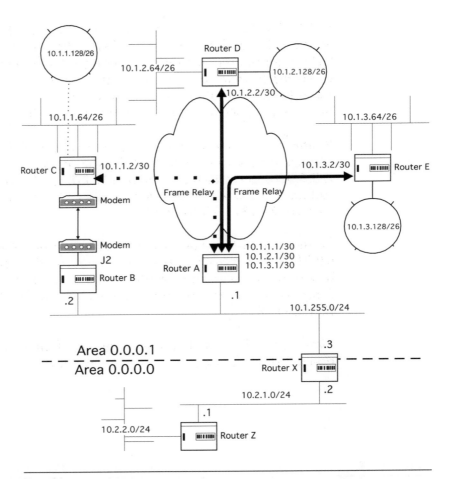

Illustration 7-11 Example Network with Static and OSPF Routing 2

Router A

Destination	Route Mask	Next Hop	Port	Metr	Typ	Src	Age
10.1.1.0	255.255.255.0	10.1.1.2	J2	1	REM	MGMT	0
10.1.1.0	255.255.255.252	10.1.1.1	J2	0	DIR	LOC	358
10.1.1.64	255.255.255.192	10.1.255.2	J1	53	REM	OSPF	243

10.1.1.128	255.255.255.192	10.1.255.2	J1	53	REM	OSPF	243
10.1.2.0	255.255.255.0	10.1.2.2	J2	1	REM	MGMT	0
10.1.2.0	255.255.255.252	10.1.2.1	J2	0	DIR	LOC	358
10.1.3.0	255.255.255.0	10.1.3.2	J2	1	REM	MGMT	0
10.1.3.0	255.255.255.252	10.1.3.1	J2	0	DIR	LOC	358
10.1.255.0	255.255.255.0	10.1.255.1	J1	0	DIR	LOC	420
10.2.0.0	255.255.0.0	10.1.255.3	J1	62	REM	OSPF	24

Router B

Destination	Route Mask	Next Hop	Port	Metr	Typ	Src	Age
10.1.1.0	255.255.255.0	10.1.255.1	J1	1	REM	OSPF	34
10.1.1.64	255.255.255.192	10.1.255.2	J2	25	REM	OSPF	243
10.1.1.128	255.255.255.192	10.1.255.2	J2	25	REM	OSPF	243
10.1.2.0	255.255.255.0	10.1.255.1	J1	1	REM	OSPF	32
10.1.3.0	255.255.255.0	10.1.255.1	J1	1	REM	OSPF	34
10.1.255.0	255.255.255.0	10.1.255.2	J1	0	DIR	LOC	420
10.2.0.0	255.255.0.0	10.1.255.3	J1	62	REM	OSPF	24

Router C

Destination	Route Mask	Next Hop	Port	Metr	Typ	Src	Age
0.0.0.0	0.0.0.0	10.1.1.1	J1	1	REM	MGMT	0
10.1.1.64	255.255.255.192	10.1.1.65	J2	0	DIR	LOC	358
10.1.1.128	255.255.255.192	10.1.1.129	J3	0	DIR	LOC	358
10.1.2.0	255.255.255.0	J4	J4	75	REM	OSPF	32
10.1.3.0	255.255.255.0	J4	J4	75	REM	OSPF	34
10.1.255.0	255.255.255.0	J4	J4	53	REM	OSPF	124
10.2.0.0	255.255.0.0	J4	J4	53	REM	OSPF	59

Router X

Destination	Route Mask	Next Hop	Port	Metr	Typ	Src	Age
10.1.1.0	255.255.255.0	10.1.255.1	J2	1	REM	OSPF	523
10.1.1.64	255.255.255.192	10.1.255.2	J2	1	REM	OSPF	521
10.1.1.128	255.255.255.192	10.1.255.2	J2	1	REM	OSPF	492
10.1.2.0	255.255.255.0	10.1.255.1	J2	1	REM	OSPF	126
10.1.3.0	255.255.255.0	10.1.255.1	J2	1	REM	OSPF	442
10.1.255.0	255.255.255.0	10.1.255.3	J2	0	DIR	LOC	1420
10.2.1.0	255.255.255.0	10.2.1.2	J1	0	DIR	LOC	1420
10.2.2.0	255.255.255.0	10.2.1.1	J1	63	REM	OSPF	352

Router Z

Destination	Route Mask	Next Hop	Port	Metr	Typ	Src	Age
10.1.0.0	255.255.0.0	10.2.1.2	J1	0	REM	OSPF	128
10.2.1.0	255.255.255.0	10.2.1.1	J1	0	DIR	LOC	1421
10.2.2.0	255.255.255.0	10.2.2.1	J2	0	DIR	LOC	1421

When Router C came up on the dial-backup link, it exchanged the link-state database (OSPF's routing information) with Router B. Router C learned the routing information for the rest of the network and was able to install routes that are more specific than the general default route that it had been using prior to the dial-backup connection.

Router B learned about the networks off of Router C and passed the link-state advertisements to all the routers that it exchanges information with. This routing information is flooded throughout area 0.0.0.1.

Router A receives the link-state advertisements from Router B and recomputes its routing table. It installs two routes,

10.1.1.64/26 and 10.1.1.128/26, in the routing table. These routes are more specific than the 10.1.1.0/24 route and will therefore be used to route traffic to the two local area networks at the Router C site.

Router X, the area border router between area 0.0.0.1 and area 0.0.0.0, receives the link-state advertisements for the routes and does two things. It recomputes its routing table and it summarizes the routing information for flooding into area 0.0.0.0. Since the summary information is subsumed by the existing summary information already being used in area 0.0.0.0, the link-state advertisement is not sent to each of the routers in area 0.0.0.0.

Router Z, the router internal to area 0.0.0.0, is unaffected by the change in topology in area 0.0.0.1. Its routing table is not recomputed.

The one thing to watch out for in this routing setup is the condition that occurs when Router B is not in a dial-backup condition and either the Ethernet (or the Token Ring) at the Router C site fails. Any packet that arrives at Router A for a destination that is homed to the failed Ethernet segment is routed according to the 10.1.1.0/24 route to Router C. Router C determines that its route to that network is down but that it has a default route to Router A that might be able to determine another route to the destination. Router C sends the packet back to Router A. Router A sends the packet to Router C. This is a routing loop, one of the hazards of static routing. The solution is to let the packet be discarded as a result of the TTL, but this is wasteful, and the cycle will repeat with every packet sent to that destination. Another alternative, supported by most modern routers, is to establish a filter that discards all packets going out of Router C on the Frame Relay interface whose destination would otherwise be local to Router C.

Classless Interdomain Routing (CIDR)

The Internet Advisory Board determined a few years back that unless some measures were taken to stave it off, the Internet was in danger of catastrophe. The globally unique address space was being allocated at unprecedented rates. The Internet had won the favor of the masses and was growing. Resources that once seemed limitless started to look insufficient. In particular, registered Internet networks that once seemed plentiful were thinning out. The Class B networks were about to be completely allocated. As the networks were allocated, they were put into service on the Internet. For almost every network that was allocated, a route was added to the Internet route tables. At the same time that the Internet was experiencing the pains from a shortage of available addresses, it was suffering from the unexpected increases to its route tables.

Supernetting

The Internet Advisory Board needed both a short-term and a long-term solution. As the short-term solution a strategy was devised that would permit aggregation of multiple smaller networks into a single larger network. This is roughly analogous to the way in which an inverse multiplexor works to take several low-bandwidth channels and combine them into a single logical channel of larger bandwidth. Making a single network out of smaller contiguous networks is known as *supernetting*. Thank goodness that it did not get the moniker of "inverse subnetting."

Up until this point network allocations were made from one of three pools of networks. The Class A pool had 126 networks, each with room for 16,777,214 hosts. The Class B pool had 16,384 networks with room for 65,534 hosts per network. The

Class C pool had 2,097,152 networks with room for 254 hosts. Except for really small or really large organizations, almost everybody wanted a Class B network. It was perceived that Class B networks were for organizations that had plans that required more than 254 and fewer than 65,534 hosts. Of course, it was possible to get allocations for multiple Class C networks, but every one of the Class C networks would increase the Internet route table, and multiple Class C networks could be cumbersome to administer.

Now, with the classless interdomain routing (CIDR) aggregation strategy, multiple Class C networks can be aggregated to form a network that supports a quantity of hosts somewhere between a Class C and a Class B. In essence CIDR has removed the significance of the network class. Illustration 7-12 shows how I have taken the IP address worksheet and modified it to illustrate supernetting.

.0/16	.128/17	.192/18	.224/19	.240/20	.248/21	.252/22	.254/23	.255/24
0	0	0	0	0	0	0	0	0
1	1	1	1	1	1	1	1	1
2	2	2	2	2	2	2	2	2
3	3	3	3	3	3	3	3	3
4	4	4	4	4	4	4	4	4
5	5	5	5	5	5	5	5	5
6	6	6	6	6	6	6	6	6
7	7	7	7	7	7	7	7	7
8	8	8	8	8	8	8	8	8
9	9	9	9	9	9	9	9	9
10	10	10	10	10	10	10	10	10
11	11	11	11	11	11	11	11	11
12	12	12	12	12	12	12	12	12
13	13	13	13	13	13	13	13	13
14	14	14	14	14	14	14	14	14
15	15	15	15	15	15	15	15	15
16	16	16	16	16	16	16	16	16
17	17	17	17	17	17	17	17	17
18	18	18	18	18	18	18	18	18
19	19	19	19	19	19	19	19	19
20	20	20	20	20	20	20	20	20
21	21	21	21	21	21	21	21	21
22	22	22	22	22	22	22	22	22
23	23	23	23	23	23	23	23	23
24	24	24	24	24	24	24	24	24
25	25	25	25	25	25	25	25	25
26	26	26	26	26	26	26	26	26
27	27	27	27	27	27	27	27	27
28	28	28	28	28	28	28	28	28
29	29	29	29	29	29	29	29	29
30	30	30	30	30	30	30	30	30
31	31	31	31	31	31	31	31	31

Illustration 7-12 Portion of CIDR Aggregation Worksheet

If you had a requirement for address space equivalent to multiple Class C addresses, you would be allocated a single network derived from Class C networks. It might look similar to that shown in Table 7-1.

Address Requirement	Class C Networks	Network Allocated
1 to 254	192.168.0.0	192.168.0.0/24
255 to 510	192.168.0.0 to 192.168.1.0	192.168.0.0/23
511 to 1022	192.168.0.0 to 192.168.3.0	192.168.0.0/22
1023 to 2046	192.168.0.0 to 192.168.7.0	192.168.0.0/21
2047 to 4094	192.168.0.0 to 192.168.15.0	192.168.0.0/20
4095 to 8190	192.168.0.0 to 192.168.31.0	192.168.0.0/19

Table 7-1   Single Network Derived from Class C Network

If you had a requirement for 6000 host addresses, you could be allocated a network such as 192.168.0.0/19, which would be a composite of 32 Class C addresses. Depending on how subnetting was intended to be engineered, you could possibly make a case for an allocation of a Class B network. The point is, however, that even though 32 Class C networks were allocated, only one route, 192.168.0.0/19, was added to the Internet route tables. Further, the utilization of the 192.168.0.0/19 supernet is as high as 0.73, whereas if a Class B network were allocated for the demand, it would achieve a utilization of only 0.09. Supernetting is clearly a much more efficient utilization of address space.

Classless Addressing

The term "classless interdomain routing" suggests that this classless strategy is applied to the Internet backbone where interdomain routing takes place. Since the goal of reducing the route table within the Internet is embodied in the CIDR strategy, it only follows that support for supernetting must be built into the exterior routing protocols. Older exterior routing protocols, such as EGP and BGP-2, lack support in the routing table for a network mask. The updates themselves do not carry network mask information but derive the mask from the class of network being advertised. BGP-4, on the other hand, supports masks different from the one implied through the inherent class of the network. Typically this would be a smaller mask than the inherent mask of the network; however, all the principles apply to cases of larger masks. This is good from the perspective that Class C address space, which accounts for less than a quarter of all address space, may be consumed faster than expected by allocation of supernets. The supernet 192.168.8.0/21 supports the same number of hosts as the subnet 172.16.8.0/21. If the Class C address space were consumed faster than expected, a single class A network could be split up into as many as 256 Class B equivalent networks, 65,536 Class C equivalent networks, or any combination necessary. Not all of the Class A networks have been allocated. In fact, half of all the Class A networks have been reserved by the IANA. This is roughly 25 percent of all globally unique address space.

Subnetting and supernetting strategies work fine for modern exterior gateway routing protocols, but what about the interior routing protocols? In the past (and in many places, the present) routers have relied on classes for assumptions about what configurations should be allowed. For instance, although CIDR permits a network such as 192.168.8.0/21 to be defined, an interior router might have difficulty with it. In reality, validity checks that once prevented a user from incorrectly configuring a network interface with an address of 192.168.9.21 using a network mask of 255.255.248.0 must be removed to permit such a configuration. The notion of classes must be removed from routers.

This is not so difficult if you are using a modern routing protocol such as OSPF. RIP version 1 is a different story. Remember that RIP makes some assumptions to compensate for the absence of subnet mask information in the route updates. These assumptions should be kept in mind when using a supernet allocation. If a RIP router were to receive an update such as 192.168.8.0 (/21), it would likely install the route in its tables and use a mask of 255.255.255.0, which would be wrong. This is not entirely different from the way some of the older exterior routing protocols mentioned earlier would react.

Address Allocation

The real problem that initiated the CIDR movement was that the Internet unexpectedly grew quite popular. As more organizations became connected, more and more addresses were being assigned by the allocation authorities. The address space became depleted and the route tables bloated. The routing tables would benefit slightly from supernetting; however, the routing tables would greatly benefit from a large-scale route aggregation plan. RFC 1518, "An Architecture for IP Address Allocation with CIDR," provides the framework for such a plan. The essence of the architecture is similar to the concepts discussed earlier in this chapter. The exception is that earlier portions of this chapter studied aggregation within an autonomous system. RFC 1518 applies aggregation techniques to the Internet backbone.

In the plan presented in RFC 1518, an entity, such as an Internet service provider or a government, is allocated a number of IP networks or supernets. Subscribers come to a provider for Internet access, and the subscriber is allocated networks from the provider's allocation. The subscriber maintains the IP network for the duration of the business agreement. A subscriber who wishes to change providers relinquishes the IP networks belonging administratively to the provider. This is an important point. Under this architecture the end users "lease" their IP addresses from the provider. If it were a purchase arrangement, the end users would take their allocation with them to a new provider. This would defeat the purpose of the aggregation strategy, since each segment of the initial provider allocation that is rehomed would have to be advertised separately on the Internet backbone in addition to the provider's aggregated route advertisement. The more this situation occurs, the less efficient the scheme becomes. The best policy for ensuring the highest degree of aggregation is to "rent" the IP addresses. It is important to note, however, that the CIDR specification does not require users to relinquish their IP networks if they change their Internet service provider. This requirement would have to be dictated by the ISP as a part of the service contract. Illustration 7-13 depicts an architecture as detailed in RFC 1518.

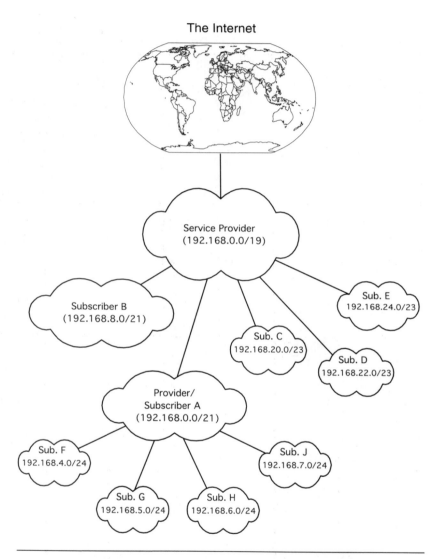

Illustration 7-13 Example Allocation for Internet Route Optimization

.0/16	.128/17	.192/18	.224/19	.240/20	.248/21	.252/22	.254/23	.255/24
0	0	0	SvcProv 0	0	Sub A 0	0	0	0
1	1	1	1	1	1	1	1	1
2	2	2	2	2	2	2	2	2
3	3	3	3	3	3	3	3	3
4	4	4	4	4	4	4	4	4
5	5	5	5	5	5	5	5	5
6	6	6	6	6	6	6	6	6
7	7	7	7	7	7	7	7	7
8	8	8	8	8	Sub B 8	8	8	8
9	9	9	9	9	9	9	9	9
10	10	10	10	10	10	10	10	10
11	11	11	11	11	11	11	11	11
12	12	12	12	12	12	12	12	12
13	13	13	13	13	13	13	13	13
14	14	14	14	14	14	14	14	14
15	15	15	15	15	15	15	15	15
16	16	16	16	16	16	Avail. 16	16	16
17	17	17	17	17	17	17	17	17
18	18	18	18	18	18	18	18	18
19	19	19	19	19	19	19	19	19
20	20	20	20	20	20	20	Sub C 20	20
21	21	21	21	21	21	21	21	21
22	22	22	22	22	22	22	Sub D 22	22
23	23	23	23	23	23	23	23	23
24	24	24	24	24	24	24	Sub E 24	24
25	25	25	25	25	25	25	25	25
26	26	26	26	26	26	26	Avail. 26	26
27	27	27	27	27	27	27	27	27
28	28	28	28	28	28	Intrnl 28	28	28
29	29	29	29	29	29	29	29	29
30	30	30	30	30	30	30	30	30
31	31	31	31	31	31	31	31	31

Illustration 7-14 Class C Supernet Worksheet—ISP to Subscriber

In this example the Internet service provider (ISP) has been allocated supernet 192.168.0.0/19, which is a composite of 32 Class C networks, from 192.168.0.0 to 192.168.31.0. The ISP reserves the supernet 192.168.28.0/22, a block of four Class C networks, for its own internal use. The remainder of the 192.168.0.0/19 supernet has been suballocated to five organizations, subscribers to the connectivity service that the ISP is providing. They are denoted as Subscribers A through E in Illustrations 7-13 and 7-14. Two blocks of networks are not currently allocated, 192.168.16.0/22 and 192.168.26.0/23.

Interestingly, Subscriber A is also a provider. Subscriber A has received an allocation of Class C networks that, when considered together, comprise the supernet 192.168.0.0/21. This provider has chosen to reserve the supernet 192.168.0.0/22 for internal purposes. The remaining four Class C networks from the initial allocation have been suballocated by Provider/Subscriber A to four organizations as individual Class C networks, 192.168.4.0/24 through 192.168.7.0/24, as shown in Illustration 7-15.

.224/19	.240/20	.248/21	.252/22	.254/23	.255/24
SvcProv 0	0	Sub A 0	Intrnl 0	0	0
1	1	1	1	1	1
2	2	2	2	2	2
3	3	3	3	3	3
4	4	4	4	4	Sub F 4
5	5	5	5	5	Sub G 5
6	6	6	6	6	Sub H 6
7	7	7	7	7	Sub J 7

Illustration 7-15 Suballocation of Networks

It is possible to add another layer of hierarchy and aggregation. This is referred to as *continental aggregation* and could happen, for instance, if all of the Internet service providers within the

United States were given their allocations out of the same supernet of Class C networks. Other geographic areas would be assigned their own supernet from which they could make suballocations to Internet service providers and subsequently to the end users.

One last note regarding subscriber-to-provider aggregation as depicted in Illustration 7-13. This architecture works particularly well when the provider is the sole Internet service provider for a particular subscriber. If a subscriber has more than one connection to the Internet, this architecture may prove inadequate. A single autonomous system would not be likely to take an address allocation from more than one ISP. There are several choices for how the IP addressing should be derived for organizations that have more than one Internet ingress/egress. Among the choices are for the organization to request a globally unique address allocation from only one of the Internet service providers. The other Internet service providers may advertise more specific routes than the ISP that provided the allocation, but the situation would not be any worse than if the organization requested its IP network allocations from the InterNIC or other authority.

Summary

The route table is the central database used to determine the next-hop address to be used in the forwarding process. It is likely that the entire database must be searched to derive a list of candidate routes during the Basic Match pruning rule. The smallest and most compact routing table will be more quickly and efficiently searched than will a large and cumbersome routing table.

- This chapter dealt with designing an IP address scheme that will result in as small a routing table as possible, given the network architecture and interior routing protocol employed in the autonomous system.

- Route aggregation was discussed as it pertains to RIP, OSPF, and static routing. In an RIP environment automatic route aggregation is a side effect of RIP updates not including a subnet mask and the assumptions that a router makes when trying to assign a route mask to a received network route update.

- In an OSPF environment in which the subnet mask information is passed in the link-state updates, route aggregation is performed at an area border router.

- In a static routing environment route aggregation can be set up as elaborately as the network administrator cares to set it up. Static routing can be one of the best ways to achieve an efficient route table. Static routing can also be used in conjunction with a dynamic routing protocol whereby the static routes are imported into a dynamic routing architecture such as OSPF. This can lead to additional levels of route aggregation.

- A new concept, called supernetting, Classless interdomain routing, or CIDR, is much more than supernetting, however. It is a strategy for curbing the growth of the route tables within the Internet and for utilizing remaining address space more efficiently.

Addressing for High Utilization of Address Space

It is important that globally unique IP networks be utilized efficiently, due to a recent boom in Internet popularity, but results from inadequate granularity in the addressing mechanisms. That is, there are essentially three classes of unicast addresses that can support discrete numbers of host addresses. A Class A network can support 16,777,216 hosts, a Class B network can support 65,534 hosts, and a Class C network can support 254 unique host addresses. This is the maximum that the class of address could support if the network were not subnetted and all hosts were on the single IP network. This is rarely the case, due to the traffic and media constraints. For all practical purposes it is necessary to subnet the network into manageable units and, at the same time, maintain a high degree of address utilization.

Estimating Address Assignment Efficiency

Christian Huitema wrote RFC 1715, "The H Ratio for Address Assignment Efficiency," in 1994 to document an approach for estimating the efficiency of an addressing scheme. In RFC 1715 the H ratio is defined as:

H = log (number of objects) / available bits

Note that the formula uses a base 10 log function instead of a base 2 log function. I prefer to present the formula first from a base 2 perspective, since I believe that it is easier to understand than the base 10 equivalent.

H = log 2 (number of objects) / available bits

To state it as simply as possible, the log base 2 of a number is, when rounded up to the nearest integer, equal to the number of bits required to represent the magnitude of the number in binary. For instance, the log base 2 of 16 is equal to exactly 4. That is, to represent 16 discrete levels in binary would require 4 bits. Take the number 38. The log base 2 of 38 is approximately 5.25. Rounding up to the nearest integer, it would require 6 bits to represent the number 38 in binary. It is easy to see from looking at the log base 2 formula that if you had 8 bits to work with and you had 256 objects, this would render an H ratio equal to 1, since the log base 2 of 256 is exactly 8. You require 8 bits and you have 8 bits available to use; therefore you have 100 percent efficiency.

The interpretation of the formula starts to get a little difficult for values of H less than 1.0. For instance, would an H ratio of 0.875 be equivalent to 87.5 percent efficiency? The answer is *no*. To illustrate, let's assume that you have 8 bits of address space available and 128 objects that need addresses. We know that you could represent 256 objects with 8 bits of address space; 128 objects in a space that could accommodate 256 objects indicates a 50 percent utilization, but our H ratio is 0.875! If I had two objects in the same address space, I would get an H ratio of 0.125, even though I have less than 0.8 percent address space utilization.

Now back to the formula given in RFC 1715:

H = log (number of objects) / available bits

This formula uses the log base 10 of the number of objects. The reason cited is "because they are easier to compute mentally." I'm not going to argue with someone who computes logarithms mentally. I have a calculator that does not compute log base 2 functions naturally. Perhaps the RFC 1715 formula would be easier for me to use. Let's take a look at a few of the calculations we worked earlier using the log base 2 formula. If you had 256 objects and 8 bits of address space available, the H ratio (RFC 1715) would be 0.301. The maximum value possible for the RFC 1715 H ratio is 0.301 and is equivalent to a 100 percent utilized address space. But 128 objects and 8 bits available renders an H ratio of 0.263 and a utilization of only 50 percent. Table 8-1 shows a comparison of the log base 2 H ratio, the log base 10 H ratio, and utilization for various numbers of hosts with 8 bits of address space available.

Number of Hosts	H Ratio (log2)	H Ratio (log10)	Utilization (%)
256	1.0	0.301	100
128	0.875	0.263	50
64	0.75	0.225	25
32	0.625	0.188	12.5
16	0.5	0.151	6.25

8	0.375	0.113	3.125
4	0.25	0.075	1.56
2	0.125	0.038	0.781

Table 8-1 Comparison of hosts, ratios, and utilization

From the table you can see that a log base 10 H ratio of 0.20 will render a utilization between 12.5 percent and 25 percent. One of the examples provided in RFC 1715 is the Internet address space. In 1994 there were approximately 3 million hosts connected to the Internet, which has an address space of 32 bits. The log base 10 H ratio is 0.202, which, as we just saw, would fall somewhere between 12.5 percent and 25 percent utilization. Now remember that a Class A network can accommodate about 16.7 million addresses, a Class B network can accommodate about 65 thousand addresses, and a Class C network can accommodate 254 addresses. The total potential address space for the Internet is more than 3.72 billion addresses. That means that 3 million addresses out of more than 3 billion potential addresses is less than 0.1 percent utilization. How can this be? Take a 32-bit address space: In order to get a 100 percent utilization, you would require approximately 4.3 billion objects. In order to get 12.5 percent utilization, you would require about 537 million objects. Now compute the H ratio (log 10) for 537 million objects with 32 available bits. The H ratio is equal to 0.273! Well, now I am really confused. The same utilization (12.5 percent) with 8 bits of available space rendered an H ratio of 0.188!

Calculating Address Assignment Efficiency

The reason for this is that the H ratio is a ratio based on the number of bits. As the number of bits increases, so too does the significance of the highest-order bit. In fact, it increases exponentially. For instance, in an 8-bit representation the seventh bit has a decimal value of 64, and the eighth bit has a value of 128, a difference of 64. In a 16-bit representation the 15th bit has a value of 16,384, and the 16th bit has a value of 32,768, a difference of 16,384. The H ratio cannot be used to indicate the utilization efficiency of an address space unless the number of bits representing the address space is a constant. Besides, who needs to work logarithms in order to estimate the efficiency of an addressing scheme? To me, the bottom line is how many hosts I can address with the networks I am allocated and how many addresses I use from the potential space:

Utilization = addresses used / addresses possible

In order to represent this as a percentage, multiply the result by 100. The "addresses possible" portion of this formula can refer to the allocated network(s), all subnets of the allocated network, or a single subnet of the allocated network. For instance, if you had a Class C address allocated to you and you wanted to determine the utilization of your addressing scheme, you would simply count the number of allocated addresses on that Class C network and divide that quantity by 254, the maximum number of hosts possible. Some folks could argue that you should divide by 256, since that is the number of addresses possible with an 8-bit field. This would suggest that the maximum utilization of a Class C address is 0.992. I believe that it is unnecessary to "dock" you for the loss of the all-0s and all-1s addresses from the start. If you noticed that the example in Chapter 2 used 256 hosts per Class C and 65,536 hosts per Class B, let me remind you that I had not discussed the special-case addresses of all 0s and all 1s by that time.

Now suppose that you had a Class C address divided into four equal-size subnets. Each subnet has the capacity to have 62 hosts per subnet. The maximum number of hosts would be 248 (62 × 4). If all addresses in each of the subnets were allocated, the utilization of the Class C network would be:

Utilization of Class C = 248 / 254 = 0.976

On the other hand, the utilization with respect to all subnets would be:

Utilization of all subnets = 248 / 248 = 1.0

When you calculate the utilization of the network, you are including the loss of efficiency due to subnetting. When you calculate the utilization with respect to all subnets, you are calculating the efficiency you have achieved within the bounds of the subnetting your network requires. To illustrate, consider the case in which you have a Class C network allocated to you and you must allocate 64 point-to-point IP networks out of it. Since there are exactly two hosts on a point-to-point IP network, there will be exactly 128 addresses used out of the 254 addresses possible on the Class C network. The utilization of the Class C network that you were allocated is 0.504. The utilization with respect to all subnets, however, is 1.0.

Addressing Efficiency and Routing Protocols

Chapter 4 discussed routing and the way that different routing protocols deal with addressing. Remember from the discussion that RIP does not convey subnet mask information in the routing updates. Conversely OSPF does reflect the masks in the link-state advertisements. It would follow that OSPF would tend to allow better address space utilization than RIP would give. Let's revisit a previous example (see Illustration 8-1).

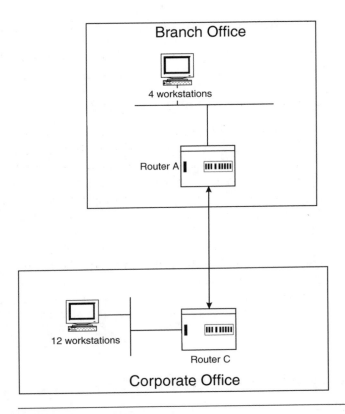

Illustration 8-1 Example Network

This network reflects two sites joined by a point-to-point numbered IP network. The corporate office site must permit at least 13 addresses on its Ethernet (12 hosts and 1 router). The point-to-point IP network requires two host addresses (one for each router), and the branch office requires five addresses on its Ethernet.

In an RIP routing environment, we are constrained to have fixed-length subnet masks. The network that has the largest address requirement is the Ethernet at the corporate office. It requires a 28-bit network mask in order to accommodate 13 hosts (it can handle up to 14 hosts). For our addressing we would need to allocate three subnets that can each accommodate 14 hosts (42 total hosts), even though we need to provide for only 20 addresses. The utilization with respect to all subnets is:

Utilization (subnets) = 20 / 42 = 0.476

In an OSPF environment you can create subnets, depending on your networking needs. In our example the point-to-point IP network required the use of a subnet that could potentially accommodate 14 hosts. That subnet alone had a utilization of only 0.143! The best choice for a point-to-point (numbered) IP network is a two-host subnet with a mask of 255.255.255.252. Illustration 8-2 shows how addressing might be set up in an OSPF environment.

.0/24	.128/25	.192/26	.224/27	.240/28	.248/29	.252/30
0	0	0	0	0	0	0
1	1	1	1	1	1	RTR A 1
2	2	2	2	2	2	RTR C 2
3	3	3	3	3	3	3
4	4	4	4	4	4	4
5	5	5	5	5	5	5
6	6	6	6	6	6	6
7	7	7	7	7	7	7
8	8	8	8	8	8	8
9	9	9	9	9	RTR A 9	9
10	10	10	10	10	10	10
11	11	11	11	11	WS A 11	11
12	12	12	12	12	WS B 12	12

Illustration 8-2   Example IP Addressing Worksheet

13	13	13	13	13	WS C 13	13
14	14	14	14	14	WS D 14	14
15	15	15	15	15	15	15
16	16	16	16	16	16	16
17	17	17	17	RTR C 17	17	17
18	18	18	18	18	18	18
19	19	19	19	WS A 19	19	19
20	20	20	20	WS B 20	20	20
21	21	21	21	WS C 21	21	21
22	22	22	22	WS D 22	22	22
23	23	23	23	WS E 23	23	23
24	24	24	24	WS F 24	24	24
25	25	25	25	WS G 25	25	25
26	26	26	26	WS H 26	26	26
27	27	27	27	WS I 27	27	27
28	28	28	28	WS J 28	28	28
29	29	29	29	WS K 29	29	29
30	30	30	30	WS L 30	30	30
31	31	31	31	31	31	31

Illustration 8-2 (Continued)

This addressing scheme has three subnets with a total capacity for 22 addresses. Since 20 addresses are used, the utilization with respect to all subnets is:

Utilization (subnets) = 20 / 22 = 0.909

You undoubtedly noticed that I did not calculate the utilization of the Class C address space. This example used only a portion of a complete Class C network. Just calculating the efficiency with respect to the subnets was sufficient to show how OSPF can facilitate efficient utilization of address space.

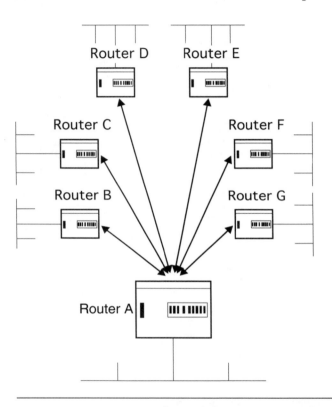

Illustration 8-3 Example Network with Six Remote Sites

Now let's look at a little different scenario, as shown in Illustration 8-3. In this example six remote sites are connected via point-to-point links to the central (hub) site. Each of the seven sites has 10 workstations connected to the Ethernet at the site. Assuming that one Class C network is available for the addressing and that numbered IP point-to-point networks must be used, let's look at how the network could be addressed using RIP and then with OSPF.

In an RIP environment, in which you are constrained to a fixed-length subnet mask, the minimum mask that will handle at least 10 hosts (plus the router IP address) is 255.255.255.240 (28-bit mask), which can accommodate up to 14 hosts. A Class C network can be divided into 16 of these subnets. The number of addresses required in this topology is:

Ethernet addresses = $7 \times (10 \text{ w/s} + 1 \text{ router}) = 77$

Point-to-point addresses = $6 \times 2 = 12$

Total addresses = 89

Of the possible 16 subnets that the Class C network could be divided into, 13 were actually used (7 Ethernets and 6 point-to-point links), and three were "wasted"—excuse me, "reserved for future growth." These 16 subnets can accommodate 14 host addresses each, for a total capacity of 224 host addresses. The utilization with respect to all subnets is 0.397, but when you consider only the subnets that addresses are allocated from, the utilization can be said to be 0.489. You might want to calculate the utilization in this way, seeing that there are indeed three subnets unused and that they could support one more remote sites like the others. The utilization of the Class C network is calculated as follows:

Utilization (Class C network) = $89 / 254 = 0.35$

Using OSPF, we can address for the same example network; however, we can pick subnet sizes as appropriate for the type of network and number of hosts. The point-to-point networks would use the traditional point-to-point numbered IP network mask of 255.255.255.252. There are six subnets of this size. The Ethernets could use a 255.255.255.240 subnet, as we used for RIP in this example. The number of host addresses in this example remains the same, at 89 host addresses. The utilization with respect to the subnets that addresses were allocated from is:

Utilization allocated subnets) = 89 / 110 = 0.809

The utilization with respect to all subnets cannot be calculated for this example, because of the number of subnet combinations that the remaining address space can be divided into. A little over half of the address space from the Class C network is available for future growth. The utilization of the Class C network address space is the same as for RIP, 0.35.

The Class C network utilization is the same for RIP as it is for OSPF in the example. The key difference is that the utilization of the subnets is much higher for OSPF than for RIP, and more important, the RIP network has room to grow equal to another remote site. The OSPF network, on the other hand, has room to grow equal to another five remote sites!

Cheating RIP to Achieve Efficiency

This section discusses an option for improving the address utilization in a fixed-length subnet environment. Although it is possible that you get involved in an OSPF network designed using fixed-length subnet masks, this section is aimed primarily at RIP routing. Consider the simple scenario shown in Illustration 8-4.

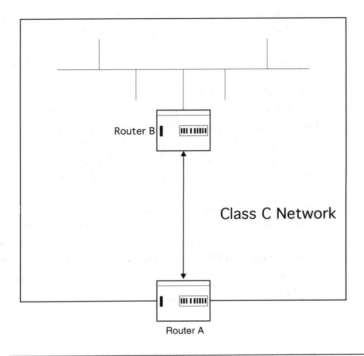

Illustration 8-4 Fixed-Length Subnets and Utilization

It is common for the equivalent of a Class C network to be allocated to a given remote site. In this example the point-to-point connection and the remote Ethernet should have addresses allocated from the same Class C network. There are two physical networks, the point-to-point network and the Ethernet. Traditionally we would cut the address space in half and give the Ethernet 126 host addresses in the x.x.x.0/25 network, and the point-to-point would be allocated 126 hosts in the x.x.x.128/25 network, with 124 host addresses on that network being wasted (really wasted this time.) What you can do instead is allocate more subnets with fewer hosts per subnet, allocate one of the subnets to the point-to-point network, and allocate the remaining subnets to the Ethernet. Table 8-2 reflects the maximum number of Ethernet host addresses and efficiency attainable when dividing the address space of a Class C network into multiple fixed-length subnets.

Number of Subnets	Hosts/Subnet	Max. Ethernet Hosts	Max. Utilization
2	126	126	0.504
4	62	186	0.740
8	30	210	0.835
16	14	210	0.835
32	6	186	0.740
64	2	126	0.504

Table 8-2 Maximum Utilization, Using Fixed-Length Subnet Masks

It is clear that the number of host addresses that can be placed on the physical Ethernet can be increased by more than 80 and that the total address utilization can get as high as 0.835. In order for this to work, however, the network must be divided up into cliques, with interclique communications handled by the multihomed router. The router must have an address in each of the clique networks in order for the cliques to share information and resources. Even though the maximum Ethernet hosts and utilization are the same for the cases in which the address space is divided into 8 or 16 subnets, it is more than likely that a larger clique size is desirable, since there would potentially be less interclique communications necessary.

Network Mask Deception—
Another Trick

This is a trick that I have tried and found to work in the instances that I have attempted. I cannot tell you whether there are conditions in which this would fail to work. It warrants a mention in this book because of the benefit it can provide. Implement it with caution!

Consider an Ethernet that has a single network allocated to it and addressing divided into multiple subnets. In other words, it has been partitioned into cliques, as was just discussed. If a host in one of the cliques is to communicate with a host in any other clique, it must be facilitated by the router, as shown in Illustrations 8-5 and 8-6.

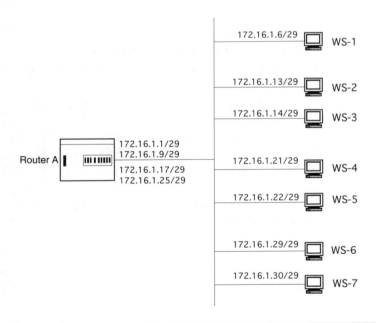

Illustration 8-5 Dividing a LAN into IP Clique

.0/24	.128/25	.192/26	.224/27	.240/28	.248/29	.252/30
0	0	0	0	0	0	0
1	1	1	1	1	RTR-A 1	1
2	2	2	2	2	2	2
3	3	3	3	3	3	3
4	4	4	4	4	4	4
5	5	5	5	5	5	5
6	6	6	6	6	WS-1 6	6
7	7	7	7	7	7	7
8	8	8	8	8	8	8
9	9	9	9	9	RTR-A 9	9
10	10	10	10	10	10	10
11	11	11	11	11	11	11
12	12	12	12	12	12	12
13	13	13	13	13	WS-2 13	13
14	14	14	14	14	WS-3 14	14
15	15	15	15	15	15	15
16	16	16	16	16	16	16
17	17	17	17	17	RTR-A 17	17
18	18	18	18	18	18	18
19	19	19	19	19	19	19
20	20	20	20	20	20	20
21	21	21	21	21	WS-4 21	21
22	22	22	22	22	WS-5 22	22
23	23	23	23	23	23	23
24	24	24	24	24	24	24
25	25	25	25	25	RTR-A 25	25
26	26	26	26	26	26	26
27	27	27	27	27	27	27
28	28	28	28	28	28	28
29	29	29	29	29	WS-6 29	29
30	30	30	30	30	WS-7 30	30
31	31	31	31	31	31	31

Illustration 8-6 IP Address Worksheet Showing IP Cliques

This example shows a single IP network, 172.16.1.0/27, that has been partitioned into four cliques—networks 172.16.1.0/29, 172.16.1.8/29, 172.16.1.16/29, and 172.16.1.24/29. Look what happens when you change the subnet mask of the workstations to 255.255.255.224 (27-bit network mask) and leave the router IP interfaces as previously defined, using the 29-bit network mask Illustrations 8-7 and 8-8.

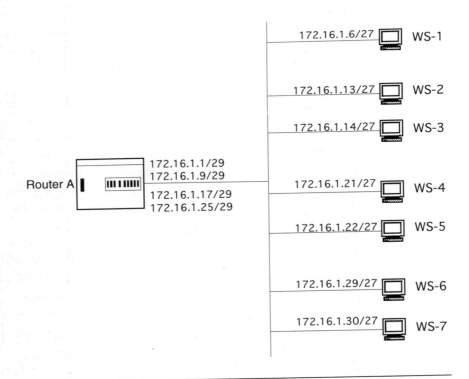

Illustration 8-7 IP Network Mask Deception

.0/24	.128/25	.192/26	.224/27	.240/28	.248/29	.252/30
0	0	0	**0**	0	**0**	0
1	1	1	**1**	1	**RTR-A 1**	1
2	2	2	**2**	2	**2**	2
3	3	3	**3**	3	**3**	3
4	4	4	**4**	4	**4**	4
5	5	5	**5**	5	**5**	5
6	6	6	**WS-1 6**	6	**6**	6
7	7	7	**7**	7	**7**	7
8	8	8	**8**	8	**8**	8
9	9	9	**9**	9	**RTR-A 9**	9
10	10	10	**10**	10	**10**	10
11	11	11	**11**	11	**11**	11
12	12	12	**12**	12	**12**	12
13	13	13	**WS-2 13**	13	**13**	13
14	14	14	**WS-3 14**	14	**14**	14
15	15	15	**15**	15	**15**	15
16	16	16	**16**	16	**16**	16
17	17	17	**17**	17	**RTR-A 17**	17
18	18	18	**18**	18	**18**	18
19	19	19	**19**	19	**19**	19
20	20	20	**20**	20	**20**	20
21	21	21	**WS-4 21**	21	**21**	21
22	22	22	**WS-5 22**	22	**22**	22
23	23	23	**23**	23	**23**	23
24	24	24	**24**	24	**24**	24
25	25	25	**25**	25	**RTR-A 25**	25
26	26	26	**26**	26	**26**	26
27	27	27	**27**	27	**27**	27
28	28	28	**28**	28	**28**	28
29	29	29	**WS-6 29**	29	**29**	29
30	30	30	**WS-7 30**	30	**30**	30
31	31	31	**31**	31	**31**	31

**Illustration 8-8 IP Address Worksheet Showing IP Network Mask
Deception**

The router believes that there are four networks with hosts on each network and advertises these networks to its "rest of the world." The workstations, however, believe that there is only one network, 172.16.1.0/27, which has all the workstations and four routers on it. Each workstation has a default gateway assigned to it that in actuality the router interface that would have been in its network had the more restrictive mask been used. The workstations see one another as local to their networks, due to ARP, and are able to communicate freely with one another. Any nonlocal routing would use the default gateway and would be handled by the router. The only case that I can think of that might cause problems is a BOOTP environment or one in which the workstation does not know its network mask for its IP interface and must learn it through ICMP, Get Mask. Let me say this again, *use caution* if you try this trick!

Network Address Translation

One of the best ways to make efficient use of assigned globally unique address space is to employ a network address translator (NAT). NAT devices were discussed earlier, so I will not go into the mechanics again. A NAT can do two things to improve utilization of address space. First, the network administrator can set up a one-to-one mapping of globally unique addresses to private addresses. The worst case is that each host that requires Internet access has a mapped globally unique address. Since the addresses are mapped and translated at the boundary between the autonomous system and the Internet, the globally unique addresses may be assigned consecutively without addressing holes. It is possible to achieve a utilization of 1.0 using this mechanism.

The second point of efficiency improvement that NAT can offer is the use of an address pool. Typically a one-to-one mapping, as just discussed, is configured for workstations offering services to the Internet, such as WWW and FTP servers. Those workstations in an organization that wish to access services on the Internet may be allocated a globally unique address that will endure only for the duration of the Internet access session. In this context these addresses may be referred to as *ephemeral addresses*, since they, like their TCP and UDP port namesakes, are short lived. Pooling globally unique addresses allows for efficiencies of scale. It is possible to furnish many more workstations with access to the Internet than there are globally unique addresses, under the premise that not all workstations that can access the Internet will require simultaneous access. This is the same premise on which tenant services and PBXs are based. To get the greatest efficiency, traffic and queueing theory could be applied, complete with call arrival rates, call duration, and blocking factors. It is possible to achieve efficiencies in excess of 1.0 through the use of a dynamically allocated globally unique address pool.

Summary

It is important to be efficient when assigning IP addresses, especially when the network allocation is made from globally unique address space. OSPF lends itself to addressing efficiency by virtue of being able to convey subnet mask information in its updates. RIP, which does not pass subnet mask information in its routing updates, relies on fixed-length masks. This will traditionally cause inefficiencies in networks that are irregular in size, since the largest number of hosts on a single network is often used to dictate the networkwide mask. Some tricks that can be used to get greater efficiencies in an RIP environment were discussed.

This chapter also discussed the use of the network address translator (NAT) as a mechanism for achieving extremely high utilization of the globally unique addresses. It is possible to exceed a utilization of 1.0 through the use of a NAT, due to efficiencies of scale.

Managing IP
Addresses

One of the objectives of any IP addressing scheme should be to optimize the manageability of the addresses that are used within the TCP/IP networks. Possibly more important constraints, such as efficiency or route aggregation, are being considered that will limit the management aspects in the addressing scheme. However, it is likely that some degree of management is obtainable. Further, the assignment of addresses to TCP/IP hosts can be made significantly easier through the use of some management-enhancing mechanisms, such as BOOTP and the Dynamic Host Configuration Protocol (DHCP). In addition, since it is likely that if you are designing a TCP/IP addressing architecture that deliberately accomplishes a goal such as the efficient use of globally unique networks or routing efficiency, you will want to maintain its effectiveness over time, regardless of change and growth. This chapter discusses these points.

Addressing for Management

Several methods for assigning addresses can contribute to over-all management of TCP/IP addressing. The key to assigning addresses for effective management is making the location or the utility of the address easy to remember without the need to refer to any documents. The ability to devise an optimal ad-dressing scheme for management is often degraded by the need to devise an scheme that optimizes network address utilization. It is simply a matter of which aspect is more important. For in-stance, if you have a Class C address, several point-to-point net-works, and a few Ethernets of various sizes, you may have to squeeze the individual subnet allocations into areas of the over-all network that might not be conducive to remembering the use of the address.

In this discussion I will assume that a private network alloca-tion is being used and that there is no concern for efficiency with regard to usage of the address space. In such a scenario I would typically choose to use the Class A network 10.0.0.0, since there is plenty of address space available for any scheme. In a hierarchical address scheme, such as a postal address, there are elements that define an area such as a country or a state, el-ements that define specific townships or sites within the area, and very specific addresses of people, buildings, or elements within the sites. Further, these elements are arranged in such a way that anybody, not just the postmaster or address adminis-trator, can locate the element being addressed. In most postal addressing schemes the odd-numbered street addresses are al-ways on one side of the street and the even-numbered ad-dresses on the other. Further, the addresses generally increase or decrease as you travel up or down a street. These are exam-ples of mnemonic devices (memory aids) that assist with the management of postal addresses.

The same concepts can be applied to TCP/IP addresses. Take the following example:

$10.x.y.z$

The x component could be used as the network identifier or area identifier. Networks can often be divided up into buildings, townships, countries, or contiguous WAN infrastructure, such as X.25, or Frame Relay networks. The x component would be used to identify that subset of the entire network. Be cautious to ensure that the granularity of the x component will not cause the available identifiers to be exhausted by growth and change. For instance, it might be better to choose to reflect countries with the x component if the network is international than to reflect municipalities.

The y component could be used as the site identifier. Depending on how the network was subdivided using the x component, the y component would reflect a further division. For instance, if the x component reflected a division by state, the y component could reflect a specific city or group of cities within the state denoted by the value of x.

The last component, z, could be used for the host addresses required to support the site defined by the y component. Not all addresses must fall within the same network. There might be several IP subnets per site, divided using fixed- or variable-length masks as necessary for the situation.

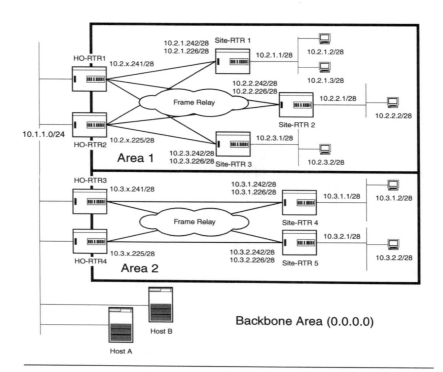

Illustration 9-1 Example of a Network Addressed for Ease of Management

Illustration 9-1 is an example of a network that is addressed using a management-oriented addressing scheme. The network uses $10.x.y.z$, where

- x = network identifier. Initially there will be four defined network identifiers:

    0 = Reserved

    1 = Home Office Ethernet (OSPF Backbone)

    2 = Frame Relay 1

    3 = Frame Relay 2

    4–254 = Unused

    255 = Reserved

- y = site identifier. Within each network (identified by the second octet) there can be a maximum of 256 sites (0 to 255). These are typically allocated sequentially, starting at 1 and working upward; however, the 0 value is legitimate and may be used.

- z = site network/host. With a 255.255.255.240 mask the last octet of address space is split in half, with each half getting 4 bits. That is, the number of hosts is restricted to 14 per network. Taking into account the uses for each octet in the address, the last octet has room for 16 networks per site. Although this may be overkill, the use of the Class A address allows for a certain amount of waste. With the ability to be wasteful and inefficient, it is possible to be administratively elegant. This addressing scheme opts for administration over frugality. If each site should require another network somewhere down the road, plenty are available without sacrificing the IP address structure defined today. In the home office networks that have a mask of 255.255.255.0, there is a maximum of 254 hosts per site ID instead of the 14-host limit used in the WAN networks.

As is evident from this example, the routes will collapse into a summary at each of the OSPF border routers. The routes in area 2 will all summarize to be 10.2.0.0/16. Route table efficiency can be a side effect of management-oriented addressing.

Another aspect of addressing for manageability is the development of a mnemonic system within each of the components of the address. This is best illustrated. In our example the x component was used to define a network identifier. The home office network uses 10.1.x.x, and the Frame Relay networks use 10.2.x.x and 10.3.x.x. It is easy to see from such a scheme that 10.3.1.1 would be a host that would be found in the Frame Relay network 2 (OSPF area 3).

Another example is where the x components represent states within the United States. The x component could be numbered consecutively from 1 to 50. The state that is first alphabetically in the list could be 10.1.0.0. The state that is the furthest west could be 10.1.0.0. The 13 original states of the union could be 10.1.0.0 through 10.13.0.0, and all the subsequent states would be numbered according to their admittance into the union. The point is, it does not matter what system you use, so long as you use a system and you work the system.

Develop and use a system when you are assigning host addresses, as well. The most important point is to be consistent. If possible, use the same addresses in each subnet for the router or for special workstations or hosts. Use the same range of addresses for all the user workstations. For instance, site 1 (10.2.1.x) in the example has five addresses defined as follows:

> 10.2.1.1 — Router Ethernet
>
> 10.2.1.13 — Mary's PC
>
> 10.2.1.14 — Joe's PC
>
> 10.2.1.241 — Home Office router Frame Relay interface
>
> 10.2.1.242 — Site-RTR1 router Frame Relay interface

The first address in each of the networks is a router. The first network of the 16 networks allocated to that site is always the local Ethernet. The last addresses in the first network are always the user hosts. The last network of the 16 formed from the last octet is always the network used on the Frame Relay network. The first address in the last network is always a router. In fact, the first address is always the router IP address that is closest to the home office Ethernet in area 0.0.0.0; other routers in the same IP network would be assigned subsequent addresses, again by proximity to the home office Ethernet. Get a plan. Work the plan. Be consistent. The more address space that is available to you and the more that you can be wasteful, the more you will be able to develop an addressing scheme that is administratively easy to use.

The IntraNIC

Whenever an IP addressing scheme is developed, the objectives and the addressing rules like those detailed previously, should be documented so that you or other folks will be able to understand the methodology at a later date. A lot of work and thought have gone into the addressing scheme. Make sure that you can maintain it into the future. For instance, if a site is added while you are on vacation, somebody should have a reference that can be used to do the addressing right, so you don't have to do it again at a later time.

Along with that, there should be a log of all assigned and available addresses. This could be a database, a spreadsheet, a word processing document, or even a handwritten notebook. Make sure that it is easy to use and keep current. I call this system the IntraNIC after its grownup counterpart, which tracks and manages the usage of globally unique Internet addresses in the United States.

Table 9-1 shows an example of a spreadsheet implementation of an IntraNIC. The information elements defined for each row are useful data for identifying points of contact and responsible parties. Even the IP addressing worksheet is a good start for an IntraNIC. Add more columns for additional data that you want to keep on each address assigned.

IP-1	IP-2	IP-3	IP-4	Location	Owner	Equip.	Mfgr.	Host Name
10	(Net)	(Site)	(Host)					
10	1	1	1	HO	Charles	PC	Compaq	CharlesPC
10	1	1	6	HO	Charles	Host	HP	Host-A
10	1	1	7	HO	Charles	Host	HP	Host-B
10	1	1	15	HO	HO-RTR1	Amazon	ACC	HO-RTR1
10	1	1	16	HO	HO-RTR2	Amazon	ACC	HO-RTR2
10	1	1	17	HO	HO-RTR3	Amazon	ACC	HO-RTR3
10	1	1	18	HO	HO-RTR4	Amazon	ACC	HO-RTR4
10	2	1	1	Site1	Site-RTR1	Danube	ACC	Site-RTR1
10	2	1	2	Site1	Mary	PC	Compaq	MaryPC
10	2	1	3	Site1	Joe	PC	Compaq	JoePC
10	2	1	225	HO	HO-RTR2	Amazon	ACC	HO-RTR2
10	2	1	226	Site1	Site-RTR1	Danube	ACC	Site-RTR1
10	2	1	241	HO	HO-RTR1	Amazon	ACC	HO-RTR1
10	2	1	242	Site1	Site-RTR1	Danube	ACC	Site-RTR1
10	2	2	1	Site2	Site-RTR2	Danube	ACC	Site-RTR2
10	2	2	2	Site2	Don	PC	Compaq	DonPC
10	2	2	225	HO	HO-RTR2	Amazon	ACC	HO-RTR2
10	2	2	226	Site2	Site-RTR2	Danube	ACC	Site-RTR2
10	2	2	241	HO	HO-RTR1	Amazon	ACC	HO-RTR1
10	2	2	242	Site2	Site-RTR2	Danube	ACC	Site-RTR2
10	2	3	1	Site3	Site-RTR3	Danube	ACC	Site-RTR3
10	2	3	2	Site3	Sue	PC	Compaq	SuePC

Table 9-1 Example of an IntraNIC Spreadsheet

Translation of IP Number to Name

It is possible that even if you develop an IP addressing scheme that is easy to administer, you would still choose to refer to a device with a name. There are two ways that you can configure a network such that you will not have to refer to devices solely by their IP addresses. Although this is valuable as a mnemonic device, it is also valuable to establish independence from positional reference. That is, a device can always have a hostname of "Buck," no matter what IP network it is homed to or its geographical location.

The first mechanism is the use of the /etc/hosts file found on all UNIX hosts and many other TCP/IP hosts. The file provides a simple mapping of IP addresses to host names, such as the following:

> 10.1.1.1CharlesPC
>
> 10.1.1.6Host-A
>
> 10.1.1.7Host-B
>
> 10.1.1.15HO-RTR1
>
> 10.2.1.1Site-RTR1
>
> 10.2.2.2DonPC

A user on the workstation where the /etc/hosts file is configured can, if desired, refer to a device by its IP address. One can refer to it by the name that is defined as an alias for the IP address. Instead of "Telnet 10.1.1.6" for example, it would be possible to use "Telnet Host-A."

Another means by which an IP address can be translated to a name is through the use of the domain name system (DNS). The effect is similar to the use of the /etc/hosts file; however, it is a distributed, hierarchical system that does not require each workstation's /etc/hosts file to be kept synchronized for consistency.

DNS operates in a client-server model. One or more DNS servers should be run in or provide services to an autonomous system. Each workstation or device that wishes to use DNS for its translation from host name to IP address should run the DNS client.

I admit that I have never had to configure or maintain a domain name service. In fact, I seldom use it, although I acknowledge that when it is available, I find it to be a tremendous boon. I would much rather Telnet to "Boston-router" than to 10.123.47.199, especially when the addressing scheme is not set up so that it is easy to remember and become accustomed to.

Administration Tools

Two mechanisms in wide use today allow a network administrator to easily assign IP addresses to workstations or other network devices. The BOOTP and DHCP mechanisms are protocols that allow a device to be automatically assigned an IP address for long- or short-term use among other things.

There is a very real possibility in many organizations that growth or change will render an IP addressing scheme inadequate, no matter how well it is planned. Using one of these mechanisms will make your job of readdressing the affected portion of the network much easier.

Bootstrap Protocol (BOOTP)

BOOTP defines a mechanism that allows a diskless workstation to be placed on a network without any prior configuration and, through the use of a BOOTP server, acquire all IP addressing parameters and boot file parameters for it to boot up and participate on an IP network. RFC 951, "Bootstrap Protocol," is the initial RFC that defines the operation of BOOTP. Although RFC 951 defines the purpose of BOOTP as a service to diskless workstations, BOOTP has been used in many network devices, such as routers, for updating configuration files or application code. BOOTP can also provide an IP address to any workstation, not just the diskless variety.

The BOOTP server is typically run on a UNIX host. The BOOTP server process uses UDP port 67, and the BOOTP client process uses UDP port 68. The BOOTP server uses a configuration file, *bootptab*, which will instruct the service in how to service a BOOTP request from a client. The following is an example of a bootptab file:

```
global.defaults:\
   :sm=255.255.255.192:\
   :hd=/tftpboot:\
   :gw=10.1.1.15:\
   :ht=ether

CharlesPC:tc=global.defaults:ha=08000323121E:ip=10.1.1.1
Site-RTR1:tc=global.defaults:ha=08000325686A:
   ip=10.2.1.1:bf=sr1.scr
Site-RTR2:tc=global.defaults:ha=08000325686B:
   ip=10.2.2.1:bf=sr2.scr
```

Although the details of BOOTP are not relevant to this book, I will present a brief overview of the operation of the Bootstrap Protocol. Illustration 9-2 depicts the standard BOOTP packet.

Illustration 9-2 BOOTP Packet Structure

The fields are identified as follows:

op   Packet op code / message type:
            1 = BOOTREQUEST, 2 = BOOTREPLY

htype   Hardware address type

hlen   Hardware address length

hops   Client sets to 0

xid   Transaction ID

secs   Seconds elapsed since started boot process

flags	Option flags
ciaddr	Client IP address
yiaddr	"Your" (client) IP address
siaddr	Server IP address
giaddr	Gateway IP address
chaddr	Client hardware address
sname	Server host name
file	Boot file name
vend	Optional vendor-specific use

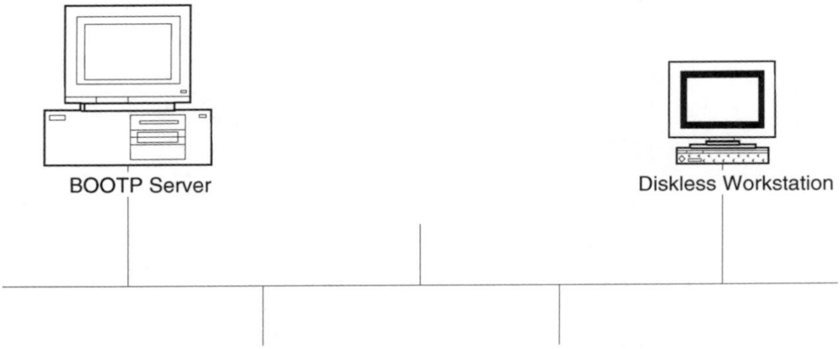

BOOTP Server   Diskless Workstation

Illustration 9-3 Example BOOTP Network

Illustration 9-3 is an example of the mechanics of BOOTP. When the diskless workstation is powered on, the workstation will send out a BOOTP request packet like the following:

destip:	255.255.255.255 (limited broadcast)
srcip:	0.0.0.0 (this host, this network)
op:	1 (BOOTREQUEST)
htype:	1 (Ethernet)

`hlen:`	6 (Ethernet)
`hops:`	0
`xid:`	23013 (randomly set by client)
`secs:`	0
`flags:`	`null`
`ciaddr:`	`0.0.0.0` (this host, this network)
`yiaddr:`	
`siaddr:`	
`giaddr:`	
`chaddr:`	`08000325686B`
`sname:`	
`file:`	
`vend:`	

Since the diskless workstation does not know the IP address of the BOOTP server, it sends the BOOTP request out as a limited broadcast, constrained to the network on which it is sent. The diskless workstation also uses the all-0s IP address as the source address in the IP datagram header.

`destip:`	`255.255.255.255` (limited broadcast)
`srcip:`	`172.16.1.1` (BOOTP server)
`op:`	2 (BOOTREPLY)
`htype:`	1 (Ethernet)
`hlen:`	6 (Ethernet)
`hops:`	0
`xid:`	23013
`secs:`	0

```
flags:      null
ciaddr:
yiaddr:     172.16.1.21
siaddr:     172.16.1.1
giaddr:     172.16.1.1
chaddr:     08000325686B
sname:
file:       /tftpboot/dws021
vend:       1,4,255.255.255.192
```

You probably noticed that the original BOOTP structure did not specify a field for subnet mask information. The use of the Vend field for this, and other purposes, is documented in RFC 1533, "DHCP Options and BOOTP Vendor Extensions."

When the diskless workstation receives this BOOTP reply from the server, it knows its IP address; however, it cannot be guaranteed that it is unique on the network. For this reason the workstation will send out three ARP requests to see whether any other device will answer up that it is the owner of the IP address 172.16.1.21. If no reply is received, in the third ARP request the diskless workstation will use a source IP address of 172.16.1.21 instead of 0.0.0.0 and announce ownership of the IP address. Then the diskless workstation sends more BOOTP requests to validate the initial response. Once satisfied that the information in the BOOTP reply is consistent, the diskless workstation initiates a TFTP file transfer of the boot file. The diskless workstation can then run the boot file and become operational.

Dynamic Host Configuration Protocol (DHCP)

DHCP can be used to provide all the parameters a host on an IP network requires to operate and exchange information on the internet to which it is attached. DHCP can also be used to manage the distribution of IP addresses within an autonomous system.

It should be possible to configure a DHCP server to provide all the parameters specified in RFC 1122, "Requirements for Internet Hosts—Communication Layers," and RFC 1123, "Requirements for Internet Hosts—Application and Support." Let's take a look at the DHCP packet structure (Illustration 9-4).

```
 0                   1                   2                   3
 0 1 2 3 4 5 6 7 8 9 0 1 2 3 4 5 6 7 8 9 0 1 2 3 4 5 6 7 8 9 0 1
+-+-+-+-+-+-+-+-+-+-+-+-+-+-+-+-+-+-+-+-+-+-+-+-+-+-+-+-+-+-+-+-+
|     op (1)     |   htype (1)   |    hlen (1)   |   hops (1)    |
+---------------------------------------------------------------+
|                          xid (4)                              |
+-------------------------------+-------------------------------+
|           secs (2)            |           flags (2)           |
+-------------------------------+-------------------------------+
|                         ciaddr (4)                            |
+---------------------------------------------------------------+
|                         yiaddr (4)                            |
+---------------------------------------------------------------+
|                         siaddr (4)                            |
+---------------------------------------------------------------+
|                         giaddr (4)                            |
+---------------------------------------------------------------+
|                                                               |
|                        chaddr (16)                            |
|                                                               |
+---------------------------------------------------------------+
|                                                               |
|                        sname (64)                             |
|                                                               |
+---------------------------------------------------------------+
|                                                               |
|                        file (128)                             |
|                                                               |
+---------------------------------------------------------------+
|                                                               |
|                       options (312)                           |
|                                                               |
+---------------------------------------------------------------+
```

Illustration 9-4 DHCP Frame Structure

Compare it to the BOOTP packet structure of Illustration 9-2. It is identical except for the last field. The Vend field in BOOTP has come to be known as the Options field in DHCP, and more bytes were allocated to the field. DHCP allows for 312 bytes in the Option field, whereas BOOTP allowed only 64 bytes in the Vend field. In fact, you will be interested to know that UDP port 67 is used for the DHCP server and UDP port 68 for the DHCP client. These are the same numbers that BOOTP uses. The reality of the situation is that BOOTP functionality is inherent in the DHCP service. It is not possible to have two different TCP/IP applications, BOOTP and DHCP, to share a UDP port. BOOTP is a subset of the DHCP implementation. It is possible for a BOOTP client to get BOOTP services from a DHCP server.

The Options field is an extension of the Vend field of the original BOOTP protocol. All extended functionality of the DHCP service is provided through essentially the same packet structure as was originally used in BOOTP.

DHCP can be used to allocate IP addresses to hosts. When a host using DHCP is powered up on a network for the first time, it negotiates with the DHCP server for an IP address. The server may provide an IP address to the requesting host under one of two premises:

- Permanent allocation: The DHCP server assigns an IP address to a host for its exclusive use.
- Dynamic allocation: The DHCP server assigns an IP address to a host for a limited time.

DHCP makes use of a term "lease," which has a value equal to the amount of time that an IP address is assigned to a given host. In general, whenever a host first comes up, it requests an IP address good for the requested lease duration. The DHCP client and server negotiate a lease duration, and the client is assigned an IP address. It is possible to assign a lease of 0xffffffff, which would allocate the IP address permanently to a client.

DHCP also has the ability to allocate a pool of addresses that are available for allocation within a given subnet. Address utilization can be improved by making the pool of addresses smaller than the number of potential clients. However, care should be taken to make sure that a host is not blocked from access to network resources by virtue of the address pool being depleted.

The bottom line is that if your hosts obtain their IP addresses through DHCP or BOOTP, it will be significantly easier to readdress the hosts, if necessary. Simply do a "find and replace" in the DHCP configuration file, and the hosts will come up on a different network the next time they are booted.

Summary

This chapter was concerned with the management of the allocation of IP addresses, as well as with the design of an addressing scheme to enhance management of the network devices. The keys to creating a network addressing scheme that enhances management are hierarchy and consistency. If a network is numbered such that there is a hierarchy to the IP address, such as 10.*net.site.host*, you will not only get the benefit of manageability but possibly also route aggregation. It is equally important that the host numbering scheme be consistent across similar subnets. This is exemplified by an intranet that has many point-to-point IP networks and in which the nearside router on the link always uses the odd-numbered address of the router pairings.

The concept of an IntraNIC was introduced. An IntraNIC is a system whereby the allocation of IP addresses is managed. The IntraNIC system relies on a database (or spreadsheet) that allows an administrator to assign "ownership" of IP addresses and subnets.

Hosts and many network devices can be assigned IP addresses dynamically through the use of BOOTP or DHCP. BOOTP, the Bootstrap Protocol, is an older protocol that was intended to provide boot services through a network connection. DHCP, the Dynamic Host Configuration Protocol, is a superset of BOOTP. Network devices can get configuration parameters automatically on boot-up, which will permit them to communicate over their internet. DHCP can also assign IP addresses, based on a lease request from a workstation.

Both BOOTP and DHCP allow an administrator to automatically assign IP addresses from a central server. This makes the management of IP address allocation a much simpler process. The two protocols also simplify the process of renumbering an addressing scheme.

Addressing for Growth and Change

This chapter introduces you to a couple of small but important topics within IP addressing architecture. These topics are anticipated growth and unanticipated change. The difference between them might seem insignificant at first; however, the key to the difference lies in the terms "anticipated" and "unanticipated."

Anticipated Growth

An addressing scheme should permit growth within the constraints of desired address efficiency. Growth that is anticipated should always be a major consideration of an address scheme design.

It almost goes without saying that if you anticipate patterns of growth within your organization, the network address scheme should allow for that growth. Excess address space should be strategically placed within the IP address plan. If I had a small branch office network with only four IP hosts allocated, I would need an IP network with 29 bits of network mask to accommodate it (up to six hosts). If I knew that that particular branch office was likely to grow as much as 400 percent over the next few years, I doubt that it would be prudent for me to use the IP network allocation scheme shown in Illustration 10-1.

.0/24	.128/25	.192/26	.224/27	.240/28	.248/29	.252/30
0	0	0	0	0	Site A 0	0
1	1	1	1	1	A-1 1	1
2	2	2	2	2	A-2 2	2
3	3	3	3	3	3	3
4	4	4	4	4	4	4
5	5	5	5	5	A-3 5	5
6	6	6	6	6	A-4 6	6
7	7	7	7	7	7	7
8	8	8	8	8	Site B 8	8
9	9	9	9	9	B-1 9	9
10	10	10	10	10	B-2 10	10
11	11	11	11	11	11	11
12	12	12	12	12	B-3 12	12
13	13	13	13	13	B-4 13	13
14	14	14	14	14	14	14
15	15	15	15	15	15	15
16	16	16	16	16	Site C 16	16
17	17	17	17	17	17	17
18	18	18	18	18	C-1 18	18
19	19	19	19	19	C-2 19	19
20	20	20	20	20	C-3 20	20
21	21	21	21	21	C-4 21	21
22	22	22	22	22	22	22

Illustration 10-1 Portion of IP Address Worksheet 1

23	23	23	23	23	23	23
24	24	24	24	24	24	24
25	25	25	25	25	25	25
26	26	26	26	26	26	26
27	27	27	27	27	27	27
28	28	28	28	28	28	28
29	29	29	29	29	29	29
30	30	30	30	30	30	30
31	31	31	31	31	31	31

Illustration 10-1 (Continued)

The problem with such an address allocation is that when the branch office "Site B" begins to grow as expected, there is no overflow. Knowing that the Site B branch office is going to experience a population boom, I might opt for a scenario such as that shown in Illustration 10-2.

.0/24	.128/25	.192/26	.224/27	.240/28	.248/29	.252/30
0	0	0	0	0	Site B 0	0
1	1	1	1	1	B-1 1	1
2	2	2	2	2	B-2 2	2
3	3	3	3	3	3	3
4	4	4	4	4	B-3 4	4
5	5	5	5	5	B-4 5	5
6	6	6	6	6	6	6
7	7	7	7	7	7	7
8	8	8	8	8	8	8
9	9	9	9	9	9	9

Illustration 10-2 Address Upgrade

10	10	10	10	10	10	10
11	11	11	11	11	11	11
12	12	12	12	12	12	12
13	13	13	13	13	13	13
14	14	14	14	14	14	14
15	15	15	15	15	15	15
16	16	16	16	16	16	16
17	17	17	17	17	17	17
18	18	18	18	18	18	18
19	19	19	19	19	19	19
20	20	20	20	20	20	20
21	21	21	21	21	21	21
22	22	22	22	22	22	22
23	23	23	23	23	23	23
24	24	24	24	24	24	24
25	25	25	25	25	25	25
26	26	26	26	26	26	26
27	27	27	27	27	27	27
28	28	28	28	28	28	28
29	29	29	29	29	29	29
30	30	30	30	30	30	30
31	31	31	31	31	31	31

Illustration 10-2   (Continued)

An entire block of 30 host addresses has been reserved for the branch office. It has been blocked out so that no other allocations can be made from that group of addresses. At least it is for now. When the branch office reaches a point at which six hosts are on the network, the address space in network 172.16.1.0/29 is exhausted. Another eight hosts can be added to the network if the subnet mask of all the hosts is changed to 172.16.1.0/28. Moving to a mask that permits more hosts per network is known as an *address upgrade*. The host IP addresses of the workstation need not change. This mask gives the branch office room for 14 hosts before the address space is exhausted and the network mask has to be changed once more, to 172.16.1.0/27 (which supports 30 hosts). If, sometime in the future, it is determined that the amount of growth was overestimated, the space that was set aside for growth of that one branch office can be freed up for other allocations.

You may be wondering why, if growth was anticipated, I did not start off by allocating the larger of the three networks. In some regards it is a matter or choice and circumstance. If address space is at a premium, perhaps because of the use of globally unique addresses, it is easier to think of entire unused networks as available room for the entire intranet. Unused address space within a network is thought of primarily as room to grow within that single IP network. If address space were plentiful, I might preallocate all address space according to the corporation's "five-year growth plan."

Attrition is the opposite of growth. When a site is shrinking, the IP addresses should be kept to the top or the bottom of the address space. See Illustration 10-3. At this moment the site requires address space from 172.16.1.0/28, since it allows for up to 14 hosts. When one more workstation is "turned off," the network 172.16.1.0/29 will suffice for all six hosts on the network. This is known as an *address downgrade*. This occurs whenever you change the network mask to permit fewer hosts per network. The benefit of an address downgrade is that an IP network is freed up for use elsewhere. In Illustration 10-3 network 172.16.1.8/29 has been made available.

.0/24	.128/25	.192/26	.224/27	.240/28	.248/29	.252/30
0	0	0	0	0	0	0
1	1	1	1	RTR 1 1	1	1
2	2	2	2	WS 1 2	2	2
3	3	3	3	WS 2 3	3	3
4	4	4	4	WS 3 4	4	4
5	5	5	5	WS 4 5	5	5
6	6	6	6	WS 5 6	6	6
7	7	7	7	WS 6 7	7	7
8	8	8	8	8	8	8
9	9	9	9	9	9	9
10	10	10	10	10	10	10
11	11	11	11	11	11	11
12	12	12	12	12	12	12
13	13	13	13	13	13	13
14	14	14	14	14	14	14
15	15	15	15	15	15	15
16	16	16	16	16	16	16
17	17	17	17	17	17	17
18	18	18	18	18	18	18
19	19	19	19	19	19	19
20	20	20	20	20	20	20
21	21	21	21	21	21	21
22	22	22	22	22	22	22
23	23	23	23	23	23	23
24	24	24	24	24	24	24
25	25	25	25	25	25	25
26	26	26	26	26	26	26

Illustration 10-3 Address Downgrade

27	27	27	27	27	27	27
28	28	28	28	28	28	28
29	29	29	29	29	29	29
30	30	30	30	30	30	30
31	31	31	31	31	31	31

Illustration 10-3 (Continued)

Unanticipated Change

There are always changes after an addressing scheme is implemented. An addressing plan should have flex points to permit changes without having to redesign completely. Flex points are essentially reservations of address space that might be used for specific purposes at some future date. In Illustration 10-2 space was reserved in case the branch office grew as anticipated. If at some point the corporate management decided that another Ethernet was justified to support a new application, the network 172.16.1.16/28 could be used. The space was originally intended to permit growth but was ultimately used as a consequence of change.

Small changes such as this one can often be absorbed into an addressing plan without too much difficulty. Large changes can be a different story. Companies are bought and subsidiaries sold. These are classic examples of large-scale unanticipated changes.

If the change is significant within an internet, it is likely that the best approach to handling unanticipated change is to reevaluate the effectiveness of the addressing plan to achieve a desired criterion. As mentioned once before, renumbering is sometimes your only choice. Of course, this job is much easier if you planned for its possibility. BOOTP and, even more so, DHCP are capable of reducing the amount of effort required to execute the renumbering of a network. These were discussed in Chapter 9.

Summary

Growth and change can be accommodated to some degree by leaving "holes" in the network addressing plan. These holes represent the reservation of space for some future need, anticipated or otherwise. Naturally the more holes that are left in the address plan, the more inefficient the plan becomes.

When addressing with the private network allocation, such as the Class A network 10.0.0.0/8, it is possible to have much more address space than ever could be conceived as possible to exhaust. Even with this overabundance of address resources, it is possible to leave flex points that are ineffective and thus completely wasteful. The flex points that are placed in an address plan should be considered carefully to maximize their benefits.

There comes a time when a network addressing plan falls apart and no longer produces the benefit it was once designed to provide. For instance, the introduction of a new wide area network mechanism leaves the old wide area network that you have designed your IP network around obsolete. In some cases it might be better to adapt the addressing scheme of the old WAN to that of the new WAN. In other cases the addressing scheme may not be so flexible. It could be "patched" with obscure IP network addressing and the once coveted route aggregation might suffer, or the entire IP address scheme could be redesigned and rejuvenated. BOOTP and DHCP can make the job much easier—if not this time, perhaps the next time.

Advanced Addressing Issues

Most of what I had to say about anything related to IP addressing has been said. What remains are two topics that will impact IP addressing.

Chapter 11 discusses multicast addressing with some details of its operation including forwarding algorithms and multicast routing protocols. The Mbone, (Multicast Backbone) in use on the Internet is also presented.

Chapter 12 introduces IP version 6. Also known as IP next generation (IPng), it is the long term solution to depletion of unique networks.

IP Multicast

One advancing protocol is IP multicast communications. A majority of the work on IP multicast began in the late 1980s and early 1990s, although it is seemingly a long way from widespread implementation. IP multicast, referred to throughout this chapter as simply "multicast" unless otherwise specified, was first introduced in this text during the discussion of IP addresses. Any IP address that has the four high-order bits set to "1110" is reserved for multicast usage. This would indicate that multicast addresses fall in the range 224.0.0.0 to 239.255.255.255, inclusive.

Simply put, multicast permits packets to be sent from one station, the multicast originator, to zero, one, or many stations, the multicast recipients. Although the main thrust of this book is to present IP addressing and ways to optimize it, IP multicast is an emerging technology that affects and is affected by addressing, specifically Class D addresses.

Multicast is a way to communicate with more than one host simultaneously, although there may be zero or one member of the group of multicast recipients. If communications were needed to only one other host, I would likely be better served by using unicasts, which permit communications between exactly two hosts. If communications were needed to all hosts, albeit rarely, I might be better served by using the more common IP broadcast capability. Indeed multicast is best used to permit communications among more than one and fewer than all hosts. Multicast itself is best used for two purposes: resource discovery and conferencing.

Resource Discovery

Multicast allows a device with no knowledge of the IP addresses of other systems on the network to ferret out all devices that have some commonality. The devices that are being searched for must be configured to listen for multicast datagrams destined for a specific Class D address. Currently the well-known multicast addresses can be found in the Assigned Numbers RFC (currently RFC 1700), an excerpt from which follows:

224.0.0.0	Base Address (Reserved)
224.0.0.1	All Systems on this Subnet
224.0.0.2	All Routers on this Subnet
224.0.0.3	Unassigned
224.0.0.4	DVMRP Routers
224.0.0.5	OSPFIGP OSPFIGP All Router
224.0.0.6	OSPFIGP OSPFIGP Designated Routers
224.0.0.7	ST Routers
224.0.0.8	STHosts

224.0.0.9	RIP2 Routers
224.0.0.10	IGRP Routers
224.0.0.11	Mobile-Agents
224.0.0.12– 224.0.0.255	Unassigned

Note that the address 224.0.0.1 is used for "all systems on this subnet." You should be aware that multicast capability is not widely implemented throughout the Internet or in commercial TCP/IP stacks, although there are a few. It would naturally follow, therefore, that it is better to consider the address of 224.0.0.1 to mean "all [multicast-capable] systems on this subnet." It would not be a good assumption that if you were to send a packet to 224.0.0.1, all hosts on the subnet would receive it. Further, you should note that the use of a subnet in this case is not consistent with the previous discussions in this text. This usage is intended to mean the physical network that the interface that is transmitting the multicast is participating in. The same discussion and caveats apply to the address 224.0.0.2.

Also note the addresses 224.0.0.5 and 224.0.0.6, which are used for OSPF routing (Interior Gateway Protocol, IGP). If a packet were to be distributed to all OSPF-designated routers within an autonomous system, this could easily be facilitated by sending the packet to 224.0.0.6. A problem is inherent to this transport, however. Sending a packet to a multicast address with the intent that it will reach only destinations on the local network is simple. Sending a packet to the same multicast address and expecting it to permeate the networks of the autonomous system is more difficult. The latter case requires the use of multicast routers, devices that can control the "flooding" of the multicast to all networks that have multicast recipients. Multicast routing capability is not inherent in all IP version 4 routers, and as such the transport of the multicast packet might be limited to the local network by necessity.

Conferencing

Another common use for multicast is the distribution of information to many hosts simultaneously. To distribute the information to hosts more distant than the local networks to which the multicast originator is connected requires multicast routers. Assuming for a moment that the backbone of the Internet and individual autonomous systems were capable of routing multicast packets, any host device would be able to receive multicasts. The uses of this are many, including audio and multimedia conferences or multicasts. Note that the term broadcast was not used, although a correlation can be drawn between a multicast conference and traditional broadcast media. If the conference were facilitated by broadcasts, the scope of the conference would be the entire Internet domain. Multicasting permits that transmission of packets to only those nodes having "registered" or "joined" the multicast group.

The following addresses are some of the well-known multicast addresses used for conferencing purposes. The list is an excerpt from the Assigned Numbers RFC.

224.0.1.7	AUDIONEWS—Audio News Multicast
224.0.1.10	IETF-1—LOW-AUDIO
224.0.1.11	IETF-1—AUDIO
224.0.1.12	IETF-1—VIDEO
224.0.1.13	IETF-2—LOW-AUDIO
224.0.1.14	IETF-2—AUDIO
224.0.1.15	IETF-2—VIDEO
224.0.1.16	MUSIC—SERVICE
224.0.1.17	SEANET—TELEMETRY
224.0.1.18	SEANET—IMAGE

In the recent past there have been several demonstrations of the multicast conferencing capability in conjunction with the Internet Engineering Task Force (IETF) meetings. The multicast addresses of 224.0.1.10 through 224.0.1.15 are used to transport the audio or video to remote participants in the IETF meetings. Illustration 11-1 is an example of the programming offered over these services during the June 1996 IETF meeting. To participate, a user would require a TCP/IP stack that supports multicasts and a service provider that is participating in the Mbone, the experimental multicast backbone. This is somewhat simplified. If you are interested in participating, please refer to the Mbone FAQ (Frequently Asked Questions) file on any of the IETF FTP servers.

MONDAY (UTC)	0930-1130 1330-1530	1300-1500 1700-1900	1530-1730 1930-2130	1930-2200 2330-0200
CHAN 1	issll	ion	mmusic	ipngwg
CHAN 2	rps	mboned	applmib	rsvp

TUESDAY (UTC)	0900-1130 1330-1530	1300-1500 1700-1900	1530-1730 1930-2130
CHAN 1	ipngwg	ion	ion
CHAN 2	rps	avt	avt

WEDNESDAY (UTC)	0900-1130 1330-1530	1300-1500 1700-1900	1530-1730 1930-2130	1930-2200 2330-0200
CHAN 1	ipngwg	mobileip	intserv	iab
CHAN 2	mmusic	rsvp	idmr	applmib

Illustration 11-1 Multicast Conference Programming for June 1996 IETF Meeting

```
THURSDAY 0900-1130 1300-1500 1530-1630  1630-1830
(UTC)    1330-1530 1700-1900 1930-2130  2330-0200
```

CHAN 1	otsv	mobileip	tech. plenary	open plenary
CHAN 2	nmarea	idmr	"	"

Illustration 11-1 (Continued)

The Mbone experimental multicast backbone is an overlay on the Internet. This is due partly to the fact that the Mbone is an experiment, and many of the commercial routers being used on the Internet do not support multicast routing. You could argue, however, that the Mbone is becoming less of an experiment and more production oriented with each passing IETF meeting. The Mbone started in much the same way that the Internet was started, as an experiment involving a handful of participants, but now has more than 3000 multicast domains. With the momentum that it is gaining, the Mbone will soon be too large to continue as an experiment much longer.

The Mbone uses the Internet for transport to each of the multicast domains. This is accomplished through the use of high-bandwidth tunnels that connect multicast routers. Currently multicast routers are commonly implemented in UNIX workstations running *mrouted*, daemon software that implements the multicast routing functions. With continued acceptance and growth of the Mbone and multicasting in general, it is likely that the multicast routing capability will eventually be integrated into the Internet backbone routers. This would permit multicast conference participation by anyone interested, not by the few who are "well connected." In some ways this would cause the demise of the Mbone, since it would no longer be required for multicast support in the Internet.

Internet Group Management Protocol (IGMP)

IGMP is the protocol that enables a host to join a multicast group or conference. The current version of IGMP is version 1 and is specified in RFC 1112, "Host Extensions for IP Multicasting." A host, using IGMP, notifies its local multicast routers of any IP multicast groups that it wishes to be a member of. The format of an IGMP message is shown in Illustration 11-2.

```
 0                   1                   2                   3
 0 1 2 3 4 5 6 7 8 9 0 1 2 3 4 5 6 7 8 9 0 1 2 3 4 5 6 7 8 9 0 1
+-------+-------+---------------+-------------------------------+
|Version| Type  |    Unused     |           Checksum            |
+-------+-------+---------------+-------------------------------+
|                        Group Address                          |
+---------------------------------------------------------------+
```

Illustration 11-2 IGMP Message Format

IGMP is a fairly simple protocol. Multicast routers are cognizant of all current multicast conferences, as well as the common, well-known multicast groups. For each multicast group that the router is aware of, it will send out a Host Membership Query. This is an IGMP message with Type = 1. It is sent to the destination of 224.0.0.1, which is the multicast address used to denote all multicast hosts on the local networks serviced by the multicast router. Each multicast host that has an interest in receiving the multicast transmission denoted by the Group Address field will respond with a Host Membership Report. This is an IGMP message with Type = 2. If at least one host on the local network is interested in receiving the multicast conversation, the router will forward the multicast packets that have an IP destination address equal to the multicast group required by the hosts on the network. Those multicast groups that are not "requested" by at least one host on a network are not propagated onto that network.

The multicast routers will occasionally send a new IGMP Host Membership Query in order to determine whether the last host interested in a multicast conversation has "discontinued its membership," in which case the router ceases to propagate the multicast packets for that particular group on that network. The periodic Host Membership Query will also indicate whether any hosts have reported a new interest in a multicast group that was heretofore not being propagated.

Multicast Routing Overview

One of the most difficult challenges of creating a usable multicast-capable internet is creating a routing mechanism for dissemination of the multicast packets to each subscriber. Multicast packets have only one destination IP address, the Class D multicast group address. There can be as few as zero or as many as (theoretically) the entire Internet community participating in a multicast conference. The routing mechanism should forward the packets to all participants without wasting bandwidth. Ideally, if the multicast group has a membership of zero, the packet should not be sent beyond the first multicast router. The packets should be distributed in a timely manner. The very nature of some of the uses for multicasting (audio and video conferencing) suggests that it is essential that delays be kept to a minimum and that any delay be deterministic.

Certainly some, if not all, of the functionality offered through multicasting is also available with less difficulty through unicast transmission. It is really just a matter of how many more resources are consumed by a unicast approach weighed against the multicast difficulty. Consider Illustration 11-3.

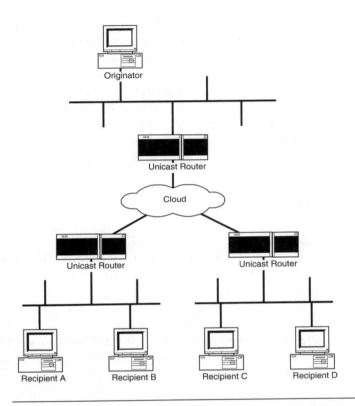

Illustration 11-3 One Originator to *n* Recipients Using Unicasting

In order for the originator station to communicate with each of the recipient stations simultaneously using unicasts, four associations would be required. Associations were defined in Chapter 1 to be:

{protocol, source IP address, source port, destination IP address, destination port}

In other words, there would have to be a TCP or a UDP connection between the originator and each recipient. Each packet that comprises the communication would have to be sent from the originator to each recipient. The Ethernet that the originator is on would see four times more traffic than in a similar situation using multicasting. Further, under the unicast configuration, if recipient A wished to assume the role of originator, perhaps in order to give an opinion on a topic, it would have to either set up an association with each of the other stations or have that communications relayed by the originator in Illustration 11-3. In order to permit every station to have both originator and recipient capabilities, the number of associations would be ($n \times (n-1)$) / 2. This, in essence, creates a full-mesh network. It is true that broadcasts could provide the functionality; however, in cases in which the participants of the conference are a minority subset of the network community, broadcasts would likely not be appreciated.

As just mentioned, the same scenario using multicasting would be much more efficient. The originator would send a multicast packet to the multicast router on its Ethernet. The multicast router would forward the multicast packet to each multicast router that needs to get the packet. The routers would, in turn, send a link layer multicast onto each of their respective Ethernets, where it would be received by the recipients. Ideally there would only ever be one instance of the multicast packet that would traverse any network.

Any recipient station that wished to assume the role of originator could do so by sending a multicast packet to the multicast group address being used for the conference. Naturally this is a simplification of the process from the perspective that a conference is often chaired and mediated to ensure that order is maintained.

Up to this point, I have only briefly covered how packets are distributed in a multicast environment. This is done through some form of distribution and routing mechanisms. First, let's cover the distribution mechanisms that might be used for multicasting.

Multicast Packet Distribution

Several mechanisms could be used to distribute multicast packets within an internet. Each has its own pros and cons. This section briefly discusses each method. For a more detailed perspective, refer to the Internet Draft document, "Introduction to IP Multicast Routing," draft-rfced-info-semeria-00.txt.

Flooding

Flooding in a multicast environment works very much as in the OSPF routing protocol. Whenever a multicast packet arrives at a multicast router, the router checks to see whether the packet has been previously seen. If the packet has not been seen by that router, the multicast router forwards the packet out all of its interfaces except the one that the packet was received on. If the multicast router has seen the packet before, it will quietly discard the packet and take no further action with regard to the packet.

Pro	Con
Easy to implement	Requires table of previous packets
Robust	Inefficient use of network bandwidth
Fast distribution	

Spanning Tree (ST)

One of the problems with flooding the multicast packets to all of the multicast routers is that the packets are sent on all links within the multicast backbone in order to forward the packet. A more optimal solution is to build a single spanning tree (ST) that includes all multicast routers but includes only enough links to permit complete connectivity. Spanning trees are loopless and have exactly one path from any multicast router in the network to any other multicast router. A host that wishes to originate a multicast packet need only forward the packet to a single multicast router. That multicast router will use the spanning tree to forward the multicast packet to all other multicast routers.

Pro	Con
Experience with implementation	Traffic concentration on links of ST
Robust	No alternate paths in ST
	ST may not use optimal links

Reverse Path Broadcast (RPB)

Reverse path broadcast improves on the basic spanning tree forwarding by creating a spanning tree for each source in a multicast group. The fundamental algorithm permits a multicast router to forward multicast packets arriving from a specific source only if the packet arrived on the interface that is considered to be the preferred interface through which that router can reach the source. See Illustration 11-4.

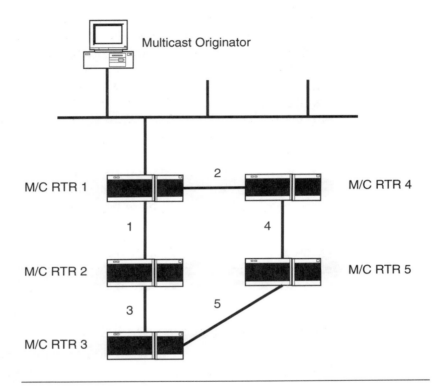

Illustration 11-4 Multicast Originator/Router Sample

Assume that the metrics for all of the numbered links are equal.
A multicast packet arrives at multicast router 3 with a source IP
address for the host system, or Multicast Originator. If the multicast packet arrives on the interface for link 3, that packet will
be forwarded to multicast router 5 via link 5. However, if the
multicast packet arrives at multicast router 3 via link 5, it will be
quietly discarded, because multicast router 3 prefers link 3 over
link 5 for routing of traffic destined to the multicast originator.

Using this basic algorithm, multicast router 3 will forward all
traffic from the multicast originator received via link 3 to multicast router 5 via link 5. It is clear, however, that using this algo-

rithm, multicast router 5 will discard that same packet just forwarded to it from multicast router 3, since link 3 is not the preferred path from router 5 to the originator. It is a natural extension to this forwarding algorithm that if a router can determine that the link it should forward a multicast packet onto is not the preferred link back to the source, it should not send the packet at all. In this case multicast router 3 should not forward the multicast packet to multicast router 5, and vice versa.

Making this determination is not as difficult as it might seem at first glance. If the routing protocol being used for the unicast packets is a link-state protocol, such as OSPF, each router in the area has an identical topology database. Multicast router 3 could compute the route entry to the multicast originator that multicast router 5 would have in its routing table. If multicast router 3 determines from the computation that it would not be the next hop for a packet sent from multicast router 5 to the multicast originator, it will not forward the multicast packet to router 5.

Distance-vector routing protocols do not require each router to have an identical topology database. They must rely on a different mechanism. In fact, in a distance-vector routing protocol the routers periodically send out updates representing their entire route tables. Adjacent routers can easily determine from these updates the information required to determine whether the multicast packet should be forwarded.

Pro	Con
Efficiently uses network bandwidth	Requires routing tables in decisions
Does not concentrate all M/C on single links	Does not consider group memberships
Fast	

Truncated Reverse Path Broadcasting (TRPB)

Truncated reverse path broadcasting (TRPB) is a slight modification of RPB. Through the use of a group membership protocol, such as IGMP, the router can determine which of the leaf networks it interfaces with have hosts that are members of the multicast group in the packet's destination address. The TRPB forwarding algorithm will not permit a multicast packet to be forwarded onto a leaf network where there are no group members. RPB dictates that multicast packets are forwarded to leaf networks. All other forwarding decisions in TRPB are the same as in RPB.

Pro	Con
Efficiently uses network bandwidth	Requires routing tables in decisions
Does not concentrate all M/C on single links	Spanning tree includes all M/C routers
Fast	
Considers group membership	

Reverse Path Multicasting (RPM)

Reverse path multicasting (RPM) is a refinement to TRPB, addressing one of the faults of TRPB, that all multicast routers within the multicast backbone are members of the spanning tree. With RPM the spanning tree includes only as many routers as are necessary to provide reachability to all members of the multicast group. Start with the spanning tree that is computed by TRPB. This spanning tree includes all multicast routers but is computed to be optimal for a specific multicast source. From each router on the periphery of the multicast backbone, determine whether there are any leaf networks that have members of the multicast group. If there are members, forward the multicast packet onto the leaf network. If there are no members, quietly discard the packet and send a "prune" message back toward the multicast source with a time-to-live (TTL) value of 1 in the IP header. The TTL value will limit the scope of the IP datagram to only one hop. Any multicast router receiving the prune message must not forward multicasts to that router in the future. This process continues, working its way back toward the source of the multicast. Eventually the spanning tree includes only the multicast routers necessary to deliver the packets to the multicast group membership. Occasionally the pruned branches of the spanning tree are reinstated to pick up any hosts that had joined the multicast group since the tree was last pruned.

Pro	Con
Efficiently uses network bandwidth	Requires routing tables in decisions
Does not concentrate all M/C on single links	Requires occasional ST reinitialization
Fast	New members may have to wait
Considers group membership	
ST includes only necessary routers	

Core-Based Trees (CBT)

The philosophy behind the implementation of forwarding using CBT differs from the other methods discussed previously. With CBT each router that can service leaf networks must be configured with a unicast address of a multicast router that will act as the core for the multicast group. Whenever a host system wishes to join a multicast group, the multicast router on the leaf network will be notified via IGMP. If the router is already a member of the forwarding tree for the multicast group, it does nothing. If it is not a member, it forwards a unicast "CBT-join" request toward the statically configured core router(s). Each router that receives this packet takes note of the multicast group and the interface that the packet was received on and forwards the packet toward the core router. If the CBT-join message reaches either the core router or any multicast router that is already on the CBT, the packet is stopped, and an acknowledgment is sent back to the source of the unicast CBT-join packet. At this point the CBT includes all multicast routers necessary to communicate to all multicast group members. There is a similar procedure for pruning unnecessary branches of the CBT when members leave the multicast group.

Pro	Con
Efficiently uses network bandwidth	Requires routing tables in decisions
Efficient joining of groups	Traffic concentration on links of CBT
Fast	
Considers group membership	
CBT includes only necessary routers	

Multicast Routing Protocols

Distance-Vector Multicast Routing Protocols (DVMRP)

The familiar interior routing protocol RIP was the basis for the initial design of DVMRP. Unlike RIP, a unicast routing protocol, the routing table the DVMRP maintains is oriented to provide next-hop information, based on the source address in the multicast datagram. Due to the differences between the routing tables used to forward unicast and multicast datagrams, a router that is capable of forwarding both types of traffic would require distinctly separate tables for each. The Mbone is mostly constructed using DVMRP routing.

The forwarding algorithm that DVMRP uses is reverse path multicasting, as described earlier. Multicast packets are initially sent to all multicast routers but then begin the process of pruning the subset of routers back to only what is required to reach all of the multicast group membership.

Similar growth problems that had to be dealt with in the earlier days of the Internet are now arising on the Mbone. A version of DVMRP is being developed that will address scalability issues. Essentially, as with the unicast Internet, the multicast backbone will be divided into small multicast autonomous systems, or domains. An exterior multicast routing protocol will handle routing multicast packets between domains.

Multicast Extensions to OSPF (MOSPF)

DVMRP used RIP as the basis for its development. MOSPF is an extension to the OSPF interior routing protocol that was discussed earlier in this book and defined in RFC 1583. These extensions are defined in RFC 1584, "Multicast Extensions to OSPF."

OSPF is an excellent choice to extend to support multicasting. Because it is a link-state routing protocol, the router maintains a topology database identical to other routers within the same area. MOSPF adds a link-state advertisement to the traditional ones supported by OSPF. This LSA is referred to as a Group Membership LSA.

IGMP is used between the host that wishes to participate in a multicast conference and a multicast router. In conjunction with the group membership LSA, the MOSPF routers are capable of computing a spanning tree that includes only the necessary routers to provide full connectivity. This computation is done on the fly with the receipt of multicast packets that describe a new multicast group. The tree is cached for use by future multicast packets using the same group as the destination address.

Summary

Certain applications could be better served by multicast architecture than by a unicast architecture with multiple associations. The applications include resource discovery and conferencing.

Resource discovery can be easier if all the resources that have similar attributes were assigned permanent multicast group addresses. A device that needed to locate those resources could send a multicast packet to the destination that specified the fixed multicast group that included those resources. The devices that received the packets and recognized that they belong to the group would respond accordingly.

Another use for multicasting is conferencing. Unlike resource discovery, which used fixed multicast groups that were related to the functionality of the device, conferencing could use common, well-known multicast addresses or transient multicast addresses. The membership would vary. A host could elect to participate and then, after determining the content of the conference, discontinue membership, essentially in the same way as you might "channel surf" the television programming.

Currently an experimental multicast backbone is overlaid on top of the Internet. This backbone, called the Mbone, is used to test applications and routing mechanisms for potential future widespread deployment. There have been several tests of conferencing over the Mbone since 1992. The IETF meetings are now regularly multicast over the Mbone in audio and video media.

Multicast routing is a subject of ongoing research. The goal of the research is to find a way to distribute multicast packets to all members of a multicast group, using the minimum amount of resources, and to allow for rapid convergence in the event of network outages. The protocol used between a host that wishes to participate in a multicast group and the local multicast router is known as IGMP, Internet Group Management Protocol. Forwarding algorithms used to distribute packets to all other members of the group may or may not use the IGMP information to improve their effectiveness. Examples of forwarding algorithms include:

- flooding
- spanning tree

- reverse path broadcast

- truncated reverse path broadcast

- reverse path multicasting

- core-based trees

Multicast routing protocols use similar algorithms as are used for their unicast counterparts. Distance Vector Multicast Routing Protocol is based on RIP, and MOSPF (Multicast Extensions to OSPF) is truly an extension of the OSPF protocol version 2, which enables routing of multicast packets in addition to routing unicast packets.

IP Version 6

Chapter 1 discussed the construction of the TCP/IP layered architecture, including the network layer, the Internet Protocol (IP). The IP header was dissected to a level necessary to promote the overall discussion of this text, IP addressing. Recall that the header takes a structure as shown in Illustration 12-1.

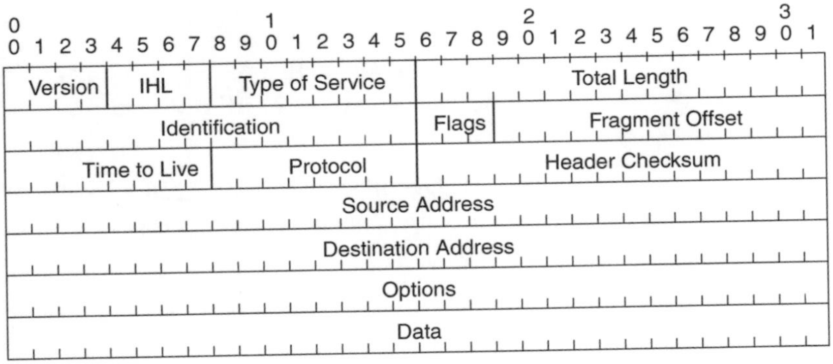

Illustration 12-1 IP Version 4 Header

273

In this chapter it is no longer sufficient to refer to this structure as the IP header. Instead it is referred to as the IP version 4 (IPv4) header. This is required because of a new Internet Protocol work-in-progress that is necessitated by the depletion of the address space. This new Internet Protocol is referred to as IP version 6, or simply IPv6, but might have been referred to in the past as IP next generation (IPng).

IPv6 is specified by RFC 1883, "Internet Protocol, Version 6 (IPv6) Specification," of December 1995. RFC 1883 states that IPv6 was created to address five issues:

- *Expanded addressing capabilities:* Addresses in IP version 6 use a 128-bit field in the IP header. IP version 4 permitted addresses that had a length of only 32 bits. It is obvious that a 128-bit address field permits an increased number of hosts possible in the global address space. In fact, a 128-bit address will allow for 3.4×10^{38} unique IP addresses, whereas a 32-bit address field allowed for only 4.3×10^{9} unique addresses! This is the focus of this chapter.

- *Header format simplification:* Since the size of the header is going to increase as a result of the size of the IPv6 source and destination address, the header was simplified to try to reduce the overhead of the new IP header.

- *Improved support for extensions and options:* Increases the flexibility of the IP datagram and reduces overhead.

- *Flow labeling capability:* This adds the ability to assign handling characteristics for particular types of data traffic, or "flows."

- *Authentication and privacy capabilities:* Extensions are added.

The last four issues, even combined, would likely not have merited a new version of IP. The clincher, as previously stated, was the need to counter the depletion of globally unique address space.

The IP Version 6 Header

Illustration 12-2 shows the fields found in the basic IPv6 header.

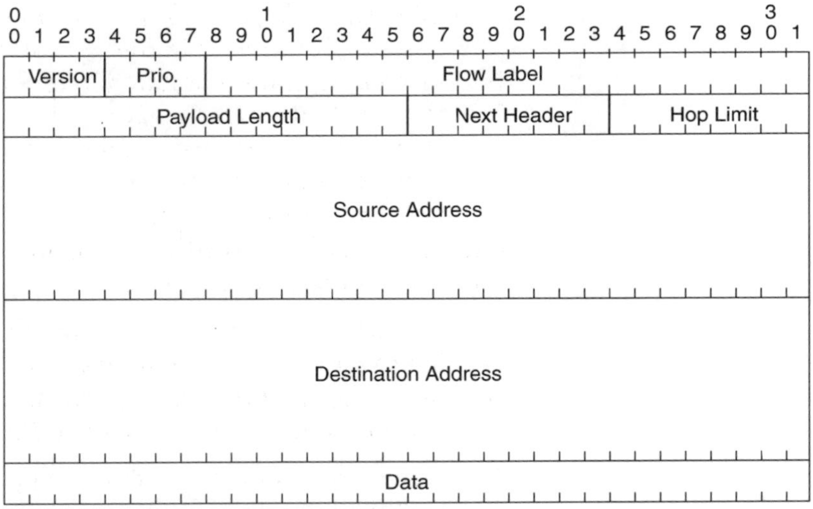

Illustration 12-2 IP Version 6 Header

- *Version*: Remember from Chapter 1 that the classic IPv4 uses a version of "4" in this field. IP version 6 uses a "6" in this field, hence IPv4 and IPv6. To date the Assigned Numbers RFC (RFC 1700) has assigned the versions shown in Table 12-1.

Decimal	Keyword	Version
0		Reserved
1–3		Unassigned
4	IP	Internet Protocol
5	ST	ST datagram mode
6	SIP	Simple Internet Protocol
7	TP/IX	TP/IX: The Next Internet
8	PIP	The P Internet Protocol
9	TUBA	TUBA
10–14		Unassigned
15		Reserved

Table 12-1 Assigned Internet Version Numbers (RFC1700)

You will no doubt note that version 6 is assigned to SIP, the Simple Internet Protocol. There were many contributors to the ideas that went into the final design of IPv6. Among the protocols advocated were SIP, SIPP, TP/IX, PIP, and TUBA (TCP and UDP over Bigger Addresses), some of which you see in Table 12-1. To some degree the final product, IPv6, was an amalgamation of the ideas proposed in these protocols.

* *Priority:* This is a 4-bit field that is used to permit administration of priorities in traffic from the same source. There are 16 distinct values permissible in a 4-bit field, 0 to 15. The lower half of the values are used for prioritization of traffic for which the source provides congestion control. The following values are recommended:

0—Uncharacterized traffic

1—"Filler" traffic (e.g., netnews)

2—Unattended data transfer (e.g., e-mail)

3—Reserved

4—Attended bulk transfer (e.g., FTP, NFS)

5—Reserved

6—Interactive traffic (e.g., Telnet, X)

7—Internet control traffic (e.g., routing protocols, SNMP)

The upper half, 8 through 15, are used to prioritize traffic for which the source does not provide congestion control. There are no recommendations for these priorities.

• *Flow label*: This is a 24-bit value used to uniquely identify traffic that should be handled using similar characteristics. This is still an experimental function.

• *Payload length*: This is a 16-bit value that represents the length in octets of the IP datagram less the length of the header.

• *Next header*: This is an 8-bit value that defines the next higher protocol found in the data portion of the IP datagram. The value expected in this field is the same as is used for the protocol field of an IPv4 header, with the exception of the value 58. ICMPv6 is an extension of the ICMP used with IP version 4, combined with the IGMP protocol, as shown in Table 12-2.

Decimal	Keyword	Protocol
0		Reserved
1	ICMP	Internet Control Message
2	IGMP	Internet Group Management
3	GGP	Gateway-to-Gateway
4	IP	IP in IP (encapsulation)
5	ST	Stream
6	TCP	Transmission Control
7	UCL	UCL
8	EGP	Exterior Gateway Protocol
9	IGP	Any private interior gateway
10	BBN-RCC-MON	BBN RCC Monitoring
17	UDP	User Datagram
18	MUX	Multiplexing
27	RDP	Reliable Data Protocol
29	ISO-TP4	ISO Transport Protocol Class 4
46	RSVP	Reservation Protocol
58	ICMPv6	Internet Control Message Protocol (version 6)
88	IGRP	IGRP
89	OSPFIGP	OSPFIGP
101–254		Unassigned
255		Reserved

Table 12-2 Sample IPv6 Next-Header Values

- *Hop limit:* This is a formalization of the fact that the IP version 4 header field, time-to-live (TTL), was a misnomer. The TTL field was actually decremented by 1 by each router that forwarded the packet. Renaming the TTL to "Hop Limit" removes any ambiguity in the naming. This field has the ability to limit the range that a packet is allowed to traverse before being discarded. This is known as "scope limiting."

- *Source address:* This is a 128-bit value used to define the node that originated the packet.

- *Destination address:* This is a 128-bit value used to define the node that is the intended recipient of the packet.

- *Data:* This is the variable-length payload of the IPv6 datagram.

IP Version 6 Address Representation

In IP version 4 there were essentially two ways to represent an IP address. You could represent an address in hexadecimal, such as 0x0A019C5B, or in dotted decimal notation, such as 10.1.156.91. Even though it is easier to remember names like "Remote_Host" than addresses like those just listed, the addresses of IP version 4 are far easier to deal with than the addresses in IP version 6. Take the following IPv6 address as an example:

0x4A3F56E466EA210729FEAE67E65FF230

No doubt this is an extreme case, but it is a valid provider-based unicast address in IPv6. To help make the addressing more palatable in IPv6, some notations that make the IPv6 addresses easier to use.

The preferred form is one in which the octets of the IPv6 address are grouped in pairs and are represented in hexadecimal format, separated by colons, as in x:x:x:x:x:x:x:x. The "x" would be replaced by the 16-tuple's hexadecimal equivalent. The previous IPv6 address would be represented as:

4A3F:56E4:66EA:2107:29FE:AE67:E65F:F230

Although this representation is no shorter than the original, it is more readable. One nice feature about this representation is that leading zeros need not be included. Suppose we have the following address:

4A3F:0000:00EA:0000:0000:0000:005F:F230

That can be reduced down to:

4A3F:0:EA:0:0:0:5F:F230

Further, any single run of all zeros in an IP address can be replaced by "::". Suppose, for example, we have the address:

4A3F:0000:00EA:0000:0000:0000:005F:F230

That can be represented instead as:

4A3F:0:EA::5F:F230

There can be only one "::" in an IPv6 address. The number of zeros can be easily deduced, based on the number of digits required to represent the number when it has been expanded.

In the transition period while both IPv4 and IPv6 addresses must be used, a mechanism exists that permits reference to IPv4 addresses from within an IPv6 address. In this case the last 32 bits can be referenced in dotted decimal notation, as was used in IP version 4. The following addresses are all equivalent IPv6 addresses with an embedded IPv4 address:

0000:0000:0000:0000:0000:0000:0A01:9C5B
::A01:9C5B
::10.1.156.91

It is obvious that with 128 bits of address, any representation, no matter how efficiently it can be reduced, might be best represented with a name via domain name services. I suspect that when IPv6 starts to make its way into production networks, it will have to be preceded with a working version of IPv6 name services.

IP Version 6 Addressing

The IP version 6 address is 16 octets, or 128 bits long. Like the Classes A through E addresses of IP version 4, a format prefix (FP) embedded in the address determines its usage. Table 12-3 lists the prefixes that have been defined at the time of this writing and the usage that the prefix denotes.

Allocation	Prefix (binary)	Fraction of Address Space
Reserved	0000 0000	1/256
Unassigned	0000 0001	1/256
Reserved for NSAP allocation	0000 001	1/128
Reserved for IPX allocation	0000 010	1/128
Unassigned	0000 011	1/128
Unassigned	0000 1	1/32
Unassigned	0001	1/16
Unassigned	001	1/8
Provider-based unicast address	010	1/8

Unassigned	011	1/8
Reserved for geographic-based unicast addresses	100	1/8
Unassigned	101	1/8
Unassigned	110	1/8
Unassigned	1110	1/16
Unassigned	1111 0	1/32
Unassigned	1111 10	1/64
Unassigned	1111 110	1/128
Unassigned	1111 1110 0	1/512
Link Local Use Addresses	1111 1110 10	1/1024
Site Local Use Addresses	1111 1110 11	1/1024
Multicast Addresses	1111 1111	1/256

Table 12-3 IP Version 6 Address Partitioning (RFC 1884)

Unicast Addresses

As you can see from Table 12-3, there are six allocations from the entire address pool that are used for some form of unicast addressing:

- NSAP allocation: OSI network service access point over IPv6 addresses

- IPX allocation: IPX over IPv6 addresses

- Provider-based unicast addresses: The allocation to Internet service providers for suballocation to other providers and subscribers

- Geographic-based unicast addresses: The allocation to geographic registration authorities for suballocation
- Link local use addresses: Local use only (routers do not forward) addresses used on a single link (network)
- Site local use addresses: Addresses used at a single site that are not forwarded by a router onto a link that is not an IP subnet of the site local network in use

Site local addresses are roughly analogous to the private internet network allocations set aside by RFC 1597, "Address Allocation for Private Subnets." The difference is that routers did not inhibit the transmission of a packet outside of the site local network in IPv4.

There are only two special unicast addresses defined in IPv6. They are:

Unspecified address: 0:0:0:0:0:0:0:0 or ::

Loopback address: 0:0:0:0:0:0:0:1 or ::1

The unspecified address is used in the same manner as the all-0s address in IP version 4. It denotes "this host" and should be used only as the source address in an IPv6 datagram.

The loopback address is used to permit a host to send an IPv6 datagram to itself. This is the same purpose that the loopback address, 127.x.x.x , was used for in IPv4. IP version 6 packets containing the loopback address should never be sent outside the node's network interface.

Illustration 12-3 depicts ways in which IP unicast addresses could be configured in IPv6. The second depiction is particularly interesting. By allocating 48 bits for the interface ID, the network manager has the ability to use the same value that the hardware address uses. At least this is possible for networks that use a 48-bit unique hardware address, such as Ethernet. At a minimum this would enhance troubleshooting methodology, since it is easier to track down an IP address than a MAC address.

n bits	128-n bits
subnet prefix	interface ID

n bits	80-n bits	48 bits
subscriber prefix	subnet ID	interface ID

s bits	n bits	m bits	128-s-n-m bits
subscriber prefix	area ID	subnet ID	interface ID

Illustration 12-3 Various IP Unicast Address Configurations with IPv6

Multicast Addresses

Table 12-3 indicates that any IPv6 address that has binary 1111 1111 in the high-order bits of the address is a multicast address. IP version 4 multicast addresses were discussed in Chapter 11. IP version 6 multicasts are slightly more structured than their IPv4 counterparts. The structure of an IPv6 multicast address is shown in Illustration 12-4.

8	4	4	112 bits
11111111	flgs	scop	group ID

Illustration 12-4 IP Version 6 Multicast Address Format

Three fields are defined within an IP version 6 multicast address:

- `flgs`: A set of four binary flags used to control the treatment of the multicast address. The flags are:

0	0	0	T

  The three high-order flags are reserved. The fourth flag, the low-order flag, is used to discriminate between addresses that are well known and assigned by the IANA (T = 0) and those that are transient addresses, or not permanently assigned (T = 1).

- `scop`: A 4-bit field used to specify to the forwarding algorithm how the multicast packet should be "scope limited." In IPv4 the only way to limit the scope of a multicast packet was to set the Time-to-Live (TTL) in the IP header to a low value. The Hop Limit field of IPv6 can still be used in this manner; however, the scope value imbedded in the multicast address has the ability to limit the scope of the multicast packet at a more abstract organizational level. The values for the field are defined as shown in Table 12-4.

Value	Field
0	Reserved
1	Node—local scope
2	Link—local scope
3	Unassigned
4	Unassigned

5	Site—local scope
6	Unassigned
7	Unassigned
8	Organization—local scope
9	Unassigned
A	Unassigned
B	Unassigned
C	Unassigned
D	Unassigned
E	Global scope
F	Reserved

Table 12-4 IP Version 6 Multicast Address Scope Values

`group ID`: A 112-bit field within the multicast address that identifies the multicast group that is the destination for the multicast IPv6 packet.

The following well-known multicast addresses have been defined in the context of IP version 6 by RFC 1884, "IP Version 6 Addressing Architecture." (note that the "x" indicates the scope-limiting field):

Reserved multicast addresses: FF0x:0:0:0:0:0:0:0

All nodes addresses: FF0x:0:0:0:0:0:0:1

All routers addresses: FF0x:0:0:0:0:0:0:2

DHCP server/relay-agent: FF02:0:0:0:0:0:0:C

Solicited-node address: FF02:0:0:0:0:1:XXXX:XXXX

IP version 6 does not define an address to be used for broadcasts. Instead it uses a broad multicast to accomplish the same function that broadcasts were used for in IPv4.

Anycast Addresses

Anycast addressing, a new concept introduced in IP version 6, allows a device to send a packet to any of one or more network interfaces (usually the closest) that have been assigned to a single anycast address. Therefore an anycast address is a special case of a unicast address. That is, if you assign the same unicast address to multiple interfaces, most likely on different devices, you will be defining an anycast address. A packet that is sent to an anycast address will be delivered to only one of the devices that has the IPv6 address specified in the datagram's destination IP address. Anycast addressing is still experimental.

IP Version 6 Address Allocation

IP version 6 is the long-term solution to address space depletion. There was another problem that was recognized and addressed by classless interdomain routing (CIDR), that of explosive route table growth in the Internet. IP version 6 does little to stave off this problem. There was some planning, however, that went into the design of IPv6 that, along with a planned allocation methodology, will reduce the route table explosion problem.

First and foremost, IP version 6 will be a fresh start. Haphazard allocations will not be made. Address allocation authority will be decentralized, and individual authorities will have to provide rigorous administration of their respective address allotments. Addresses will be allocated based on one of two schemes. If they are allocated based on the service provider, they will be allocated from the IPv6 addresses that begin with "010." If they are allocated based on the geographic home of the network, they will be allocated from the IPv6 addresses that begin with "100."

The addresses will be allocated in such a way that they will collapse into as small a route as possible for advertisement on the IPv6 internet. This may sound an awful lot like CIDR. This is for good reason; RFC 1887, "An Architecture for IPv6 Unicast Address Allocation," was edited by the same folks who edited RFC 1518, "An Architecture for IP Address Allocation with CIDR," Yakov Rekhter and Tony Li. A great many of the allocation and aggregation concepts presented in RFC 1518 made their way into RFC 1887. In fact, it is so similar that I will forego a discussion on the topic here.

Summary

IP version 6 was created with the primary purpose of creating an address space architecture that could handle significant growth of the Internet and globally unique addresses well into the future. There were, however, four other items that were accomplished during the renovation:

- header format simplification
- improved support for extensions and options
- flow labeling capability
- authentication and privacy capabilities

This chapter focused only on the implications of the new, larger, 128-bit addresses in IPv6.

IP version 6 defines three types of addresses. Unicast addresses are used for one-to-one node communications. Multicast addresses are used for one-to-many node communications. Anycast addresses are used for one-to-any node communications. Anycast addresses are new in IPv6. Broadcasts have been made obsolete in IPv6.

Two problems noted in 1992 prompted considerable action. One was that the address space was being depleted at a much more rapid pace than expected. IP version 6 addresses this problem by expanding the address space. The other problem was that the Internet backbone route tables were growing and becoming unwieldy. IP version 6 has mechanisms built in, such as provider- and geographic-based address allocations, that in conjunction with an allocation strategy will curb the growth of the Internet route tables.

The IP Address Helper Application

As a purchaser of this book, you have access to a piece of software that I wrote for being able to understand IP addresses. This software is written for Microsoft Windows 3.1 and is available for download from Academic Press's Web site at the following URL:

http://www.apnet.com/approfessional/

The files you will need to run it are archived in a ZIP file. To extract the files, use an unZIP utility, such as PKUNZIP or WinZIP. These are common utilities, so you should have little problem finding them if you do not already have one of them. The files included in the archive are:

VBRUN300	DLL	398,416	07-24-95	12:00a
IP-HELP	EXE	22,849	06-17-96	9:23a
THREED	VBX	64,432	07-16-93	12:00a
README	TXT	1,326	06-17-96	9:45a

It is possible that the dates or the sizes may vary. The important thing is that the files are present.

Installation

Installation of the IP Address Helper application is manual. Please follow the steps indicated in the "readme.txt" file.

Running the IP Address Helper Application

Once the IP Address Helper application has been installed, you can run it by double clicking the application icon for IP-Helper. The application has a single window, as shown in Illustration A-10. It is fairly self-explanatory. There are three sections: IP Address, Subnet Mask, and Hexadecimal Equivalents. Some miscellaneous information is at the bottom of the window.

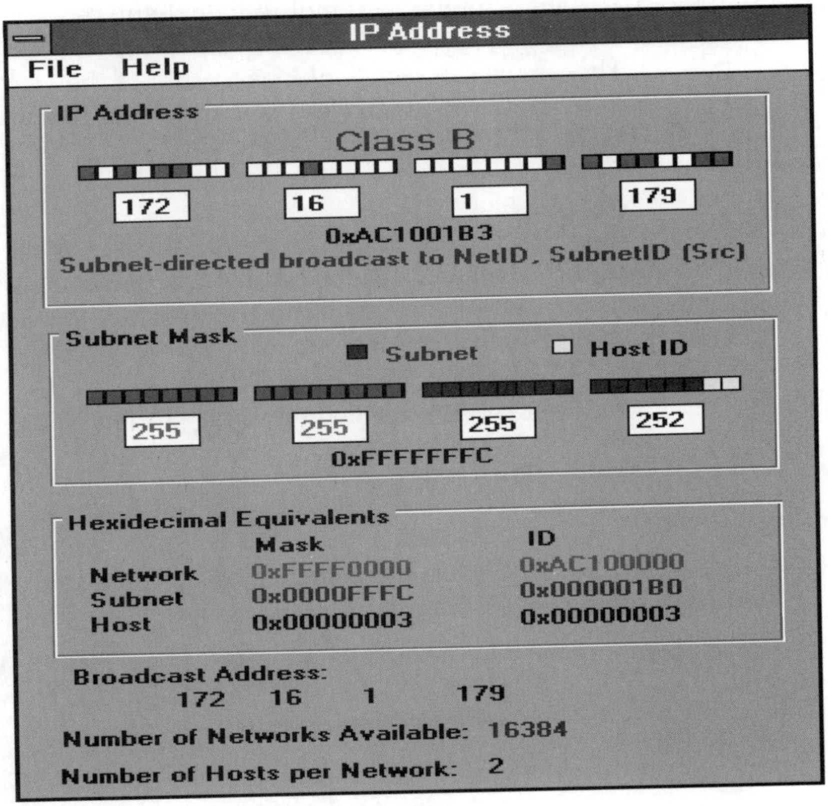

IP Address

Class B

172   16   1   179

0xAC1001B3

Subnet-directed broadcast to NetID, SubnetID (Src)

Subnet Mask

■ Subnet   □ Host ID

255   255   255   252

0xFFFFFFFC

Hexidecimal Equivalents

	Mask	ID
Network	0xFFFF0000	0xAC100000
Subnet	0x0000FFFC	0x000001B0
Host	0x00000003	0x00000003

Broadcast Address:
172   16   1   179

Number of Networks Available: 16384

Number of Hosts per Network: 2

Illustration A-1 Window for IP Address Helper Application

IP Address Section

In the IP Address section are four text entry boxes. They will accept values in the range 0 to 255. If you type anything outside of that range, the application will ask you to reenter the value. You can tab between the text entry fields.

As you type the value into the text entry field, the eight small boxes directly above the active text entry field will change. These boxes reflect the binary value of the number in the text entry field. In Illustration A-1 the value in the first text entry box is 172. The shaded boxes above it represent 1s and the blank (white) boxes 0s. The binary value for 172 is "10101100," as indicated.

You can also click in the binary representation with the mouse, using the left mouse button to toggle the bit on or off. The change will be reflected in the respective text entry box.

As the IP address is changed, either through typing in the text entry boxes or through altering the bits with the mouse, several things will happen:

- The class of the address will be computed and displayed in the top middle portion of the IP Address section.

- The hexadecimal value of the IP address will be computed and displayed just below the text entry boxes in the IP Address section.

- Special-cases situations will be calculated and displayed just below the hexadecimal representation of the IP address.

- The inherent mask of the IP address will be computed, and the Subnet Mask section will be altered to reflect this mask.

- The values in the Hexadecimal Equivalents will be recomputed.

- The Broadcast Address will be recomputed.

- The number of networks and the number of hosts per network will be computed and displayed.

Subnet Mask Section

Based on the address entered in the IP Address section, the subnet mask will have some information predetermined. In our example the IP Address section contains a Class B address. As a result, the first two (high-order) octets cannot be altered. This is indicated by the values of 255 in the first two text entry boxes being "grayed out" and the two high-order octets of the binary representation being "all red."

The remainder of the host portion bits of that network mask can be altered by typing values into the text entry boxes or by selecting the bits to be included in the mask, using the mouse and its left or right button. Selecting a "bit" with the left mouse button will include that bit and all bits more significant than it in the network mask.. Selecting a "bit" with the right mouse button will toggle the bit in the mask on or off. This functionality was added because RFC 950 permitted noncontiguous subnet bits.

As the network mask is changed, either through typing in the text entry boxes or through altering the mask bits with the mouse, several things will happen:

- The hexadecimal value of the network mask will be computed and displayed just below the text entry boxes in the Subnet Mask section.

- Special-case situations will be calculated and displayed just below the hexadecimal representation of the IP address in the IP Address section.

- The values in the Hexadecimal Equivalents will be recomputed.

- The Broadcast Address will be recomputed.

• The number of networks and the number of hosts per network will be computed and displayed.

Hexadecimal Equivalents Section

Some values used during the calculations are made visible to the user in the Hexadecimal Equivalents section. It is likely that you will not require the use of any of them. I have had occasion to use this section only once in the course of IP address consulting. It had something to do with a debugging problem using a network analyzer. The values are there for your use, should you require them.

Miscellaneous Fields

Three values are presented at the bottom of the IP Address Helper window:

• *Broadcast Address*: The subnet-directed broadcast address that would be used to broadcast a packet to all hosts on a specific subnet.

• *Number of (sub)Networks Available*: The quantity of subnetworks that can be used for the specific class of address identified in the IP Address section with the network mask in the Subnet Mask section. In the example there are 14 subnet bits in use, which permits up to 16,384 unique subnets. The value assumes that you *can* use the all-0s and all-1s subnets. You will have to subtract 2 from this number if that is not the case in your network.

- *Number of Hosts per Network*: The quantity of hosts that can be uniquely identified in the host portion of the network mask. The value already considers that you cannot use the all-0s and all-1s host addresses.

Improvements

I am always considering improvements that can be made to this utility. Feel free to contact me with any ideas that you might have for this or other related software. If you need the software for other platforms—MAC, X windows, OS/2—please drop me a line. If I get enough requests, I just might do it.

You can reach me via the e-mail address in the readme.txt file or through Academic Press.

IP Network
Number
Request
Template

[URL ftp://rs.internic.net/templates/internet-number-template.txt]   [08/95]

*********************** PLEASE DO NOT REMOVE Version Number ********************

Network Version Number: 2.0

***************** Please see attached detailed instructions ******************

1a. Approximate date of Internet
     connection....................:
1b. Name of Internet access
     provider (if known)...........:

Technical POC
2a. NIC handle (if known)..........:
2b. Name (Last, First).............:
2c. Title..........................:
2d. Postal address.................:

2e. Phone Number...................:
2f. E-Mailbox......................:

```
3.    Network name..................:


4a.   Name of Organization...........:
4b.   Postal address of Organization.:


5.    Previously assigned addresses..:

      Explain how addresses have been
      utilized, to include:

5a.   Number of hosts.................:
5b.   Number of subnets...............:
5c.   Subnet mask.....................:


Justification

Host Information
6a.   Initially.......................:
6b.   Within 1 year...................:

Subnet Information
6c.   Initially.......................:
6d.   Within one year.................:


7a.   Number of addresses requested...:
7b.   Additional supporting
      justification...................:

If requesting 16 C's or more, you are required to submit the
network topology plan in the format of the example below:

-----------------------------------------------------------------------------
Subnet#   Subnet Mask      Max   Now   1yr   Description
-----------------------------------------------------------------------------

1.0       255.255.255.224   30    8    16    Network Group (use 0!)
1.1       255.255.255.224   30   17    22    Engineering
1.2       255.255.255.224   30   12    12    Manufacturing
1.3       255.255.255.224   30    5     9    Management
1.4       255.255.255.224   30   10    15    Sales
1.5       255.255.255.224   30    7     8    Finance
1.6       255.255.255.224   30    0     0    (spare)


-----------------------------------------------------------------------------
          Totals           210   59    82
-----------------------------------------------------------------------------
```

If requesting a Class B or 256 C's (/16 prefix) a network diagram
should also be included with your request.

8. Type of network.................:

              INSTRUCTIONS FOR REQUESTING INTERNET (IP) NUMBERS

The internet-number-template.txt must be completed as part of the
application process for obtaining Internet Protocol (IP) Network Numbers.
To obtain one or more Internet numbers, please submit the template
via electronic mail, to HOSTMASTER@INTERNIC.NET. In the subject of the
message, use the words, "IP REQUEST".

Once Registration Services receives your completed application we will
send you an acknowledgement, via electronic mail.

If electronic mail is not available to you, please mail hardcopy to:

                    Network Solutions
                    InterNIC Registration Services
                    505 Huntmar Park Drive
                    Herndon, VA 22070

                          -- OR --

                    FAX to (703) 742-4811

Please do not modify the form nor remove the version number.

European network requests should use the european template located
at (ftp://ftp.ripe.net/ripe/forms/netnum-appl.txt). Please follow
their instructions for submission.

Networks that will be connected/located within the geographic
region maintained by the Asian-Pacific NIC should use the APNIC
template located at ftp://ftp./apnic/docs/english/apnic-001.txt.
Please follow their instructions for submission.

 ***PLEASE READ THE FOLLOWING INFORMATION PRIOR TO REQUESTING AN
IP NUMBER FROM THE INTERNIC:

Due to technical and implementation constraints on the Internet routing
system and the possibility of routing overload, certain policies may
need to be enforced by the major transit providers in order to reduce
the number of globally advertised routes. These potential policies
may include setting limits on the size of CIDR prefixes added to the

routing tables, filtering of non-aggregated routes, etc. Therefore,
addresses obtained directly from the InterNIC (non-provider-based,
also known as portable) are not guaranteed to be routable on the Internet.

It is for this reason, you are encouraged to request an IP address
from your service provider. If you have not selected a service provider,
but plan to connect in the future or your network will never be
connected to the Internet, you are encouraged to use IP numbers
reserved for non-connected networks set forth in RFC1597 until
you can utilize address space from your chosen Internet provider.

Also, please note, your organization will only be assigned address
space for their immediate to one (1) year requirement. A prefix longer
than /24 may be issued if deemed appropriate.

Section 1 - Internet connection

    Please supply information on the approximate date of your
    connection to the Internet and the name of your Internet
    access provider, if known. Again, if you have a service
    provider, you should be contacting them for IP addresses.

Section 2 - Technical Point of Contact

    The technical POC is the person who tends to the technical
    aspects of maintaining the IP addresses. This person should
    be able to answer any utilization questions the InterNIC may have.

    Each person in the InterNIC database is assigned a "handle" -
    a unique tag consisting of the person's initials and a serial
    number. This tag is used on records in the database to
    indicate a point of contact for a network, domain, or other entity.

    If the technical POC's nic handle is unknown, please leave
    question 2a. blank.

    When completing question 2b, place the city, state, and zip code
    on a separate line. Use a comma to separate the city and state.
    Do not insert a period following the state abreviation. For example:

        Organization address.: Street or PO Box
                               Herndon, VA 22070

    If the organization is in a country other than the United States,
    please include the name of the country on the last line by itself.

    Contacts must list phone numbers and e-mail addresses.

Section 3 - Network name

Supply the SHORT mnemonic name for the network (up to 12 characters).
This is the name that will be used as an identifier in
internet name and address tables. The only special character that
may be used in a network name is a dash (-). PLEASE DO NOT USE
PERIODS OR UNDERSCORES. The syntax XXXX.com and XXXX.net are not
valid network naming conventions and should only be used when
applying for a domain.

Section 4 - Organization name and postal address

    Identify the name and geographic location of the organization
    that will be utilizing the network address. Please make
    sure your response on 4b is to the right of the colon.

Section 5 - Previously assigned addresses

    Please list all IP addresses previously assigned to your entire
    organization. Also give the specifics regarding the utilization
    of those addresses in questions 5a thru 5c.

Section 6 - Justification

    Estimate the size of the network to include the number of hosts and
    subnets that will be supported by the network. A "host" is defined
    as any device (PC, printer, etc) that will be assigned an address
    from the host portion of the network number. A host may also be
    characterized as a node or device.

Section 7 - Number of addresses requested

    Please state exactly how many addresses you are requesting along
    with any additional justification necessary. As stated on the
    template, if you are requesting 16 C's or more (/19 prefix) you
    will need to complete the network topology plan in the format
    shown on the template.

    If you are requesting 256 C's or a Class B (/16 prefix) or more,
    please include a copy of your network diagram.

    Your organization is strongly encouraged to subnet where
    feasible.

Section 8 - Type of network

Networks are characterized as being either Research, Educational,
Government-Non Defense or Commercial. Which type is this network?

For further information contact InterNIC Registration Services:

        Via electronic mail: HOSTMASTER@INTERNIC.NET
        Via telephone: (703) 742-4777
        Via postal mail: Network Solutions
                              InterNIC Registration Service
                              505 Huntmar Park Drive
                              Herndon, VA 22070

IP Addressing Worksheet

The following four pages constitute a worksheet that can be used to assist with subnetting a Class C or equivalent network. The usage is detailed in the introduction to Section II of this text.

I encourage you to photocopy these sheets and cut and paste the four pages together. I think that you will find this to be a valuable tool.

.0/24	.128/25	.192/26	.224/27	.240/28	.248/29	.252/30
0	0	0	0	0	0	0
1	1	1	1	1	1	1
2	2	2	2	2	2	2
3	3	3	3	3	3	3
4	4	4	4	4	4	4
5	5	5	5	5	5	5
6	6	6	6	6	6	6
7	7	7	7	7	7	7
8	8	8	8	8	8	8
9	9	9	9	9	9	9
10	10	10	10	10	10	10
11	11	11	11	11	11	11
12	12	12	12	12	12	12
13	13	13	13	13	13	13
14	14	14	14	14	14	14
15	15	15	15	15	15	15
16	16	16	16	16	16	16
17	17	17	17	17	17	17
18	18	18	18	18	18	18
19	19	19	19	19	19	19
20	20	20	20	20	20	20
21	21	21	21	21	21	21
22	22	22	22	22	22	22
23	23	23	23	23	23	23
24	24	24	24	24	24	24
25	25	25	25	25	25	25
26	26	26	26	26	26	26
27	27	27	27	27	27	27
28	28	28	28	28	28	28
29	29	29	29	29	29	29
30	30	30	30	30	30	30
31	31	31	31	31	31	31
32	32	32	32	32	32	32
33	33	33	33	33	33	33
34	34	34	34	34	34	34
35	35	35	35	35	35	35
36	36	36	36	36	36	36
37	37	37	37	37	37	37
38	38	38	38	38	38	38
39	39	39	39	39	39	39
40	40	40	40	40	40	40
41	41	41	41	41	41	41
42	42	42	42	42	42	42
43	43	43	43	43	43	43
44	44	44	44	44	44	44
45	45	45	45	45	45	45
46	46	46	46	46	46	46
47	47	47	47	47	47	47
48	48	48	48	48	48	48
49	49	49	49	49	49	49
50	50	50	50	50	50	50
51	51	51	51	51	51	51
52	52	52	52	52	52	52
53	53	53	53	53	53	53
54	54	54	54	54	54	54
55	55	55	55	55	55	55
56	56	56	56	56	56	56
57	57	57	57	57	57	57
58	58	58	58	58	58	58
59	59	59	59	59	59	59
60	60	60	60	60	60	60
61	61	61	61	61	61	61
62	62	62	62	62	62	62
63	63	63	63	63	63	63

64	64	64	64	64	64	64
65	65	65	65	65	65	65
66	66	66	66	66	66	66
67	67	67	67	67	67	67
68	68	68	68	68	68	68
69	69	69	69	69	69	69
70	70	70	70	70	70	70
71	71	71	71	71	71	71
72	72	72	72	72	72	72
73	73	73	73	73	73	73
74	74	74	74	74	74	74
75	75	75	75	75	75	75
76	76	76	76	76	76	76
77	77	77	77	77	77	77
78	78	78	78	78	78	78
79	79	79	79	79	79	79
80	80	80	80	80	80	80
81	81	81	81	81	81	81
82	82	82	82	82	82	82
83	83	83	83	83	83	83
84	84	84	84	84	84	84
85	85	85	85	85	85	85
86	86	86	86	86	86	86
87	87	87	87	87	87	87
88	88	88	88	88	88	88
89	89	89	89	89	89	89
90	90	90	90	90	90	90
91	91	91	91	91	91	91
92	92	92	92	92	92	92
93	93	93	93	93	93	93
94	94	94	94	94	94	94
95	95	95	95	95	95	95
96	96	96	96	96	96	96
97	97	97	97	97	97	97
98	98	98	98	98	98	98
99	99	99	99	99	99	99
100	100	100	100	100	100	100
101	101	101	101	101	101	101
102	102	102	102	102	102	102
103	103	103	103	103	103	103
104	104	104	104	104	104	104
105	105	105	105	105	105	105
106	106	106	106	106	106	106
107	107	107	107	107	107	107
108	108	108	108	108	108	108
109	109	109	109	109	109	109
110	110	110	110	110	110	110
111	111	111	111	111	111	111
112	112	112	112	112	112	112
113	113	113	113	113	113	113
114	114	114	114	114	114	114
115	115	115	115	115	115	115
116	116	116	116	116	116	116
117	117	117	117	117	117	117
118	118	118	118	118	118	118
119	119	119	119	119	119	119
120	120	120	120	120	120	120
121	121	121	121	121	121	121
122	122	122	122	122	122	122
123	123	123	123	123	123	123
124	124	124	124	124	124	124
125	125	125	125	125	125	125
126	126	126	126	126	126	126
127	127	127	127	127	127	127

128	128	128	128	128	128	128
129	129	129	129	129	129	129
130	130	130	130	130	130	130
131	131	131	131	131	131	131
132	132	132	132	132	132	132
133	133	133	133	133	133	133
134	134	134	134	134	134	134
135	135	135	135	135	135	135
136	136	136	136	136	136	136
137	137	137	137	137	137	137
138	138	138	138	138	138	138
139	139	139	139	139	139	139
140	140	140	140	140	140	140
141	141	141	141	141	141	141
142	142	142	142	142	142	142
143	143	143	143	143	143	143
144	144	144	144	144	144	144
145	145	145	145	145	145	145
146	146	146	146	146	146	146
147	147	147	147	147	147	147
148	148	148	148	148	148	148
149	149	149	149	149	149	149
150	150	150	150	150	150	150
151	151	151	151	151	151	151
152	152	152	152	152	152	152
153	153	153	153	153	153	153
154	154	154	154	154	154	154
155	155	155	155	155	155	155
156	156	156	156	156	156	156
157	157	157	157	157	157	157
158	158	158	158	158	158	158
159	159	159	159	159	159	159
160	160	160	160	160	160	160
161	161	161	161	161	161	161
162	162	162	162	162	162	162
163	163	163	163	163	163	163
164	164	164	164	164	164	164
165	165	165	165	165	165	165
166	166	166	166	166	166	166
167	167	167	167	167	167	167
168	168	168	168	168	168	168
169	169	169	169	169	169	169
170	170	170	170	170	170	170
171	171	171	171	171	171	171
172	172	172	172	172	172	172
173	173	173	173	173	173	173
174	174	174	174	174	174	174
175	175	175	175	175	175	175
176	176	176	176	176	176	176
177	177	177	177	177	177	177
178	178	178	178	178	178	178
179	179	179	179	179	179	179
180	180	180	180	180	180	180
181	181	181	181	181	181	181
182	182	182	182	182	182	182
183	183	183	183	183	183	183
184	184	184	184	184	184	184
185	185	185	185	185	185	185
186	186	186	186	186	186	186
187	187	187	187	187	187	187
188	188	188	188	188	188	188
189	189	189	189	189	189	189
190	190	190	190	190	190	190
191	191	191	191	191	191	191

192	192	192	192	192	192	192
193	193	193	193	193	193	193
194	194	194	194	194	194	194
195	195	195	195	195	195	195
196	196	196	196	196	196	196
197	197	197	197	197	197	197
198	198	198	198	198	198	198
199	199	199	199	199	199	199
200	200	200	200	200	200	200
201	201	201	201	201	201	201
202	202	202	202	202	202	202
203	203	203	203	203	203	203
204	204	204	204	204	204	204
205	205	205	205	205	205	205
206	206	206	206	206	206	206
207	207	207	207	207	207	207
208	208	208	208	208	208	208
209	209	209	209	209	209	209
210	210	210	210	210	210	210
211	211	211	211	211	211	211
212	212	212	212	212	212	212
213	213	213	213	213	213	213
214	214	214	214	214	214	214
215	215	215	215	215	215	215
216	216	216	216	216	216	216
217	217	217	217	217	217	217
218	218	218	218	218	218	218
219	219	219	219	219	219	219
220	220	220	220	220	220	220
221	221	221	221	221	221	221
222	222	222	222	222	222	222
223	223	223	223	223	223	223
224	224	224	224	224	224	224
225	225	225	225	225	225	225
226	226	226	226	226	226	226
227	227	227	227	227	227	227
228	228	228	228	228	228	228
229	229	229	229	229	229	229
230	230	230	230	230	230	230
231	231	231	231	231	231	231
232	232	232	232	232	232	232
233	233	233	233	233	233	233
234	234	234	234	234	234	234
235	235	235	235	235	235	235
236	236	236	236	236	236	236
237	237	237	237	237	237	237
238	238	238	238	238	238	238
239	239	239	239	239	239	239
240	240	240	240	240	240	240
241	241	241	241	241	241	241
242	242	242	242	242	242	242
243	243	243	243	243	243	243
244	244	244	244	244	244	244
245	245	245	245	245	245	245
246	246	246	246	246	246	246
247	247	247	247	247	247	247
248	248	248	248	248	248	248
249	249	249	249	249	249	249
250	250	250	250	250	250	250
251	251	251	251	251	251	251
252	252	252	252	252	252	252
253	253	253	253	253	253	253
254	254	254	254	254	254	254
255	255	255	255	255	255	255

References

Request for Comments (RFC)

RFC 791, "Internet Protocol," STD 5, Postel, J., USC/Information Sciences Institute, September 1981.

RFC 792, "Internet Control Message Protocol," STD 5, Postel, J., USC/Information Sciences Institute, September 1981.

RFC 826, "An Ethernet Address Resolution Protocol," STD 37, Plummer, D., MIT, November 1982.

RFC 894, "Standard for the Transmission of IP Datagrams over Ethernet Networks," Hornig, C., Symbolics, April 1984.

RFC 903, "A Reverse Address Resolution Protocol," Finlayson, R., T. Mann, J. Mogul, and M. Theimer, Stanford, June 1984.

RFC 950, "Internet Standard Subnetting Procedure," STD 5, Mogul, J., and J. Postel, USC/Information Sciences Institute, August 1985.

RFC 951, "Bootstrap Protocol (BOOTP)," Croft, B., and J. Gilmore, Stanford University, Sun Microsystems, September 1985.

RFC 1058, "Routing Information Protocol," Hedrick, C., Rutgers University, June 1988.

RFC 1112, "Host Extensions for IP Multicasting," STD 5, Deering, S., Stanford University, August 1989.

RFC 1122, "Requirements for Internet Hosts—Communication Layers," STD 3, Internet Engineering Task Force (R. Braden, Editor), USC/Information Sciences Institute, October 1989.

RFC 1123, "Requirements for Internet Hosts—Application and Support," STD 3, Internet Engineering Task Force (R. Braden, Editor), USC/Information Sciences Institute, October 1989.

RFC 1293, "Inverse Address Resolution Protocol," Bradley, T., and C. Brown, Wellfleet Communications, January 1992.

RFC 1466, "Guidelines for Management of the IP Address Space," Gerich, E., May 1993.

RFC 1518, "An Architecture for IP Address Allocation with CIDR," Rekhter, Y., and T. Li, T.J. Watson Research Center, IBM Corp., Cisco Systems, September 1993.

RFC 1533, "DHCP Options and BOOTP Vendor Extensions," Alexander, S., and R. Droms, Lachman Technology, Bucknell University, October 1993.

RFC 1583, "OSPF Version 2," Moy, J., Proteon, March 1994.

RFC 1584, "Multicast Extensions to OSPF," Moy, J., Proteon, March 1994.

RFC 1597, "Address Allocation for Private Internets," T. J. Watson Research Center, Rekhter, Y., B. Moskowitz, D. Karrenberg, and G. de Groot, IBM Corp., Chrysler Corp., RIPE NCC, March 1994.

RFC 1627, "Network 10 Considered Harmful (Some Practices Shouldn't Be Codified)," Lear, E., E. Fair, D. Crocker, and T. Kessler, July 1994.

RFC 1700, "Assigned Numbers," STD 2, Reynolds, J., and J. Postel, USC/Information Sciences Institute, October 1994. This document is periodically updated and reissued with a new number.

RFC 1715, "The H Ratio for Address Assignment Efficiency," Huitema, C., INRIA, November 1994.

RFC 1735, "NBMA Address Resolution Protocol (NARP)," Heinanen, J., and R. Govindan, Telecom Finland, ISI, December 1994.

RFC 1812, "Requirements for IP version 4 Routers," STD 1, Baker, F., Cisco Systems, June 1995.

RFC 1883, "Internet Protocol, Version 6 (IPv6) Specification," Deering, S., and R. Hinden, Editors, Xerox PARC, Ipsilon Networks, December 1995.

RFC 1884, "IP Version 6 Addressing Architecture," Hinden, R., and S. Deering, Editors, Ipsilon Networks, Xerox PARC, December 1995.

RFC 1887, "An Architecture for IPv6 Unicast Address Allocation," Rekhter, Y., and T. Li, Cisco Systems, December 1995.

IETF Internet Draft Documents

"Core Based Trees (CBT) Multicast: Architectural Overview," <draft-ietf-idmr-cbt-arch-03.txt>, Ballardie, A. J., University College London, February 1996.

"Core Based Trees (CBT) Multicast: Protocol Specification," <draft-ietf-idmr-cbt-spec-05.txt>, Ballardie, A. J., S. Reeve, and N. Jain, University College London, Bay Networks, April 1996.

"Internet Group Management Protocol, Version 2," <draft-ietf-idmr-igmp-v2-03.txt>, Fenner, W., June 1996.

"Introduction to IP Multicast Routing," <draft-rfced-info-semeria-00.txt>, Semeria, C., and T. Maufer, 3Comy Corporation, March 1996.

"Network Renumbering Overview: Why Would I Want It and What Is It Anyway?," <draft-ietf-pier-renum-ovrvw-00.txt>, Ferguson, P., Cisco Systems, June 1996.

"Router Renumbering Guide," <draft-ietf-pier-rr-01.txt>, Berkowitz, H., PSC International, June 1996.

"Why Consider Renumbering Now," <draft-ietf-pier-consider-00.txt>, Manning, B., Cisco Systems, June 1996.

Textbooks and Other

Comer, Douglas E., *Internetworking with TCP/IP Volume 1 Principles, Protocols, and Architecture*, Second Edition, Prentice Hall, Englewood Cliffs, 1991.

Huitema, Christian, *Routing in the Internet*, Prentice Hall, Englewood Cliffs, 1995.

Huitema, Christian, *IPv6, The New Internet Protocol*, Prentice Hall, Upper Saddle River, 1996.

Nemeth, Evi, Garth Snyder, Scott Seebass, and Trent R. Hein, *UNIX System Administration Handbook*, Second Edition, Prentice Hall, Englewood Cliffs, 1995.

Perlman, Radia, *Interconnections Bridges and Routers*, Addison-Wesley, Reading MA, 1992.

Shoch, John, "Internetwork Naming Addressing and Routing," *Proceedings of COMPCON*, 1978.

Stevens, W. Richard, *TCP/IP Illustrated: Volume 1 The Protocols*, Addison, Wesley, Reading MA, 1994.

Index

A

Address, 34, 245
Address Assignment Efficiency,
    199-218
    Ephemeral Addresses, 218
    NAT , 217
    OSPF, 204
    RIP, 204
    RIP, 210
Address Downgrade, 245
Address Management, 221-239
    BOOTP, 221, 230
    DHCP, 221, 230, 236-238
    IntraNIC, 227
    Mnemonic Devices, 222
Address Resolution Protocol, 8
Address Terminology, 37
Address Upgrade, 245
Administration Tools, 230
Aggregation, 166
Area Border Router, 105
Area Route Summarization, 101
ARP, 111
Association, 29, 259

B

BGP, 191
Bridges, 69
Broadcast Address, 85

C

CIDR, 58, 154, 187, 191
Class D, 45, 251
CSMA/CD, 8

D

DEC LAT, 69
Designated Router, 146
DHCP, 236-238
    DHCP Lease, 238
    Dynamic Allocation, 238
    Permanent Allocation, 238
DLCI, 142

E

EGP, 191
Ethernet, 134
Ethernet Types, 7
Ethernet Vendor Address, 6

F

Firewalls, 156
FP (Format Prefix), 281
Frame Relay, 141-148
   (Full Mesh), 143
   Hub and Spoke, 146
   OSPF, 145
   Partial-Mesh Frame Relay,
    148
   PVC, 142
   RIP, 145

G

Gateways, 74

H

Hand Tracing a Route, 112
Hardware Addresses, 5
Hop Limit, 279
Hosts, 64, 65

I

ICMP, 16, 30, 108
IEEE 802.3, 8
IETF, 255
IGMP, 16, 30, 257
Internet Connection, 151-157
   InterNIC, 154
   Legal Address, 152
   Registered IP Network, 153
   Supernetting, 153

Internet Datagram Frame, 12
Internet Version Number, 13
InterNIC, 157
IP (Internet Protocol), 30, 33-63
   Class A Address, 42, 63
   Class B Address, 43, 63
   Class C Address, 44, 63
   Class D Address, 45, 251
   Class E Address, 46
   Class of an IP Address, 40
   Destination Address, 35
   Network Mask, 36
   Prefix Code, 36
   Source Address, 35
   Unicast Address, 46
IP Address Helper
   Application, 291-297
IP Address Worksheet, 124-133,
   305
IP Network Number Request
   Template, 299
IP Version 6, 13, 273-288
   Anycast Address, 287
   IP Version 6 Address
    Allocation, 287
   IP Version 6 Addressing, 281
   IP Version 6 Header, 275
   Loopback Address, 283
   Multicast Address, 284
IPng (IP Next Generation), 274
ISDN, 107, 139
ISO (International Organization
   for Standardization), 66
ISP, 152, 193

J

John Shoch, 34

L

LAN Transit Networks, 136
Local Bridge, 70
LSA (Link State Advertisement),
  104,106

M

MAC Addresses, 5
Magic Cookie, 213
Mask Mathematics, 53-56
    Boolean Algebra, 53
    Boolean AND, 54
    Boolean NOT, 54
    Mask Mathematics, 53
Mrouted, 256
Multicast, 251-269
    CBT (Core-Based Trees), 266
    Conferencing, 254
    Flooding, 261
    IGMP, 257
    IP Multicast Communications,
      251
    Mbone, 256
    RPB (Reverse Path Broadcast),
      262
    RPM (Reverse Path
      Multicasting), 265
    Spanning Tree, 262
    TRPB (Truncated Reverse

    Path Broadcasting), 265
Multicast Group, 45
Multicast Routing Protocols,
  268-269
    DVMRP (Distance-Vector
      Multicast Routing
      Protocols), 268
    MOSPF (Multicast
      Extensions to OSPF), 269

N

Name, 34
Netbios, 69
Network Address Translators,
  156
Network Analyzers, 75
Network Convergence, 96
Network Management Systems,
  74

O

OSI Reference Model, 66-76
    Application Layer, 67
    Link Layer, 67, 69
    Network Layer, 67, 71
    Physical Layer, 67-68
    Presentation Layer, 67
    Session Layer, 67
    Transport Layer, 67
OSPF (Open Shortest Path First),
  101, 105, 145, 176, 183, 192,
  204, 225, 253, 269

OSPF Backbone Area, 176
OSPF Border Routers, 225

P

PING (Packet Internet Groper), 70
Point to Point (Numbered), 49, 137
Point to Point (Unnumbered), 49, 138
Pooled Dial-in Access, 139
Ports, 24-25
    Destination Port, 24
    Ephemeral Ports, 25
    Source Port, 24
    Well-known Port, 24
PPP, 5, 139
Private Internet Exchange (PIX), 157
Private IP Networks, 154
PUP (PARC Universal Protocol), 34

R

Radia Perlman, 34
RARP, 111
Remote Bridge, 70
Repeaters, 68
RFC 1058, 94
RFC 1112, 257
RFC 1122, 236

RFC 1123, 236
RFC 1518. 192, 288
RFC 1533, 235
RFC 1583, 102
RFC 1584, 269
RFC 1597, 155, 283
RFC 1715, 200
RFC 1883, 274
RFC 1887, 288
RFC 792, 110
RFC 826, 111
RFC 950, 48, 63
RFC 951, 231
RIP Version 1, 94, 145, 168,192, 204, 210
RMON (Remote Monitor), 76
Route, 35
Route Aggregation, 159-197
    CIDR, 187
    Classless Addressing, 191
    Continental Aggregation, 196
    OSPF, 176, 183
    RIP Routing, 168
    Route Summarization, 160
    Static Routing, 178
    Supernetting, 187
Route Table Efficiency, 159
Routers, 71
Routing, 79-116
    Autonomous System, 93
    BGP (Border Gateway Protocol), 93

Default Route, 83
Distance Vector, 93
EGP (Exterior Gateway
   Protocol), 93
Exterior Routing Protocols, 92
Forwarding Information Base,
   80, 84, 87
Forwarding Process, 85
Hierarchical Network Prefix
   Routes, 83
Host Routes, 83
ICMP, 92, 108
Interior Routing Protocols, 92
Link State, 93, 102
Loopback Route, 84
MetriC, 91
Optimal Route, 86
Pruning Rules, 87
RIP (RIP Version 1), 94
Routing Table, 80, 84
Static Routing, 107
Type of Service, 90
Routing Table, 80, 84, 87

S

SLIP, 5, 139
SNMP, 74
Socket, 29
Spanning Tree, 71
Special-Case Addresses, 60-61
   Directed Broadcast, 61

Limited Broadcast, 61
Loopback Address, 61
Static Routing, 107, 178
Subnet Masks, 50, 56
Subnet Terminology, 57
Subnets, 47, 63

T

TCP, 6-23
   Checksums, 20
   Reliable Transport ServiceS, 19
   TCP (Transmission Control
Protocol), 22
   TCP Frame, 23
TCP/IP Connections, 27-29
TFTP, 235
The Link Layer, 4-11
The Network Layer, 12-19
The Physical Layer, 4
Token Ring, 134
Traceroute, 116
Translational Bridges, 69
Trusted Neighbor, 95
TTL (Time to Live), 85, 86, 266

U

UDP (User Datagram Protocol),
   16-26
   Checksums, 21
   Destination Port, 26

   Source Port, 26
   UDP Well-known Port, 26
   Unreliable Transport Services
     20
Unnumbered IP Interfaces, 49, 138
Utilization, 207